Political Sociology for a Globalizing World

Political Sociology for a Globalizing World

Michael S. Drake

polity

First published in 2010 by Polity Press

Polity Press
65 Bridge Street
Cambridge CB2 1UR, UK

Polity Press
350 Main Street
Malden, MA 02148, USA

ISBN-13: 978-0-7456-3755-6
ISBN-13: 978-0-7456-3827-0 (pb)

A catalogue record for this book is available from the British Library.

Typeset in 10.5 on 12 pt Plantin
by Servis Filmsetting Ltd, Stockport, Cheshires
Printed and bound in Great Britain by MPG Books Group, UK

The publisher has used its best endeavours to ensure that the URLs for external websites referred to in this book are correct and active at the time of going to press. However, the publisher has no responsibility for the websites and can make no guarantee that a site will remain live or that the content is or will remain appropriate.

Every effort has been made to trace all copyright holders, but if any have been inadvertently overlooked the publishers will be pleased to include any necessary credits in any subsequent reprint or edition.

For further information on Polity, visit our website: www.politybooks.com

Contents

Detailed Contents

Introduction

This book is not intended as an encyclopaedic survey of knowledge but rather as a commentary on recent tendencies in the development of knowledge as the discursive construction of a field of analysis that, in turn, feeds back into politics. It is intended as a book to be discussed, contested, challenged and, for students, tested against the everyday reality of political events at every level from the grandest to the most socially microscopic. It is intended to be read not in academic isolation but in engagement with the political through awareness of the range and depth of political issues in contemporary society. For students, this could mean testing its ideas against current newspaper or other media reports, albeit with an understanding that these sources have their own slant in selection, description and interpretation of an event.

The book is organized around the way that three major processes of social transformation have changed the issues, actors, practices and effects of politics, extending the parameters of what we can call the 'political' beyond what can effectively be addressed by existing political institutions. The book argues that massive social transformation, ongoing since the second half of the twentieth century, has not only rendered much of the old politics of modern times irrelevant, but has also produced new ways of acting and thinking politically which almost inevitably appear to threaten existing institutions. Those institutionalized forms and forces have also developed new strategies of government and control that address the new context, but in ways which often effectively prevent political action in new ways, channelling any dissent into forms which can be accommodated and absorbed without fundamental change.

Postmodernization is used as a catch-all term to refer to all the processes through which both society and our understanding of society have become 'de-centred' with the decline of the 'production paradigm' which structured and organized industrial society, both formally and informally. Globalization refers to the ways in which 'society' no longer maps onto the self-contained nation-state, and securitization refers to the way in which political issues increasingly become presented as issues of security. These three processes are indicated by three global events. The student revolts of 1968 were emblematic of a general revolt against authority and challenged the link between politics and the class structure of modern society, suggesting alternative ways to act and alternative conceptions of power in society. The Eastern European revolutions and the Chinese democracy movement of 1989 established the conditions for the development of subsequent globalization processes beyond the bipolar and ideologically aligned world order of the Cold War (communism and Soviet-style government vs. capitalism and Western democracy). The 9/11 terrorist attacks of 2001 mark the acceleration point of securitization processes, after which these become global rather than merely national or international issues. These cross-cutting themes enable thinking across and between the more conventional divisions of the study of the relations between the political and the social into which the book's chapters are organized.

1

Political Sociology and Social Transformation

In José Saramago's novel *Seeing* (2007), a government is confronted with a city that refuses to participate in the electoral process of sustaining political elites and returns an overwhelming majority of blank ballot papers, though without any apparent conspiratorial organization among its citizens. The novel produces many insights into the contemporary political condition, but this basic premise can be read as an allegory of the relation between modern politics and society, in which a rupture has opened between political institutions and politicians, on the one hand, and the societies they supposedly represent, on the other.

Crouch (2004) tells a similar story of declining political participation in advanced democracies, but provides an analytical explanation for this in the very success of the democratic political system in producing economic prosperity and individualization. This, he argues, undermines the collective political project of democracy, resulting in the decline of mass political parties and other forms of organized representation such as trade unions, a collapsing exercise of the electoral franchise, and disinterest in and even antagonism towards collective provision of services, public institutions and collective rights. This familiar scenario is also addressed by Hay (2007), albeit with a different explanation and conclusion, for Hay acknowledges that social actors do not simply collapse into post-political mass passivity. Rather, they develop different styles of political engagement that bypass political institutions and thus escape the conventional measures used to analyse political activity. Furthermore, even withdrawal into privatized lifestyles produces a politics, as Giddens (1991) explained, though this may not correspond to the conventional conception of what politics and political issues consist in. Furthermore, new political issues and the politicization of social life per se produce new public spheres and new forms of political organization, as has long been analysed by those studying the 'new social movements' that emerged in the 1970s (Scott 1990).

The watershed year was 1968, when students rioted on the streets of Paris and major cities across the world, making demands for freedoms that had often not been articulated before. Even in Eastern Europe, 1968 marks the appearance of new thinking and new movements for change that no longer looked either to the Communist Party or to the legacies of pre-communist political organization, but sought to think through new routes for political emancipation which spread silently and invisibly beneath the surface until the revolutions of 1989, when they erupted as if spontaneously. Such movements themselves articulate their relation to society in normative ways, in terms of what should be, but they also generate an analysis of what there is. Though social and political science conventionally distinguish between the 'is' and the 'ought', these two moments of articulation are not separate in political practice. Social movements have thus played a major part in resituating the parameters of the political, by politicizing the social.

Changes in the relation between the political and the social as a result of processes such as globalization and post-industrialization highlight the changing structural determinations of politics, but the effect of the actions of new social movements on society emphasizes agency and contingency. These shifts also, however, confound the assumed distinctions between a political science concerned with actions and a social science concerned with structures. What we mean by the political and the social have both undergone radical transformation, beginning with the rupture of 1968.

Rather than constructing a historical spectacle of '68, the function of the events of that year here is simply to serve as a well-known marker of much more widespread changes which challenged existing authority across the breadth of society, from the international scale of superpower domination to the micro-social scale of manners in gender and family relations and norms of individual body management, such as the length of men's hair. The year 1968 serves to indicate processes which have transfigured and continue to transfigure the political and the conditions of politics. To use the contemporary phrase *la lutte continue* does not mean that the same (now old) struggles go on interminably as a post-'68 traditional political agenda; at least some of the issues of that time have passed into irrelevance, superseded by subsequent events. As the Situationist Viénet (1992) argued in reference to the Paris events of 1968, we need to look to the continually renewing conditions and styles of struggle.

To help understand how the relation between sociology and political studies has changed as a result of this reconfiguration of the relations between the social and the political, we can look at a snapshot taken at the very moment in which these assumptions began to unravel. In 1967, meetings of the American Political Science Association convened to discuss the relation between political science, then considered to be in crisis, and other disciplines, such as sociology, seen at the time as in dynamic growth, with its relevance firmly established – a situation which is often seen as reversed today. The discussion appears to have become extended over the ensuing year, when the sociologist Seymour Martin Lipset edited a collection of papers from the meetings (Lipset 1969). It is perhaps significant that the essays published in the book give no indication of the radical challenges to legitimacy and authority that broke into open rebellion around the world in that intervening year and which now, in retrospect, appear as the singular significant event of the time. However, despite the subsequent construction of 'the events of '68', it is not the events themselves that are sociologically important, but the wider processes that they merely indicate and mark.

I will concentrate on two essays which enter into direct correspondence with one another: Lipset's 'Introduction' and a paper by the political scientist Giovanni Sartori, 'From the Sociology of Politics to Political Sociology' (Lipset 1969: vii–xxii, 65–100). Both authors argue that political sociology properly understood is in fact closer to political theory than to political science. They write against the background of a social developmental paradigm typical of modernization theory, in which what Adorno (2001) critically termed 'the totally administered society' had become the objective of all progressive development, characterized by the planned welfare state as the vehicle for society to integrate functionally hitherto distinct spheres of life. Sociology and political science are usually distinguished as the study, respectively, of social structure and of political-governmental institutions, but Sartori and Lipset both argue that political sociology can be more than the application of sociology to politics. Sartori contrasts both the conventional study of social variables in politics (the sociology of politics) and the science of political institutions in society with a political sociology which would look at political as well as sociological reasons for action, and at how political institutions such as parties are a function of social factors but also affect those factors. In Sartori and Lipset's political sociology the distinction between cause and effect breaks down, as social factors are revealed as effects of political action and political action is revealed as a function of social factors.

Although this may help us to grasp what political sociology can be in relation to sociology and political science, the definition remains abstract. It is significant to note that the authors' concrete examples reveal how the year of rebellion in between the conference and the publication of the papers had begun to undermine the terms of the discussion even before it was in print. For instance, as examples of political action, Lipset and Sartori refer to political parties, the very institutional form that was bypassed by the rebellions of '68, thus enabling the actors of those revolts to reinvigorate politics, finding new ways around the sclerotic paths of the administered society by contentiously politicizing hitherto uncritically accepted aspects of social life. To follow these developments, sociological theorists have taken seriously many of the new approaches in political theory that have emerged from the subsequent pluralization of the political.

Situating political sociology

We can thus begin from the understanding that the separation of the study of the social and the political has a history. The distinction derives from the different ways that the academic study of politics and of society has developed in the modern world, and, if political sociology is basically the study of the relation between politics and society, it has to take account of how both these elements, and the way in which we analyse them, undergo change.

Politics and society were not always considered separately. In early modern Europe, the kind of thinking and writing that we would today call political theory concerned both political and social life. At that time, the dominance of religious ideas about how people should live was being eroded by secular thought, which developed non-religious criteria for evaluating the organization of collective human life, such as productivity, security and stability, as well as ideals that had taken on religious sanction in the Middle Ages, such as justice and universality. Some of those criteria were practical and others were ideal, but most political theory, even that of such notorious 'realists' as Niccolò Machiavelli, ultimately tried to unite the ideal, or normative, and the practical, or objective, dimensions into one unitary project. The ultimate objective was a society that would be both just and efficient, so modern political ideas fused traces of mainly Christian theology with notions of the materialist interests of a community.

Max Weber (1978) argues that all salvation religions, such as Christianity, are the outcome of a compromise between an evangelical tendency, which aims only at the salvation of the soul – what Max Weber has called an 'other-worldly' orientation – and a pastoral tendency, which aims at the development and reproduction of a community of believers that produces a more this-worldly orientation. From the pastoral point of view, evangelical excesses such as giving all of one's possessions to the poor and dedicating one's life to prayer represent a threat to community, while from the evangelical perspective the institution of a church invested in earthly community is a sacrilege. The tensions between these polarities were managed through the institutions of monasticism and church hierarchy, which together formed a system of social order for medieval Europe that functioned alongside the political order provided by such secular authorities as princes and communes.

Modern political thought developed through this tension, not least through the contention of both church and princely authority in the Reformation, most clearly exemplified in the development of the doctrine of resistance by French Huguenot theorists, driven by the Protestant emphasis on conscience. Conscience-based resistance thus translated the evangelical tendency in religion into secular political terms, producing a very different basis for revolt against authority from that of the millenarian ideas that had justified most previous revolts. Interestingly, this historical moment also marked off a break between the modern and medieval worlds with the introduction of the notion of feudalism to characterize the integrity of secular and religious authority of the earlier era (Skinner 1978).

Max Weber, in his distinction between the modern political orientations of an ethics of conviction and an ethics of responsibility (Weber 1946), observed how the tension between other- and this-worldly religious perspectives carried over into modern politics. The major ideologies of the modern political world contained these tensions and provided frameworks through which they could be related to one another, if not exactly reconciled. However, it is perhaps characteristic of politics in the early twenty-first century that these two poles are no longer expected to correspond. Today, instead, they represent twin tracks for political rhetoric, as the rhetoric of hope (or redemption) has become a performative prerequisite for establishing authority to undertake the practical, technical performance of (pastoral) government, as was explicit in the 2008 US presidential election campaign of Barack Obama.

Political science and political studies are concerned with these formal, explicitly political functions, analysing political rhetoric (usually as some kind of discourse analysis), studying institutions such as governments and parliaments and formal political processes such as elections, legislation and policy-making, focusing on formal political agents such as sovereign nation-states and political parties, all within the framework of a structure of clearly defined political ideas – primarily ideologies. As such, political studies tend to neglect social context and the social origins of political issues and movements. At best, these are often reduced to economic conditions or cultural identities (e.g. ethnicity, nationality) that are accepted as they present themselves, rather than questioned. Political science is relatively unconcerned with the social forces behind political action, or with how political action effects social forms. Operating on the plane of political institutions and formalized processes, political science often proceeds as though 'politics' takes place in a stratospheric, rarefied realm high above, abstracted from society.

This analytical separation of politics from society for the purpose of study mirrors conventional modern divisions of knowledge and also reflects the way that modern political liberties were defined as separate from social life, as observed by the young Karl Marx. Marx developed a critique of the enshrinement of the Rights of Man in the French constitution, where he pointedly argued that the constitution created the illusion that political identities and relations were distinct from social identities and relations, that all citizens are free and equal when in reality inequality persists, and most people's lives are actually ruled not by the constitution but by economic necessity. Marx argued forcefully that the new political ideology had displaced religion as the supposed universal truth but had actually replicated the structure of religious doctrine, setting up the political sphere as equivalent to heaven – an ideal, illusory condition. Since the French Revolution at least presented itself as the overthrow of religion, his critique represented a new, secular equivalent to blasphemy (Marx [1844] 1992). Marx argued that, in the absence of real emancipation from economic servitude, the proclamation of ideals such as the Rights of Man merely reproduced in the concept of citizenship the religious idea that each human being was imbued with a sacred soul, setting up the political domain as separate from actual life, just as in religion the idea of heaven is separate from earth.

By the twentieth century, that political sphere had become more filled out. Rather than just the constitution and the formal political identities it defined, a complexity of institutions, relations and forms had emerged, linking politics to society in ways that Marx had not foreseen. Emile Durkheim, for instance, pointed out how the ideal of the individual, the subject of the Rights of Man, provided a common value for complex, socially diverse modern societies in which solidarity no longer arose mechanically from the sense of sameness that had characterized earlier, less complex societies. Social solidarity in the modern world had to be represented in a symbolic form that reflected the social structure of the complex division of labour in society. The notion of the individual, he argued, provided a modern equivalent to the primitive totem, in which society represented itself to itself and thereby generated social solidarity and ontological security for all of its members as a sense of being part of something greater than themselves (Durkheim [1898] 1969).

From the late nineteenth century onwards, alongside such ideological forms as individualism and citizenship, parties, classes and nation-states provided focal points for the development of political sociology as the study of links between the political and the social, rather than simply the study of political institutions and forms themselves. In this framework, political sociology developed through two main strands, Marxism and elite theory, which we can cover briefly.

Marxist political sociology begins from the fundamental understanding that politics is ultimately determined by the economic structure of capitalism, so that the structural antagonism between the interests of capital and labour underlies all political struggles. Secondly, Marxist political sociology takes a functional view of the state as the 'executive committee of the ruling class' (though it is a major problem for Marxism to show empirically the link it draws in theory between dominant economic interests and the political direction of the state). Thirdly, Marxism has developed a theory of ideology in the sense of the world-view of a particular class which provides a coherent explanation of society, its problems and its possibilities. Thus, for Marxism, ideals and even social knowledge articulate class interests as universal truths.

Marxism is often accused of being economistic, in that all social and political conflict is ultimately traced back to the struggle between labour and capital. The main rival to Marxism in the development of political sociology simply stripped out the economic element, arguing that society is largely politically passive and so is always ruled by politically active elites. Elite theory developed in the early twentieth century as the main rival to Marxism in political sociology, in the works of Pareto, Mosca and Michels, but was already implicit in Machiavelli's Renaissance analyses of the form of a republic.

The conceptual structure of elite theory is that society is ruled over by a minority which changes over time, either in internal factional struggles between interest groups, through recruitment from wider society, or as the replacement of one elite by another. The theory of the 'circulation of elites' explains regime change as revolution or coup d'état, but it can also be applied to the analysis of modern democracies, where the struggle between elites is mediated by an electoral process that remains always limited to a choice between competing factions. Mass parties simply reproduce the same structure of elite domination and circulation internally, but can also function as a mechanism through which elites reproduce themselves, recruiting and elevating the more ambitious, able and politically active members from the wider passive society. Like the Marxist model of class-divided society, elite theory does not claim to analyse any particular political form, but generalizes from its basic premise of a distinction between elite and society to develop law-like propositions for universal application – just as Marxism sees all capitalist political systems as simply different forms of the domination of society by the capitalist class.

Resituating political sociology

Contextualizing and historicizing the development of political sociology enables us to see that these approaches were developed as tools to analyse a political field that consisted of classes and parties in the framework of internally socially stratified national states. Both elite theory and Marxism share that assumption about the field of politics, which since the 1960s has been multiply disrupted by manifold changes. Globalization ruptures the frame, postmodernization changes actors and actions, while securitization displaces the objectives.

For instance, the serial events around the G-nations' summits, and indeed the summits themselves, from Seattle to Genoa to Edinburgh and beyond, are inexplicable in terms of nineteenth- and twentieth-century modern political sociology. These summits did not involve classes or parties as significant actors in the discussions, the press releases and media representation of the formal events, or in the equally significant 'informal' events on the streets around them. Rather, formal participants, protesters and even the police authorities providing security aspired to operate as global rather than national actors, on a stage provided by the media. Similarly, the 9/11 attack on the Twin Towers in New York, the 2004–5 public transport suicide bombings in London and Madrid, and the 2008 gun attacks in Mumbai were conducted by transnational terror networks in global cities with casualties of multiple nationalities, on targets selected for their national significance only in so far as those nations operated as global actors. These attacks were thus quite distinct in scope, aim and significance from operations of war between sovereign states, and from the earlier bombing campaigns of nationally oriented movements such as the Provisional IRA or ETA.

The erosion of the significance of the national frame can be read also in more mundane political events. International treaties have radically transformed the relations of national states not only with each other but also with their own citizens, most notably in the EU. Elections are often fought without rhetorical reference to the old political ideologies of communism, socialism, liberalism and conservatism, which contested the national distribution of resources (where these remain as labels, they often designate something very different to the content of the ideology, both in democracies – as with New Labour in the UK – and in other forms of regime – such as the People's Communist Party of China).

Though many new approaches have been developed to engage sociologically with particular aspects of these political developments, the term 'political sociology' adheres to the old field of politics, often more as a 'sociology of politics' than in the sense of a political sociology as envisaged by Lipset and Sartori. One response has been to abandon the term 'political sociology' in favour of a new designation, 'cultural politics' (Nash 2001; Held et al. 2008). This term is intended to encompass the politicization of culture in all senses, from practices such as art to the taken-for-granted background assumptions embedded in patterns of everyday life. However, it is difficult to see why those concerns could not be addressed by a political sociology that took up the developments of the 'cultural turn' demanded for the analysis of contemporary social life, in which the cultural dimension becomes something that social actors reflect on and use in new ways, so that it becomes a theatre for a new politics of representation. Unless 'the cultural' is conceived so widely that the term loses specificity (to include, for instance, the contention of developments in bioscience, religious affiliations, tourism and commodity production) in comparison with a new political sociology, cultural politics actually seems to narrow rather than extend the scope of study.

A new political sociology in fact needs to look not only towards cultural theory but also, as Sartori and Lipset suggested, to political theory, which has retained broader philosophical or conceptual concerns that overlap with those of social theory. Radical political theory in particular has retained a focus, both critical and positive, on the socially constitutive effects of political action. This concern is shared by contemporary political sociology (Nash and Scott 2001) and differentiates it from a sociology of politics that would continue to relate the political and the social to each other as interacting but essentially separate fields of enquiry.

Political sociology can be much more than a concern with the social background and implications of formal political processes. If we understand the political as the question of how we can and should live, then it can be concerned with the social forces behind political action or with the social context of politics understood as the contention of given authority, identities, relations and structures, as an attempt to change social reality. Political sociology in this sense can be contrasted to political science, which studies the formal institutions of politics, often in isolation from social context. Political sociology is also both an intervention in and a reflection of contemporary forms of political action. It is structured and affected by society and by political activity, but may also have some influence over them, even if indirectly, providing frames of understanding for political action. Thus, political sociology originally developed based on frameworks from the nineteenth and twentieth centuries, when politics had become configured in terms of classes and parties acting in the context of the nation-state, which in turn existed in a nation-state system – i.e. a world defined by the boundaries and interests of sovereign nation-states. This situation was the outcome of long-term historical processes, but was often treated teleologically, as the inevitable and final outcome of those processes, with perhaps a final stage of development of a world state posited in the future. However, the certainty of such progressivist perspectives has come into question since the 1960s, and, in the longer term, that modern configuration may even appear as a historical anomaly.

Questioning progressivism was a key tenet of postmodernist arguments in the late twentieth century, and, although postmodernists often overemphasized their arguments (one thinks particularly, for instance, of Baudrillard's frequent claim that transformations he observed had already occurred, that we were already living in the world that he speculated theoretically), this book argues that we cannot today, in post-postmodernist perspective, recover the positive progressivism of the past. Sociological debates with postmodernism historicized modernity, which means that now we must understand the social and political configuration in which political sociology developed as a *particular* and even as a historical configuration.

In order to do that, we need to go back to the eighteenth century, and specifically to the French Revolution, which overthrew the old order in which social identity (status) and social order and power were identical with power and the political order. The French Revolution, and the parallel rise of the democratic franchise elsewhere in Europe over the course of the nineteenth century, sundered that relationship between social and political order, establishing instead a political state in which all (men) were equal, regardless of status.

However, as Marx pointed out, political equality in the formal political sense, in the state, was only a minor or even a fantasy part of actual life. Political equality in the state ignored 'the social question', the latent inequality of social order. All that democratic revolutions and reforms had done, Marx argued, was to split the political from the social order. Over the course of the nineteenth century, politics became concerned primarily with 'the social question'. The problem was how to develop political means to ensure the progress of society. The solutions to that question took two main forms: either a laissez-faire approach, in which society was left to market forces – which were considered as the most effective means of ensuring the best possible outcome for all – or a state-interventionist approach, in which politics were used to intervene in society.

Modern politics thus became about the *social distribution* of goods and services. The state as a permanent apparatus of administration had already taken shape under the old regimes of Europe, and the corollary of the different responses to the social question was the issue of whether the proper function of the state was to organize distribution directly or to enable the market to operate optimally. Even revolutionary Marxism can be seen as a sub-set of state intervention, since it aimed to establish a workers' state to administer society – i.e. to manage distribution in place of the market. Social classes had distinct objective interests regarding that distribution, so politics became a matter of contending responses to the social question by mass parties which were formed as the collective representation of class interests.

The same period, following the French Revolution, also saw the acceptance of the nation-state as the most effective and therefore the proper frame within which the state could either organize distribution or enable the market to function. Even up to the mid-nineteenth century, the unitary nation-state was only one form of political rule among others. The geographical areas of Germany and Italy, for instance, were still fragmentary patchworks of different regimes, while large parts of Central and Eastern Europe, the Middle East and China were still organized politically as empires. Nationalism arose in Europe in the nineteenth century as a popular reaction to the Napoleonic attempts to extend the new political order of the French Revolution as an imperial project to emancipate the continent from its old regimes. Popular resistance to this imperialism took the form of an assertion of the same principles and revolutionary ideals, but in a national rather than a universal framework. This process was repeated subsequently in China, and in the twentieth century across all the world that had been dominated by the European imperialisms which had promised to deliver progress through colonial administration. Even international Marxism collapsed back into the nation-state framework, as the main parties comprising the Second International broke into national blocs during the First World War and the Third International formed by the residual minority became subordinate to Russian foreign policy by the 1930s.

The politics of the twentieth century thus took the form of mass parties representing the interests of social classes, contending the social distribution of goods and services in the context of a nation-state which was considered essential for their effective delivery and thus claimed an overriding allegiance. Over the twentieth century, this arrangement came to be seen as the normal outcome of historical development, and the ideologically oriented, class-aligned, bureaucratic, hierarchical party became the form of political organization. Parties were defined by programmes and policies deriving from a particular view of society, a political ideology which could identify social problems and devise remedial policies. Those policies were conceived as variations of the political administration of the nation-state, and so ideologically derived party politics representing the interests of social classes fed into the spread of the nation-state and nationalism on a world scale, as imperial domination came increasingly to be contested by national liberation movements organized on party lines. By mid-century, the entire planet was clearly becoming comprised of nation-states in which politics was conducted through parties and addressed primarily the two questions of national security and social distribution (of food, housing, health, education, work, life opportunity, leisure time, consumer goods, and even the right to sexual relations and reproduction).

This configuration appeared to sociologists as the end-point of social and political development, as the normal outcome of social evolution. However, when set in longer-term perspective, it can appear as singular, even anomalous. For instance, we can debate whether modern national sovereignty ever actually became ubiquitous. It can be argued that empire persisted throughout the later twentieth century in an unspoken form in what were effectively Soviet and US empires, and economic and cultural imperialism in Asia and Africa outlived the disappearance of formal imperial administration. Similarly, the objective nature of social class formations may be seen as an effect rather than the source of political organization, Such long-term perspectives enable us to re-engage with the political today as a continuously emergent field, rather than as a fixed set of institutions, principles and practices.

Changing context, changing politics and the politics of change

We can begin by tracking some of the changes that undercut the perspective of classical political sociology. Firstly, the 'end of ideology' thesis advanced at the end of the 1980s argued that, with the collapse of the Soviet communist bloc, liberalism was triumphant, announcing the dawn of a new era in which ideological conflict would disappear as a source of political contention on a global scale (Fukuyama 1993). This positive liberal vision is often conflated with more critical postmodern pronouncements about the end of ideology as a source of politics (Callinicos 1990), but there is no necessary connection between the two arguments. The analysis of politics in terms of underlying ideologies which implicitly provide action with a coherence and logic no longer produces effective insights, and may even give rise to quite misleading illusions, but liberalism does not appear to have survived unscathed more than any other. References to the 'hegemony of neo-liberalism' in economic globalization processes misread those processes themselves, since they are not free market outcomes, but rely heavily on the infrastructure provided by states at national levels and on the superstructure of international trade regulation that is itself possible only as a result of the ongoing activities of states as actors within globalization (Hirst and Thompson 1999). Put more simply, economic globalization is dependent on political internationalization and regulation. As a project, economic globalization requires a pragmatic orientation to contingency that takes its cues from business practice, not ideology. Rather than pursuing ideological projects, institutional political practice today is informed by and refers itself to technically prescriptive objectives, as a problem-solving exercise encapsulated in the post-ideological, technocratic concept of 'governance'. Even more crudely, it refers to the immediate instrumental requirements for retention of power.

This decoupling of politics from the ideological frame does not, however, indicate a depoliticized society. Rather, social life has become increasingly politicized in the sense that it is open to contention or challenge. So the second point is that what we consider as 'political' has over the past four decades undergone massive shifts that have created a disjuncture between political institutions and ideologies, on the one hand, and the newly politicized issues and forces of contention, on the other. Politicians' abandonment of ideologically coherent policies and their unprincipled scramble for populism are simply a symptom or an effect of this disjuncture rather than its cause, and the obsolescence of much nineteenth- and twentieth-century political sociology similarly reflects this shift in the scope of the political away from the politics of distribution in the context of the nation-state. The political has always been about shaping how people live, but there has been little fundamental change since the 1970s in the institutions of politics, in the form of the state or in political ideologies and parties, while the same period has seen massive social, economic and cultural transformation to which political practice has responded in new ways.

Those changes can be summarized under a number of headings, some of which are often enrolled under the term of 'postmodernization' (Crook et al. 1992; Lash and Urry 1994, 2008). Firstly, the diminishing coherence of political ideologies and the collapse of the mass political parties that had developed around them have left a vacuum that has been partially filled by the discourse of identity and the politics of its expression and representation, including the revaluations of social identities of gender, sexuality, race or ethnicity, and so on. The politics of representation have to some extent displaced the politics of distribution that characterized the modern political field.

Secondly, the period following the economic crisis of the 1970s has seen massive economic restructuring, which has been variously conceptualized as post-industrialization (Bell 1973) or post-Fordism (Harvey 1989). Economic recovery from the 1970s was led by the development of the service-sector economy. While that development is particularly characteristic of the hitherto 'advanced industrial economies' of the West (or what was previously known as the First

World), the restructuring of the global economy since the 1970s could not be reduced to the simple model of a new global division of labour in which the First World became post-industrial and the Third World industrial. Rather, the relations of development in the 'new capitalism' correspond to the process observed by Leon Trotsky in the early twentieth century, in the context of the industrialization of Russia, which he termed 'combined and uneven development' (Trotsky [1906] 2007). The development of new economies such as China and India in the post-1970 period has taken a mixed form, combining post-industrial development on a par with the First World with rapid and massive industrialization at a range of levels through to high-tech manufacturing. These developments leave behind a large and increasingly marginalized residuum of the poor, 'redundant populations' for whom both return to pre-industrial subsistence economy and access to human rights are blocked. Thus, gangsterism and the 'black economy' emerge in these bypassed developmental interstices, not necessarily ghettoized and isolated, but often coexisting with global economic development, producing new forms of inequality and even slavery (Bauman 2003; Bales 2004).

Such backwaters, the stagnant lagoons of undevelopment, exist not only in the Third World but appeared as a function of economic restructuring itself in the midst of post-industrial plenty, in the form of entire de-industrialized areas. The abandoned wastelands of old industries that scar cities across the world are the spatial correlate of 'redundant' labour. Post-1970s economic restructuring was characterized by the appearance of an 'underclass', a concept linked to arguments about race and criminality in the USA (Murray et al. 1989). The liberal, moralist connotations of that work obscured the real economic disenfranchisement of this population fraction behind the normative rubric of 'long-term unemployed working class' in mainstream sociology, which even today tends to deny that the old industrial categories of social class are at least objectively compromised and perhaps even completely irrelevant to conceptualize social relations in the global economy.

The third factor in 'postmodernization' is the erosion of stratification by class and the effective division of society instead by multiple lines of division and inequality along the more general lines of social identity, and with it both the erosion of a sense that our lives are structured and the development of the sense that social identification can be proactive, socially assertive. In this scenario, class persists as a lifestyle identification or a marker of cultural affinities rather than of economic relations. Class identification is now comparable to other categories of identity politics, for instance in the UK today producing the identification of 'working class' with white, 'local' ethnicity and a particular exclusive nationalism. In a series of strikes by construction workers in the UK oil industry that spread across the country in 2009, this compound Weberian status marker for the organization of collective self-interest operated not in resistance to exploitation, but to demand an exclusive right to exploitation under the slogan of 'British jobs for British workers'. Nationalism is a particularistic, exclusive identification that is asserted as well as ascribed, but simply dismissing it as a reaction against globalization neglects the extent to which its opposite – cosmopolitanism – is itself an outcome of the recognition struggles of social identity categories. Those struggles have transformed the political by opening to question the taken-for-granted object of interest politics. The new politics of representation is concerned not with the distribution of power to decide, but with the constitution of power in a much wider sense, as the power to define. That new index of the political is not reducible to the axis of progressive–reactionary or left–right on which the politics of interest could be analytically mapped.

Nationalism, though not all identity politics, appears anachronistic in the context of globalization, arguably the fourth dimension of the great transformation that has reconfigured the background, the field and the practice of politics since the 1970s. The definition and scope of globalization has been as sharply contested and as inconclusively argued as the debates over class decomposition and postmodernization. The different strands of this debate have used the term in slightly different ways. Globalization has been used to indicate a programme of economic neo-liberalization, and this sense of the term produced the debate of the 1990s between pro- and anti-globalization forces, but it has been clear from the outset that the 'antis' represent an alternative globalization rather than a return to nationalism or any other exclusive identification (Held and McGrew 2007). 'Globalization' then appears as an 'essentially contested concept' (Gallie 1964), meaning different and even opposite things to different proponents. In historical terms, it has been unclear whether globalization refers only to late twentieth- and twenty-first-century processes of increased scope and intensity of global interconnectedness, or whether we have to consider those developments as conditional upon and even as a continuation of earlier phases of transcontinental links and influences in a 'world-system', of which the nation-state system was merely a particular phase (Wallerstein 2004). This debate has converged with the emergence in the social sciences and humanities of postcolonial perspectives which offer an alternative to the Western-centredness of social and political theory as it has developed since the Enlightenment, in which the rest of the world has always been represented as the Other of modernity, as irrational, undemocratic, traditional, and so on (Said 1988; Goody 2007). Further debates have questioned the content and dynamic of globalization, moving from economic determinism, through a more causally mixed hypothesis (Scott 1997), to perspectives highlighting the cultural aspects of globalization (Featherstone 1990; Featherstone et al. 1995) and those which see it as a plurality of processes or flows, whether centred or de-centred (Harvey 1989; Appadurai 1996). At its most radical, the concept of globalization suggests that, in order to understand our new, global reality, we must abandon the tools of social science developed in the context of the nation-state (Urry 2003; Beck 2005).

These four sets of changes have of course proceeded at different speeds and in some cases even in different directions in different societies; however, what is important here is not the universality or directionality of change, but the politicization of social identities and issues that were hitherto considered below or outside the scope of the political. All these changes appear to take place outside the institutions of politics as they have developed over the twentieth century and impinge upon them only through their interface with wider society. Linked to a decomposition of modern structures of social class in the context of economic transformations of capitalism, there has been a de-alignment over the same period of time of the class–party link (Crook et al. 1992; Lash and Urry 1994). As well as decoupling from class, modern political parties have undergone a threefold reconfiguration themselves, albeit unintentionally. Designed to represent collective class interests, their mass memberships have collapsed as the old class structures that generated those interests have eroded, and differentiation between parties decreases as they abandon ideologies which no longer relate to collective social interests in favour of attempts to infer a popular public consensus to guide their policy-making. Finally, a general long-term decline in electoral participation appears to indicate a crisis of legitimation for political authority as embodied in the liberal democratic political system.

However, these trends have been accompanied by the appearance of new forms of political activity, new collective actors and the emergence of new, postnational theatres of political action, both for actors 'from above' and for those 'from below'. In response, new political sociologies have developed to recognize and reflect these shifts. The old political ideologies represented the interests of a particular section of society as political options for class-based societies in the context of national 'containers', but they are also 'grand narratives' in the sense that they all base their diagnosis of the social question on a narrative of social development. However, as Lyotard observed over two decades ago, the immense proliferation of information as a result of digital technology produced demands for the constant revision of knowledge and the continuous reassertion of the legitimacy of expertise which resulted in the compartmentalization of knowledge into self-enclosed specialisms, rendering grand narratives implausible and hence unsustainable.

If we ask what now binds collective political actors together in the place of ideology, we are likely to see social identities, socially recognized frameworks for the self, as providing that function. Religious, cultural and lifestyle identities all provide a frame and a sense of meaning for action in the same way that ideology functioned in modernity. Social identities may be imaginary, but they are real in effect, and, rather than interpreting society as though it existed independently of them, we can understand social identities as comprising the social fabric itself. The revival of nationalism after 1989 can be seen as one aspect of this wider substitution of the politics of identity and its representation in place of political ideologies of social distribution.

The obsolescence of ideology means that the objectives of politics have also changed. Ideologies were to be implemented via the management of distribution of goods and services in society, but the struggles over social distribution have been displaced, or at least complicated, by struggles over the recognition of social identities. There are many different forms this can take, just as the struggles over distribution took the form of a very wide range of different policy instruments in the state, proposed and contested as discrete packages by mass political parties.

Those particular means for the realization of objectives have also come under increasing strain: the state as container, parties as representative of collective interests, ideologies as the articulation of those interests, and policy as a way of delivering objectives, with its tendency to rationalize rather than to submit decisions to political debate. As well as a reflection of social changes, the demise of ideology and party differentiation can be seen as the outcome of processes inherent in mass democratic politics, where there was a tendency for the government of society to become reduced to the expert implementation of a political plan, as the displacement of politics by reason of state (Hay 2007: 9). In that process, all issues tended to become rationalized, to become problems for solution by experts, with the corollary that politics became reduced to policy and party programmes became presented as functionally necessary responses rather than political choices, described as the 'technicization of politics' (Miller and Rose 2008: 77). At the same time, however, the displacement of the mass subject of politics by new individualized consumerist subjects has opened up a gulf between political power and political subjection that is reflected in falling participation in formal political institutions and a decline in identification with ideological values that have been described as the appearance of 'post-democracy' (Crouch 2004).

The disjuncture between ideology and politics and between political action and its subjects has produced new strategies of executive political action that cut across the old ideological spectrum. Those new strategies have been analysed as 'liberal governmentality' (Dean 1999), in which political power becomes exercised by acting upon subjectivities, on people's sense of who and what they are, rather than through direct government intervention on the old model of sovereign decision-making. The criteria for political success and virtue then shift from the performance of decisiveness required of old political actors to the performance of receptivity and service provision increasingly demanded of political actors in 'post-democracy', where the benchmarks for effective political performance reflect wider criteria for the legitimation of authority in society, like the performances demanded by human resource management (Sennett 2006). Political rhetoric then becomes 'emotional labour' much like any other performance in a service economy, as illustrated by the power of the emotional appeals of Barack Obama's speeches in the 2008 US presidential election campaign.

However, sovereign decisiveness and technocratic imperatives have reappeared since 9/11 in the form of political reason that translates issues into the discourse of security (Buzan et al. 1998). This tendency has been conceptualized as 'securitization' and, although the tendency is most pronounced in the use of anti-terror legislation, the concept extends across a much wider field of state interventionary action. Framing issues in terms of security produces very different effects from the frame of the politics of distribution, extending executive concerns to new areas of social life which become subject to intense attention, such as the practice of minority religion, chanting at football matches or the exhibition of artworks. Some of the key issues of the politics of distribution become neglected because security is presented as the essential precondition of all other freedoms and actions, such as consumption and political participation. Securitization appears to rescue the functions of sovereign power from the challenge to authority that comes from below in identity politics, new social movements and the politicization of everyday life. Therefore, the political emphasis of the executive duty to ensure public security has been seen as a deliberate and cynical strategic ploy on the part of political elites to reassert effective power and authority in conditions that have undermined the conventional legitimacy of political domination (Mullard and Cole 2007).

Identity politics have challenged the displacement of politics by policy expertise because they contest the ascription of needs, desires and interests on which such expertise rests. Policies of social integration (such as assimilation) in particular have been contested by identity-based movements. However, the politicization of identity occurs outside the framework of institutions that hitherto comprised the theatre of politics, through new forms and processes (in the media, in culture, in everyday social interaction). Identity is also politicized in a new sense that is less concerned with the distribution of resources but rather has at its core the issue of the right of social identities to speak for themselves and to define themselves – i.e. the issues of recognition and representation. Ultimately, these changes raise the question of what counts as 'political', and that question itself can be seen as one of the major fault lines of contention between established political actors and institutions and new political movements which seek effectively to redefine the political, so that the nature of politics itself becomes politicized in the sense that it is opened to contention (Mouffe 2005).

From situational to transformational political sociology

Mouffe provides a clear distinction between the political as 'the dimension of antagonism . . . constitutive of human societies' and politics as the 'practices and institutions' of organization of the field produced by the former (Mouffe 2005: 9). However, she speculates a contingent rather than a deterministic relation between the political as 'originary acts of political institution' and the social as the 'realm of sedimented social practices', since the content of these categories – what can be considered as social and what as political – is dependent on context: 'The frontier between the social and the political is essentially unstable.' We are thus dealing with two variables, as Lipset and Sartori argued. The political is not to be conflated with the institutions and practices of politics, and the social is not to be understood as an objective structural reality pre-existing action (ibid.: 17–18).

A political sociology which takes as its subject the shifting parameters and definitions and the mutability of practices that we call 'political' is very different from a political sociology which takes its subject as given in either formal political institutions or structural social formations. A new political sociology is needed to focus on how these shifts in politics and the political are related to social forces and social change, relations which operate in either direction. However, this study cannot follow earlier political sociology.

There is thus no continuity to be addressed in the transition to new political sociology. We are faced with a rupture which first opened four decades ago but has not been addressed by the 'old' political sociology because it lacks the perspectives and the tools to do so. New developments since the 1970s in fields such as social movement theory, cultural studies, political theory and security studies have attempted to grasp these shifts in politics, and they have developed new tools with which to do so, since changes in society have been complemented by concomitant theoretical developments – in the analysis of power, social identity, political action, sovereignty and statehood, globalization, individualization, revolution, risk and security.

There is of course a two-way relationship between theory and the movements that have actively transformed society over the past thirty years. New analyses of power inform new political practices, and also enable us to see the new spaces and processes of political action that they open up. If the underlying struggle today consists in the question of what counts as 'political', then it can be measured by the extent to which those new forms bear fruit, or are incorporated into the older institutions of established politics and power.

The question of whether old forms can be adapted or need to be jettisoned is reflected as a division in the new political sociology that has developed to study the new configurations of the political. David Owen (2001) has pointed out that the developments in political sociology are divided into two broad approaches. On the one hand, some of the new political sociology looks for new social structures, relations or forces behind new forms of political action. This approach is represented in the work of a wide range of theorists, including Giddens, Beck, and Lash and Urry. These developments tend to define themselves as part of the sociology of late modernity, rejecting postmodernism. On the other hand, another set of developments, which Owen identifies as postmodern or postmodernist, abandon the search for hidden social forces underlying political action. This second approach instead accepts political actions as social forces in themselves, as activity which is itself a source of identity and solidarity, constituting rather than merely representing or reflecting interests. This approach is characterized by the work of theorists such as Foucault, Mouffe and Melucci. As we shall see, this division is refracted again and again, both in political struggles and in debates in political sociology and political theory.

Owen's distinction between a political sociology of late or postmodernity and postmodern political sociology will provide one axis of the analytical grid of this book. The other consists of the contention of what counts as political, which is most clearly studied in the theorization of current struggles, not in terms of a stand-off between different positions that can be aligned on a progressive–repressive axis, but in terms of a confrontation between entirely different power relations, conceptualized as constituted power – where power is established, a force of control, of a capacity make things happen – and constitutive or constituent power – which is power in its sense of potential, embodied in forces that open onto new and undetermined social and political possibilities. Unlike positional distinctions, these 'powers' do not relate to one another directly but represent both two moments of power and two quite incommensurable conceptions of the political, often in today's world facing one another in incomprehension, like the government and state, on the one hand, and the blank votes and civil life of the city's populace in Saramago's novel, on the other.

2

Theorizing Power

In Saramago's novel, which is intended as a speculative reflection through fiction on tendencies in the relation between political institutions and social life today, the officials of the city continue to do their jobs, despite the withdrawal of the government, reminding us of the distinction between the state as a permanent administrative apparatus and the decision-making executive of modern politics. The people refuse power, and in so doing render the executive powerless. Administration continues without any executive. People continue to produce and consume, to read and discuss events, though the newspapers have little to print and so are easily manipulated by the self-exiled government.

Commentators such as Crouch and Bauman have argued that it is precisely the affluence of modern society that has undermined participatory democracy. The assumption is that people prefer to consume rather than to undertake political action. Saramago gives this assumption a novel twist by extrapolating its logical consequences, in which the people, denied any real choice by the convergence of political programmes, make a choice of not choosing, thereby undermining power through an aggregate refusal to participate in the political game, even to the extent of declining to articulate any explicit opposition.

The idea that political interests are displaced by consumer desires is theoretically articulated by critical theory to explain the apparent eclipse of modern political reason since the mid-twentieth century (Adorno and Horkheimer [1947] 1997; Lefebvre [1968] 1984; Debord [1967] 1992), but Saramago suggests in his allegory that everyday life is always political anyway, while the formal dimension of 'real' power may be an illusion. Saramago questions not only where power lies, but also what it is.

Power and theory

Since the late twentieth century, power as a phenomenon has become increasingly a matter of theoretical contention, reflecting the way that it has increasingly been subject to challenge since the generational revolts of the 1960s undermined many of the old forms in which social domination and control had previously gone unchallenged, whether in the name of traditional religion, patriarchy, racialism or authority. This was not a Western phenomenon but was associated with modernization across the world, for instance in the Cultural Revolution in China, where a similar generational revolt was fomented and utilized by one elite faction against others, but simultaneously swept away many residues of traditional culture, ironically clearing the ground for the development of twenty-first-century Chinese capitalism. The rise of religious fundamentalism may also be seen as part of the same phenomenon, with its superficial anti-modern ideology a function of its own de-traditionalizing force. These anti-authoritarian challenges effectively undercut many basic assumptions about power, since they have shown how it is embedded (and therefore can be contested) in culture, as well as exercised through formal political structures such as the state.

The sociological analysis of power often begins by attempting to distinguish between different forms, or different meanings of the term, to develop from these discussions a closed definition of the concept. Different approaches are then assessed according to how well they explain this *a priori* conception. This is the approach taken by Steven Lukes, who defines the concept in the formulation 'A exercises power over B when A affects B in a manner contrary to B's interests' (Lukes 2005: 37). He then elaborates his three-dimensional framework for analysis and assesses the validity of rival approaches, which are rejected if they cannot be reduced to this formulation. In response, Barry Hindess has pointed out that, while many other approaches can indeed be reduced to this formulation, requiring all valid statements about power to conform to this criterion would reject 'the conception of power as resting on consent . . . which has been at the centre of Western social and political thought throughout the modern period' (Hindess 1996: 10).

In the second edition of his classic work, Lukes admits that the topic of his book, 'power as domination, is only one species of power' (Lukes 2005: 12). However, his text still attempts to reformulate all power under the one heading, with the argument that other forms of power are simply misunderstandings of social relations in which consent is ultimately 'the imposition of internal constraints', so retaining both the narrow conception of power as domination and the methodological individualism of his original formulation. Lukes assimilates this to a variant on his 'underlying conception', but Hindess's critique seeks to separate out the notion of power as legitimation, to re-establish it for investigation in its own right as a kind of power distinct from domination. However, even Hindess's dualist framework of 'power as a capacity and power as a right' does not seem to exhaust the possibilities if we also want to consider power that is not the property of agents, but seems to be inherent in social structures or discourses, such as Bryan Turner's concept of 'medical power/knowledge' (Turner 1995).

Contrary to the *a priori* approach, the very fact that the languages of social and political theory do not provide a conceptual 'fix' on power indicates its indeterminacy. Instead of trying to fix it conceptually, we can set different analytical formulations in their historical context to see how those ideas reflect contemporary conditions. These different ways of thinking about power are not fully comparable, and therefore it is problematic to evaluate their analyses against one another. However, once we recognize that they refer to different understandings of power, we can see how each can be used most effectively for critical analysis.

The idea that the world has undergone a process of postmodernization highlights how the classical sociological analysis of politics presupposes particular assumptions about power – what it is and how it works – which today seem only partially adequate. In a society pervaded with images, in which ideological representations proliferate, and which is subject to successive displacements of expertise, power today cannot be considered as simply the power to decide and to influence the decisions or actions of others; it has thoroughly permeated the grounds and the context of all decision-making and action, such that our understandings of who we are and of what is possible become a function of diverse representations, which can be summarized as 'discourse'.

Further changes in context are indicated by the concept of globalization, which highlights how the classical political sociology of power tends towards a state-centric view that is increasingly untenable today, when tendencies of development and their implications work in the other direction, away from the national level, either diffusing into the local or taking off into the global. A further shift in context can be traced in the prevalent preoccupation in political practice with security and in the wider social consequences of framing issues in that way.

The contrast enables us to identify a transition in thinking and action that will be further developed in subsequent chapters, moving from old understandings of how power works to new approaches, from the old scope of politics to the new, from old forms of action (political parties, national liberation movements, political ideologies) to new forms (direct action, but also consumer campaigns and religious or cultural movements such as fundamentalism) and from old issues which were framed within the nation-state (inflation, unemployment, racial purity, crime rates, etc.) to new concerns such as climate change, transglobal migration, cultural practices or global terrorism).

Power, part 1

Power as possession: elite theory

Common-sense approaches to power assume that some have it and some are subject to it, provoking the sociological question of whether there are social qualities peculiar to groups that become powerful. Sociologically, elites are distinguished from the rest of society simply by their organization. Pareto's binary analysis of groups which behave, respectively, like foxes and lions, with power always shifting from one kind of group to the other as each gains advantage from the weaknesses of the other when it is in power (Finer 1966), implies that the contention of power is restricted to elites, distinct from the rest of the population. The idea that a 'circulation of elites' as a 'counter-elite' replaces an established elite can be traced back to Machiavelli's observations of the political system characteristic of the Italian Renaissance city-states, which he in turn analysed on the model of the ancient Roman republic to engage his analysis with the key political issue of his own time – the question of whether a monarchical, oligarchical or republican form would best govern human society.

In the classical elite theory of Vilfredo Pareto and Gaetano Mosca, the concept of an elite does not designate a purely political class floating free of social determinants. A ruling elite is considered as representative of a broader layer of society and, for Mosca, is divided by the social forces it represents, but, for both, the sphere in which they operate has a degree of independence from economic relations, enabling modern elites to be sustained by meritocratic recruitment from below. However, while elite theory can be sociologically embedded in contemporary social structures, it reasons from a fixed notion of power that some kind of elite domination is always inevitable (Bottomore 1993: 3–14; Mills 1956: 23).

Elite theory appears to have renewed relevance with the ebb of class identifications in voting behaviour since the late twentieth century. It enables us to relate the political cliques evident in internecine intra-party politics much more clearly to specific social fractions. Thus, for instance, the Conservative Party in the UK consists of a relatively closed political elite based on the cultural network of gentlemen's clubs and old school ties, sometimes known as 'Tory grandees', plus a socially distinct, more open elite recruited as 'new blood'. Similarly, the British Labour Party still retains elements of its old constituency of trade union functionaries, plus new, 'Blairite' elements representing the 'new middle class' of professionalized public-sector and media workers. Struggles for positions of dominance within each party and contention for office between the parties produce cycles in which elites circulate in and out of direct power. We can read British political history since the 1970s as such a cycle of elites, with each successive party of power being led by an elite which gradually loses its grip, to be overthrown by its internal rivals when the party loses power. In the USA, such groupings can take the form of ideological alignments, such as Bush's neo-conservative faction in the Republican Party, or may develop from a dynastic basis, such as the Kennedy family, a form that has also provided a core for democratic political elites in India and Pakistan.

There is no hard and fast dividing line between elite analysis and class analysis, since the former theorizes not an autonomous 'political class', but links between such a class and social interests. Sklair (2000) used the concept of class to identify an emergent transnational social fraction which, by virtue of their close imbrication with the steering offices and institutions of global capital, effectively determines the framework of options for national political actors, with an overlapping membership. Scott Lash and John Urry traced how new developments in capitalism and the emergent sector of cultural production (i.e. the conditions of postmodernity) in the 1990s appeared to be producing a distinctive class fraction identifiable by new consumption patterns, cultural identifications and social attitudes, relating very clearly to the rise of New Labour in the same period (Lash and Urry 1994).

Elite theory has the advantage of not requiring theoretical explanations to link economic to political power, acknowledging instead that elites can be very open about their activities. The sociologist Richard Sennett used serial invitations to the annual Davos meetings of the 'transnational capitalist elite' as the basis for a critical analysis of how this corporate elite thinks (Sennett 1998). The term was also used by the US sociologist C. Wright Mills to refer to the 'military-industrial elite' he saw as governing the USA in the Cold War period, adding to the concept's analytical dimensions of group psychology and state–society relations the dimension of interlocking social structural institutions which united an elite 'who occupy the command posts' (Mills 1956: 23). Mills's work appears to have renewed relevance today, as a reinvigorated US presidential executive authority seeks to use military power as its primary means in a grand strategy to establish a novel global authority, especially given the closely linked interests of figures in the administration of the last president, George W. Bush, to military-industrial corporations (Chatterjee 2004).

Elite theory suggests political power needs no special base, but can be simply a function of political organization and strategy. Elites do not require long-term grand strategies, but respond to contingency and utilize the 'local' narratives peculiar to contingent situations, rather than adhering to grand-narrative ideological scenarios. The contrast in viewpoints and analysis can be illustrated by reference to the US presidency. Taking the viewpoint of ideological and class analysis, some critics have argued that, rather than articulating a self-interested elite conspiracy, the neo-conservatism of the Bush regime had deep roots in the insecurity of US capital as it developed during the Cold War via continuous state investment in the permanent arms economy. The result was a distinct programme in the shape of the 'Project for the New American Century', most of whose contributors subsequently formed the White House administration of George W. Bush (Callinicos 2003).

The elite theory analysis is close to Max Weber's concept of 'Caesarism', an analysis based on the outcome of the ancient Roman republic in Caesar's dictatorship (Weber 1994; Casper 2007). In Rome an elite ruled but depended on the votes of the citizen masses (the male plebs, who voted to veto or assent to any new law). Weber argued that, in the absence of a dynamic public sphere, modern mass democracy tends to be reduced to a similar 'plebiscitary' process, producing simply a streamlined yes/no vote on closed issues. The ruling elite therefore refers to the masses only when they are likely to gain assent for their proposals, with the advantage of 'spin' (the creative presentation of an issue as a non-issue, or vice versa). In this way, an elite or a leader in government can control their own party by using the ultimatum of resignation 'as a means of intimidating office holders, such as Parliamentary representatives, from acting against one's will' (Eliaeson 2000: 140). The same tactics can even be used to manipulate entire electorates, as in George W. Bush's successful campaign in 2004 for re-election, which effectively constructed the vote as a referendum on his regime's security policy responses to the crisis initiated by the al-Qaeda terrorist attacks of 9/11.

Elite theory understands power in terms of sovereignty, and of politics solely as the contention of that sovereignty by elites. For elite theory, power is something that is possessed, held by a select group, and exercised over everyone else. Power is simply the property of elites. Even this simple concept, however, has to be supplemented because, in order to be durable, power has to be accepted as legitimate by those over whom it is exercised, otherwise we are left with no distinction between power and force and no way of distinguishing temporary from more permanent relations of power. There is clearly some qualitative difference between a bank robbery and a tax bill, and if political sociology cannot distinguish between the two then it is not able to provide adequate explanations of the social world. Weber pointed out that domination through physical force alone could not sustain itself; in order to be stabilized, domination had to be complemented by legitimation. It had to be translated into authority which people would obey willingly, and that could occur in one of three ways: through tradition, through charisma (an extraordinary personal quality of a leader) or through rational legality – usually involving some form of bureaucratic administration.

Max Weber and the instrumental concept of power

Most sociological approaches to power take some orientation from Weber's more abstract writings (which reflected his training as lawyer), working through the development of a priori definitions and their testing through challenging examples. Weber's definition – power as the authority of command, with its obverse as obedience – is strictly instrumental, but hedged with qualifications which effectively exclude many examples that his preceding discussion acknowledged as social relations of power. This normative methodological framework established a template that has been followed by subsequent sociological analysts such as Lukes, Giddens and Mann, who alter some of the caveats about what to include in the category of power, but adopt Weber's methodological framework of exclusive a priori definition and his instrumentalist understanding. For Weber, power is to be understood generally in the sense of domination, 'the possibility of imposing one's will upon the behaviour of others' (Weber 1978: 942).

Weber differentiates domination as a structural attribute, 'by virtue of a constellation of interests', from 'power to command and duty to obey', arguing that only the latter can be considered as power. While the former may be identified in almost any kind of social relations, be they charitable, athletic, scholarly or even erotic, such a broad definition would 'render the term "domination" scientifically useless' (Weber 1978: 943). The target here is evidently Marxism, since the examples Weber works though to exclude from his analysis are all economic market relations. Though he acknowledges that such power may be experienced most forcefully by those subject to it, he rejects this concept in favour of 'that narrower sense which excludes from its scope those situations in which power has its source in the formally free interplay of interested parties'. Domination implies autonomous command and dutiful obedience, so that the concept of power is restricted to instances where it is used as an instrument.

Weber further narrows that scope of the sociological approach to power, since his instrumentalist definition effectively excludes the use of immediate force as an unsustainable form of power which therefore has no long-term sociological effect. In the text known as 'Politics as a Vocation', he presents these legitimations of domination in summary form as three 'pure types' of 'inner justification' of obedience: traditional authority, charismatic authority and legal-rational authority. Charisma, the most volatile and revolutionary source of authority, is unstable and tends over time to become formally or informally institutionalized, either as traditional or as legal-rational authority. The latter tends to sweep aside traditional authority by virtue of its adaptive capacities and legitimizes 'domination exercised by the modern "servant of the state", requiring of the office-holder no extraordinary personal qualities' (Weber 1946). Furthermore, Weber's claim that we live in 'a house of power' indicates a particular model of power peculiar to the nation-state framework of thinking – it implies that power is inescapable, that it enters into all areas of life, but also that it is contained within a static structure which gives it particular forms. Weber's analysis thus lends itself to normative, progressivist modernization theory in which all authority ultimately tends towards the legal-rational and the modern state appears as the ultimate form of social and political development.

Albeit in different terms, Anthony Giddens similarly acknowledges that the wider notion of 'transformative capacity' vested in all structurated agency implies the power to redefine social situations, identities or relations, and is hence potentially political, but restricts his discussion of power to a sub-category 'where transformative capacity is harnessed to actors' attempts to get others to comply with their wants', so collapsing the concept back into the Weberian restricted definition of instrumental power, or power over (Giddens 1985: 93). This enables Giddens to go on to theorize 'power containers' as a form of Weber's house of power, but with dynamic rather than static properties. As Giddens puts it, 'power containers generate power' as a property of their capacity to enable 'the concentration of allocative and authoritative resources' (ibid.: 13). The density of concentration in turn depends on four conditions: surveillance of information and activities, extra-economic organizational capacity, the instrumentalization of force as coercion, and the legitimation of domination through ideology.

Giddens's analysis of power is deliberately embedded in modernity, but that of Michael Mann aims at a more historically transcendent approach. Dividing an exclusively instrumental notion of power as capacity to effect the actions of others into political, military, ideological and economic sources enables Mann to apply his approach to a much wider historical and geographical scale than Giddens, but at the cost of sacrificing explanatory capacity. Furthermore, Mann's notion of political power is very narrowly associated with the state, producing what has been referred to as a 'politics without the people' (Trentman 2006). Mann's analysis also models all belief systems on the political ideologies of modernity, reducing culture to the level of an interchangeable variable and thus neglecting the radical differences in reasoning constituted by cultural factors such as religion.

In application, Mann's fourfold analysis of power evades explanation, because each source of power is conditioned by others. One commands power by controlling one of the sources of power, which begs the question of how one has the capacity to control – a question always referred to another source. It is therefore questionable exactly how much insight this analytical division can produce; applying it to US global domination under the Bush presidency produces only the conclusion that the Second Iraq War was fought for control of the oil supply (Mann 2003), a conclusion independent of the analytical framework. This example also illustrates the nominalism of the analytical framework that Mann employs, as his ideological, political and military sources become inextricably entwined when considering the other force of Islamism, leading us to ask whether their separation in 'the West' is not culturally contingent. Poggi (2001) questions Mann's distinction between political and military sources of power, but we could equally question the distinction between any of the categories, which simply reflect the functional distinctions that characterize modern society and the social sciences, elevated to the status of historically and culturally transcendent categories of the sources of power.

Classical political sociology was forged in the time of the nation-state, as an attempt to provide theoretical explanations of how power worked in modern societies, but today we have to question whether this framework does not distort our understanding of power in a global context which, since it produces fundamental changes within national societies, challenges the validity of such theoretical models (Beck 2005; Urry 2003). This aim no longer motivates the development of some new theories, which address power in a global context and pay attention to specific, 'local' narratives.

Lukes's analysis of power *can* be used independently of the nation-state system and its party politics to look at power relations in sub-, inter- and even transnational contexts. However, his methodological individualism posits actors at any given level as a collective, singular entity, with fixed 'real' interests. He begins from the pluralist premise that all social life is contentious, and therefore there is always more than one course of possible action for any collective body (whether it is a government, a company corporation, a political party or a golf club), and since society consists of a plurality of interest entities there will be conflict over what decisions are taken in any given situation. This pluralist framework provides the basis for his analysis of three 'dimensions' of power: the first dimension in which the outcome of direct conflict is decided (the power to make or influence decisions), the second in which issues and options for decisions are determined (the power to set the agenda) and the third in which objectives, ideals and possibilities are described (the power of scene-setting) (Lukes 2005).

The last 'dimension' of power is very close to the Marxist analysis of ideology as a social force shaping popular thoughts and desires, though Lukes restricts the concept of power to its instrumental sense, despite the scope to extend the third dimension to include representations and culture which shape social order indirectly and independently of social actors. While Marxists do not share his methodological individualism, the Marxist analysis of society as an economic system is similarly grounded on the notion of collective actors in antagonistic social relations pursuing their own interests. Marxism is normatively committed to the instrumental conception of power and so cannot abandon the figure of the ruling class in its formulations of capitalism, however abstractly structural those become.

Pierre Bourdieu similarly refuses the implications of his own sociological relativization of class cultures and values to argue that, ultimately, one value-system is given priority over others and is accepted as the norm for the society as a whole, determining a hierarchy to the distinctions that people use to identify themselves and others, though there is no basis in his sociological analysis for this *a posteriori* assertion that only some culture is ideological. The instrumental concept of power has to be bolted on to Bourdieu's structuralist sociology, and Lukes's boundary work on what power is seems no less artificial, a requirement of normative commitments in theory rather than the logic of theory itself.

Marxism, ideology and the structural concept of power

Marx as he is classically read by structural sociologists presents a theory of primarily economic power – in which power consisted in the capitalist system. This insight can be traced through Marx's early writings, specifically his critique of the French republican constitution (Marx [1844] 1992), where he points out that, in the context of domination and subordination in economic life, the political equality offered by the liberal democratic constitution is no more real than the religious fantasy of heaven in contrast to earthly life. For Marx, power should be identical with social justice, so that, in a truly communist society, it would become entirely distributed throughout society as the power of human self-realization, and the state (as a concentration of power) would wither away. However, Marx never developed a general analysis of power, and one of the problems facing subsequent generations of Marxist thinkers has been to explain how economic predominance translates into political power, since the interests of economic and political actors, of business and of the state, are so often at odds.

Even Marx recognized that economic power was managed through the state. This insight was developed particularly by Lenin, in his work *The State and Revolution*, where he argues that the state consists of 'special bodies of armed men' (Lenin [1918] 1992), essentially a kind of 'executive committee' on behalf of the interests of the ruling class as a whole. However, Lenin's theorization of the state as primarily an organ of repression fails to explain the everyday, mundane acceptance of capitalist relations of exploitation by the vast majority of the working class, to account for which twentieth-century Marxists developed the theory of ideology. Those developments span the full range of ways in which the term 'ideology' can be used: to refer to explicit political statements such as party manifestos, to refer to the deliberate misrepresentation of the world in favour of the interests of a particular group, to refer to the world-view of a particular group expressed as universal truth, and, in its widest sense, to refer to any kind of social representation, such as images or text in newspapers, art, TV, music, or even clothing, which can all be seen as 'ideological' in the sense that they convey some socially meaningful statement about the world we live in.

The Marxist theory of ideology is an explanation of how power works through ideas as well as economic relations and armed force, and this provided Marxism with an account of how capitalism survived and flourished despite the objective interests of the working class to emancipate themselves from exploitation under capitalism. Marx and Engels ([1845–6] 1987) formulated the germ of their theory of ideology in the phrase 'the ruling ideas in any epoch are those of the ruling class', but it was only in the twentieth century, as a response to the failure of its economistic pronouncements, that Marxism produced explanations of how class domination persists. The Marxist analysis of the power of ideology refers to the way in which the real interests of subordinate classes are masked by the false consciousness promoted by the ruling class through their (mis) representations of the world. Since the media of representation are owned and controlled mostly by the ruling class, like any other means of production in capitalist society, so the false understanding of the world that they promote has become predominant in society. Terry Eagleton explains this succinctly when he says that Marx and Engels conceptualized ideology as 'thought false to the true situation' (Eagleton 1991: 104).

Abercrombie, Hill and Turner (1980) developed a systematic critique of this 'dominant ideology thesis'. In pre-modern societies, they argue, the means of communication were insufficiently developed for a dominant ideology to penetrate far into the subordinate classes, who were mostly illiterate. The pre-modern orders of society in medieval Europe were thus mostly left each to their own separate belief systems, so long as the subordinate orders recognized the legitimacy of the dominant, in material and symbolic forms such as tithe payments and seasonal church attendance. In modern capitalist society, dominant ideology is difficult to identify because ideology generally appears internally divided and contested and therefore cannot offer the totalizing picture of the world that the dominant ideology thesis supposes. Abercrombie, Hill and Turner suggest that the apparently 'dominant' ideology in any society functions more as a source of cohesion for the dominant class than as a means of repression of the interests of other classes. The acquiescence of subordinate classes is secured by simple negative economic compulsion rather than positive ideological motivation.

For some Marxists, such as Lukács, ideology was not determinant but the world-view of a particular class, understood by them as true and expressed as a universal truth. Ideological struggle for the class consciousness of the proletariat became the central question for Marxist theory (Lukács [1922] 1971). However, in Lukács's lifetime, this struggle was repeatedly trumped by nationalism which seemed immediately associated with no particular class interests, as it took socialist, fascist and liberal-democratic forms, implying that it had greater purchase than purely political ideology because it had a cultural purchase through the homogeneity assumed and proclaimed by the nation-state. Culture could function as a medium for the expression of political interests, and thus its control could be contested. However, culture as an issue and arena of contention in itself was never seen as politically significant because power was understood as concentrated in the state. It was only with the extension of the concept of ideology in Marxist theory, especially with the recovery of the work of Gramsci in the 1960s and 1970s, that culture began to be theorized sociologically as a zone of struggle or contention, in the context of a generational revolt against authority that frequently took a cultural form.

Ideology performs the same function for the Marxist theory of power as legitimation does for Weber's theoretical explanation: it enables us to explain how power operates without requiring continuous force and how compliance is secured. For Marxist theory, ideology transforms economic and armed domination into hegemony; for Weberian theory, legitimation transforms domination into authority. In both cases, subordination becomes consent. However, more recent work has attempted to theorize the consequences, sources and new possibilities of the changes marked by the watershed indicator of 1968, and has sought to free itself from the limitations and circularities of modern political and social thought and practice. From its security in the concentration of 'power over' vested in the modern state, the concept of power has again become 'essentially contested', as it was at the end of the feudal era in the revolutions of the seventeenth and eighteenth centuries.

The description of power as a contested concept indicates a politics of the analysis of power itself. It is not possible or valid to abstract political sociology (or any other social science) from its context, and that context is inherently contentious. Theory is therefore developed

to inform practice and to influence ideas in society, however indirectly, and thus normative ideas (about what power ought to be) are
easily confused with analytical ideas (about what power is). It is often
strategic to conflate the two in academic just as in political discourse.
Marx and Weber were both, in very different ways, advocates of partisan political programmes, and their advocacy often renders their
work into political theory, where the normative/analytical distinction
remains unmade. Subsequent political sociology developed in an
academic context that became increasingly distanced from political practice after the Second World War and, more recently, in the
context of new social movements and of processes of postmodernization, globalization and securitization. Political theory, rather than
political sociology, has been the source of most theoretical developments around the theme of power.

Power, part 2

Power revisited

So far we have dealt with theories of power as something that is
held, possessed, but the last thirty years has seen the development of
theories that begin to think about power in rather different ways. I
have suggested that these developed in a corrosive context for stable
structures of power. We can trace this shift in thinking through the
very different reception accorded to Lukes's original publication of
his analysis of power in 1974, when it radically challenged many
assumptions in both theory and practice, opening a bridge between
pluralist academic political sociology to revolutionary Marxist social
critique and informing the practice of politics by widening the scope
of strategic vision, through to the relative conservatism of its second
edition in 2005, when it appears to police the parameters of what
we consider as power and the political against intervening theoretical developments and new political practices. Thus, the reception of
Lukes's work over this time enables us to chart the shifting parameters of the politics of the analysis of power itself, to see how the
'essentially contested concept' has been reconfigured by enormous
shifts in the theoretical and practical context. It was upstaged by new
approaches which focused instead on the conditions of consent, or
obedience, looking at power in terms of its effects.

From ideology to discourse

Sociological analysis of this dimension of power has been heavily influenced by the work of the Marxist theoretician Antonio Gramsci in his *Prison Notebooks* (Gramsci 1971). The circumstances of the production of the text perhaps provide us here with some insight into the work itself – even in his imprisonment by Mussolini's fascist dictatorship, power did not constitute total domination of the will or determination of intellect: Gramsci negotiated opportunities to write in the hope that his words would inform future struggles.

The main idea drawn from Gramsci's work is the concept of hegemony, though the term is often used to indicate any form of domination where direct coercion is not present, losing much of its original meaning. The term was developed from the Latin word used to describe the strategy by which the ancient Roman republic became dominant throughout Italy, in which tribes that it conquered or subordinated retained their freedom rather than being enslaved, but had to provide armed contingents to assist Rome in all its further struggles, thereby constructing a relation in which the subject tribes would develop common defensive interests and come to identify with the city-state. Gramsci used the term to indicate that the working class are similarly subjected under capitalism, which can give them a sense of common interest in the stability and continuity of structural social relations in which they are exploited. Gramsci's work was developed in the 1970s by Marxists who were keen to break both with the deterministic analysis of ideology that had been repopularized by Louis Althusser and with the Leninist implications of Lukács's analysis of the struggle for proletarian class consciousness.

Contrary to common-sense assumptions of the individual as a given ontological and natural entity and identity which pre-exists its social representation, in Althusser's most influential essay on ideology (1971) the subject found at the core of liberal or capitalist ideology, the apparently singular, unitary individual as source of agency and identity, is an effect determined by ideological representations. In Althusserian terms, 'common sense' is simply a part of dominant ideology and even evidence of its construction of reality. It is difficult from this to comprehend how any form of resistance could arise, and Althusser's framework was ill-suited to the analysis of social reality, most clearly after the events of 1968, where identities were problematized and where resistance to dominant ideology seemed to arise spontaneously.

In contrast, Gramsci's analysis of ideological hegemony, rediscovered in the late 1960s, argued that the working class (or indeed any subordinate group) are won over to consent to the ideological viewpoint of the dominant social group in an ongoing contest of ideas which takes place primarily in the cultural domain, where values and identities are represented. Hegemony does not mean that those ideas are received uncritically or unaltered, or even that they are assimilated into the world-view of the subordinate groups; it simply means that they accept the ultimately prevailing validity of those ideas or representations of the world and do not attempt to unseat them. As in Willis's case studies of working-class culture in the 1970s (Willis 1977), the subordinate group may retain and even develop its own critical ideology or culture, but that will develop in such a way that it offers no real threat to the prevailing order, and ultimately depends on and acquiesces to that order, even if it defines itself oppositionally. Bourdieu (1986) has similarly shown that classes in modern society appear to have distinct cultures embodying distinct sets of values, which become the 'natural' way of acting and thinking for individual members of a class, though he too asserts that, in a given society, the values of a particular dominant group are ultimately accepted as universal, even by those who do not share those values in everyday social practice, so that the existing class hierarchy is reproduced. Gramsci, Willis and Bourdieu thus all eventually collapse their arguments into structural determinism, conceding that politics and culture are in the final analysis an expression of economic relations, though showing that culture, like politics, also constituted an arena of struggle for ideological hegemony in society.

The analysis of ideology becomes cultural analysis when the term 'ideology' is used in its widest sense to refer to any kind of social representation that makes some statement about the world in which we live in a way that is effectively powerful in the sense of Lukes's third dimension, in shaping our expectations and framing our desires This last sense of the term has been deployed by feminist as well as Marxist analysis, to reveal gender ideologies, and has been used to uncover implicit, encoded racism, disablism and ageism in both official and popular 'texts' of all kinds, from written documents, to films and posters, to the structure of archives and museum displays.

Particularly influential in this development has been the methodological work of the cultural theorist and sociologist Stuart Hall, who argued that we should define 'ideology' in the widest sense to mean any kind of representation of the world or of identities, an approach adopted by the Marxist analyses of popular culture undertaken in the 1970s at the University of Birmingham Centre for Contemporary Cultural Studies, which pioneered the sociological analysis of popular and youth cultures by interpreting their artefacts and forms as ideology in the widest sense. The term 'ideology' used like this is sometimes superseded by the term 'discourse', which indicates a way of thinking, a set of ideas and concepts, often associated not with a class but with a particular domain of expertise (such as 'medical discourse').

Michel Foucault

Foucault's work began by showing how the human sciences construct their subject, rather than emancipating a pre-given human subject from superstition and tradition, as the Enlightenment model of knowledge and the theory of ideology suppose. Discourse (what is written and said about something) is powerful in this sense, that it constructs the subject of its expertise; it is not merely expression, but is 'performative' (Miller and Rose 2008: 57). Authoritative discourse can be quite distinct from and even in conflict with power in its instrumental sense, but it has constitutive social effects, producing particular social identities and models of man in general that come to function as social norms, giving rise to expectations of behaviour and informing formal authority such as the law, health and education services, social work, etc. Foucault explored this construction through a series of books in which he refines and develops his concept of discourse and his methodology (Foucault 1972, 1974, 1984, 1988). Although he historicizes the construction of knowledge and its human subject, his work rejects the idea of progressive historical development; rather, discursive change proceeds epistemically, through discontinuous formations of knowledge each with distinct general rules of what can (and cannot) be authoritatively said.

Foucault thus rejects the model of knowledge-as-progress which had informed the politics of distribution as though it were power-neutral, with critical implications for political practice and the scope of what is considered as political. His work effectively politicized expert discourse and knowledge, problematizing the idea that there is a given human subject for the Enlightenment project of emancipation. This made it unacceptable to most ideologically driven political movements, which posit an essential humanity that needs to be liberated from the distortions of ideological visions of the world. Foucault's theoretical insights arose from a context in which radical movements across a wide range of specific struggles had begun to encounter both ideological projects and authoritative expert knowledge as power, confronting them with normative expectations of behaviour, conduct and subjectivity in the new fields of contention that opened following the 1968 revolt against authority, such as sexuality, gender, mental health and disability. Expert knowledge in these fields anticipated what was best for people, and such technocratic knowledge increasingly informed the formal political administration of the distribution of goods and services according to ideological frameworks that added further normative assumptions. Such constructions were encountered by those involved in post-'68 radical movements as limitations on the question of how we could live differently.

Foucault (1980) draws out the implications of his work for these movements, arguing that the analysis of politics and power still needed to 'cut off the king's head', as had been done in practice in the French Revolution. He meant that academic analysis and political thinking needed to catch up with the political practice of the movements, which were challenging 'disciplinary power' as it was diffused throughout society in the form of expert knowledge and its social effects, particularly its construction of normative social identities and subjectivity, while the theoretical analysis of power persisted in understanding power only on the model of sovereignty, of a singular, ultimately determinant power which was usually seen as vested either in the state or in capital.

From the perspective that modernity was characterized by particular structures of knowledge, Foucault developed a more thorough critical perspective on modernity as characterized by a particular modality of power. Thinking of modernity in this way, in terms of characteristic operations and relations of power, frees us from the theoretical straightjacket of thinking in terms of institutions (such as the state) and of structures or forms (such as capitalism) and liberates us from the trap of oppositional thinking in terms of ideologies. We no longer have to relate any practice to a great conspiracy of rational co-ordination or to think of everything in terms of its function for (or as an effect of) more fundamental social relations that supposedly comprise a 'base' to which the superstructure (everything else) must be related in some way. We no longer have to identify social struggles with ideological positions as though they can always be located on a continuum extending from reactionary to progressive positions.

Foucault (1977) developed this approach as a broad critical analysis of the 'disciplinary apparatus' underpinning modernity, extending his analysis outwards from the exemplar of Bentham's plan for a model prison, which serves for Foucault as an analogy of the modern modality of power. Foucault's analysis of disciplinary power is frequently and mistakenly assimilated to the instrumental understanding of power, but, in his analysis of Panopticism, no one has and no one gains power in the sense required by the instrumental concept. Overseers throughout such disciplinary institutions (teachers, prison guards, social workers, the police, etc.) are themselves subject to hierarchical bureaucratic surveillance through monitoring, inspections, reports, etc., while the rules of the institution do not enact the will of a sovereign legislator but arise from the knowledge developed in observations of those subject to the institution, as a normative construction of that subject. Misunderstanding arises because commentators tend to neglect Foucault's more express intention to look at power as domination not from the perspective of the power-holder, but from below; to study it in terms of its effects rather than to look for its sources. Foucault thus took up the aspect of Weber's work which formulates power as a social relation, looking at the obverse side of domination, the construction of obedience rather than of authority.

Giddens has developed perhaps the strongest critique of Foucault's accomplishment, by acknowledging this perspective and taking seriously the spatial metaphors on which much of Foucault's argument depends. Giddens (1991) argues that, in modernity, a sizeable portion of everyday life is spent outside the institutional containers of disciplinary apparatuses. Foucault's argument, however, extends beyond the model of social control as constraint assumed by Giddens's criticism, to the subjectivity that is produced by the structures and processes he has analysed.

This aspect of power as socially diffuse, as constituting its subject, had already been explored by writers in the social interactionist tradition in the process of 'internalization' as part of the process of 'labelling', by which the subject of social norms, and even stigmatizing constructions of self, adopts that social identity as their own self-identity, sometimes in a struggle that is played out in the inner life of the subject and of the institution (Goffman 1970). Such work highlights a capacity for resistance that Foucault is frequently criticized for neglecting. Though *Madness and Civilization* (1965) ends and *Discipline and Punish* (1977) begins with a revolt, an escape from discursive and disciplinary constructions into a space unstratified by social norms, Foucault indicates that such a subjectless condition is unsustainable. We are always subject to power, and without it we are not subjects in the sense of being able to order our world. In his later exploration of the historical emergence of this sense of selfhood in reflective practices around desire, Foucault (1984) explored the way in which the subject as such is tied to power/knowledge. He traced a longer genealogy through religious practices of self-surveillance and reflection that have produced, today, our 'confessional culture', in which the capacity to open one's life completely to the public gaze has become the highly valued asset of celebrity, while a capacity for continuously self-monitoring introspective ethical self-adjustment (reflexivity in Giddens's terms) has become a general social norm.

By the late twentieth century, many of the means promoted as emancipatory in the politics of distribution themselves became targets of radical social movements because of their normalizing practices. The welfare state, psychiatry and psychoanalysis, social engineering, medicine, and even the 'sexual revolution' all appeared also as modes of power, of normalization, even though they promised emancipation from oppression. What was needed was a critical analysis of these, too, which did not reduce them to epiphenomena of either capitalism or the state. How, for instance, were public health services neither a functional adjunct of capitalism nor merely a rational extension of the state, and yet not emancipatory? We could specify this more discretely: How was 'health' a function of *power*? In his later work, Foucault wrote about what he calls 'bio-power' as a complement to discipline (Foucault 1979, 1984). Both modalities of power appear in the eighteenth century, in which the power over death was displaced by power over life and the significance of the juridical system of law was displaced by the social norm (see table 2.1).

Where sovereign power in the Middle Ages operated through a right of seizure, deducting its due in terms of taxes, and lives, in early modern Europe there emerged a new discourse and principle of government, which aimed instead to ensure order, to maximize the wealth of its dominion, to increase the numbers of its subjects, and finally to enhance the health of its population. This positive economy developed an entire science of 'police', the sense that: '"police" is the

Table 2.1   The complementary modalities of power in modernity

Disciplinary power	Bio-power
Focus on society as a machine	Focus on society as a biological process
Control	Regulation
Anatomo-politics of the body	Bio-politics of population
Schools, prisons, armies, factories	Demography, public health, housing, social work
Training, education, reform	Censuses, statistics, inoculation, sanitation

ensemble of mechanisms serving to ensure order, the properly chan-
nelled growth of wealth and the conditions of preservation of health
"in general"' (Foucault 1984: 277). This 'police science' developed
techniques such as surveys and statistics, producing the basis for
disciplines such as demography, epidemiology and sociology by
mapping the distribution of age, life expectancy, disease, mortality,
wealth, housing conditions, criminality, food quality, and so on. In
the tabulation and analysis of the statistics produced by these new
mechanisms of government, there appear patterns which develop and
change over time independently of sovereign power and the execution of the law – i.e. a *social* body, with its own 'laws' and its own
'problems'.

Surveys and statistical analysis were also carried out by non-state
agencies such as professional associations, charities and civic individuals, addressing multiple sites and operating on widely different
scales, so we cannot see these developments solely in terms of the
rational development of the modern state. As early as the eighteenth
century, the mixed procedures of 'police' began to become more
clearly defined specialisms, many of which, like medicine, invoke not
merely functional but implicitly moral judgement in their identification of social and individual problems. For instance, a discourse of
welfare focused on the pauper, but this subject was transformed as the
discourse shifted from passive provision of support (as in the English
regime of poor relief up to the early nineteenth century) to more
positive modes of intervention that aimed to transform the 'indigent
poor' into useful labour, a drive which continues to be refined even
today, operating through a range of agencies across state, voluntary
sector and private services and through many disciplines, including medicine, but also sociology, psychology, occupational therapy,
planning regulation, management, etc. Similarly, the shifting definition of the family came to be conceived as a parental unit only in the
eighteenth century, when it was ascribed a pedagogical function, as
an apparatus for raising children, and so became the target of forms
of moralizing intervention such as medicine, the education system
and charitable social work.

The term 'bio-power' conceptualizes this extensive shift in the way
that knowledge and power constituted political issues, emergent in
the eighteenth century and intensifying through the refinement of
technologies and strategies in the nineteenth, while the field in which
it operates, that of life ultimately reduced to its biological dimension
– 'bare life' – is termed the bio-political, a concept that has been
applied critically to the growth of security measures since 9/11, in

which bodies are reduced to 'bare life' for the purpose of ensuring public, national and global security in the war on terror (Agamben 2000). So, in a process that can be traced through early modernity from the Renaissance through to the eighteenth century, Foucault argues that changes in the way power was exercised changed power itself, from a power over death to a power addressing life, producing a new, bifurcated order of power which operated through disciplinary apparatuses, on the one hand, and through techniques and practices addressing the object of the biological population, on the other.

The history of political thought conventionally focuses on the development of purely political reason, the tradition of thinking about the rule of the polis or political community. However, Foucault argued that the religious techniques of Christian practice from late antiquity through to the Reformation constituted another tradition of rule, with quite different principles, on the model of the shepherd and the flock rather than of the polis of fraternal citizens. This pastoral tradition of care for the souls of believers, Foucault argued, had fused from early modernity with the tradition of political reason in a new discourse of government (Foucault 1988, 2002).

Up to and including the work on bio-politics, Foucault had looked at the obverse of domination in Weber's terms, but his later work recognizes that power/knowledge never begins with a blank slate (Foucault 1982, 2002). His work on governmentality engages his genealogy of techniques of the self with his work on modern political strategies and, in so doing, reconnects again with Weber. Obedience requires freedom, if power is to be sustainable. Such freedom, however, is itself subject to power in the sense that Weber had identified but had rejected from his considerations, power as a 'constellation of interests' inherent in a wide range of social relations (Weber 1978). As Weber suggests, we are all aware of the powerfulness of such constellations, of how our own interests and projects are mediated by society. We are less aware of the extent to which the subject of these interests – ourselves – is a social construct, an effect of reflexive practices.

Foucault (1991) argued that modern practices link together two techniques of rule that are also techniques of the self – political and pastoral, the government of the city and of the soul – which come together to form a general practice of rationality, at once a technique and a moral imperative. He calls this governmentality, and it operates upon the subject of the constellation of interests described by Weber, the free subject of modern societies. Although government in this sense shapes the desires of subjects, since Foucault is tracing techniques and mentalities of rule through practices rather than ideal models of society, ideology recedes into the background. As Miller and Rose put it, 'the term "governmentality" sought to draw attention to a certain way of thinking and acting embodied in all those attempts to know and govern the wealth and happiness of populations' (Miller and Rose 2008: 54).

Foucault was consistently concerned to avoid recasting the state as the sovereign source of power in modernity. His lectures make a long digression to show how sovereignty has a history as the discursively produced and reproduced effect of particular practices and technologies of power, rather than their source (Bartelsen 1995; Foucault 2007). In the work 'On Governmentality', Foucault (1991) writes of a 'governmentalization of the state', such that the task of ruling, rather than focusing only on the state, comes increasingly to concern itself with the production of wealth and population in society, and aligns itself with a wide array of 'expert knowledges' in the development of technologies that are widespread and sometimes merely implicit, intended 'to act upon and instrumentalize the self-regulating propensities of individuals in order to ally them with socio-political objectives' (Miller and Rose 2008: 51).

Foucault's earlier analysis showed the shift from sovereign to disciplinary power, exemplified in the contrast between the spectacular execution of the regicide Damiens, where power reached down from on high to seize the body and exact punishment by destroying it, and the prison of the nineteenth century, where power seemed dispersed in the routine, the architecture, and even the self-reflections of the prisoners themselves. It is complemented in his later work by the concept of bio-power and by the analysis of governmentality. Because Foucault's work responded to emergent political and social forces, these later parts of his analysis do not fit easily together and do not, alongside the work on discourse and disciplinary power, form a fully articulated framework. The work on governmentality was specifically a response to the shift of operation in political power away from the technocratic, disciplinary power/knowledge nexus that informed the project of social administration, towards new governmental strategies which addressed a new object – no longer so much society as the individual, no longer ruling through the aim of the realization of social objectives but governing by framing individual self-realization.

Foucauldian political sociology is sometimes criticized for its apparent refusal to specify normative grounds for resistance. However, Foucault does provide an analysis of resistance which accounts for his refusal to develop normative foundations for critique. With the

shift in the modalities of power, he argues, resistance is also transformed. In pre-modern society, resistance took the form of opposing
sovereign power with the concept of an ancient, even primordial,
law (the ancient constitution, or the law of God) and called for its
reinstatement against the absolutist tendencies of sovereign power.
In modern society, resistance takes up the oppositional theme of
human potentiality and human need and addresses possible means
for human liberation, though, like the constituted power they
oppose, these ideologies are grounded in norms of their own. So, for
Foucault, resistance is the obverse of power, a claim which problematizes the emancipatory project that the radical and revolutionary traditions inherited from the eighteenth-century Enlightenment. Since
the humanist emancipatory project is inherently bound up both with
disciplinary knowledge and with those forms of knowledge that are
produced in bio-power, Foucault sought to keep his distance from
these ideologies, which can be traced from the liberal revolutions of
the eighteenth century through to the Marxism of the twentieth.

Two themes were common to that emancipatory counter-tradition
of modernity. Firstly, the emancipatory tradition always situated itself
in opposition to power over the individual and over the social, aiming
to liberate them from oppression, as though there was something
essential there to be liberated. Second was the idea that emancipation could and would be embodied in some institutional vehicle, such
as the free market or the workers' state. Foucault earned himself the
denunciation of that entire tradition when he declared that there was
no subject pre-existing power relations (i.e. no pre-existing human
essence that was repressed, and thus no essence to be liberated), and
that liberty was not and could not be a state of affairs, a form of social
organization, since these simply reinstituted power relations as normative prescriptions, but rather that 'freedom is a practice', a doing
rather than a having or a being.

Constituted and constituent power

Foucault succeeds in showing how power operates well beyond
the 'house of power' in which Weber saw us as living only when
we entered into the formal political domain, but with Foucault it is
as though we are trapped in this wider 'house of power' wherever
we turn. However, there is another critical tradition which perhaps
does enable us to make relational distinctions between powers. This
tradition of analysis derives ultimately from the Western tradition of
political thought which runs through Rousseau, Max Weber, Walter

Benjamin and Hannah Arendt, and today through a current of Italian political theory developed since the 1990s (Virno and Hardt 1996) that has been more widely taken up through the work of Hardt and Negri (2001) to inform new modes of struggle in the context of globalization. Angus Stewart develops an anglicized version of this traditional distinction in his book *Theories of Power and Domination* (2001).

Stewart (2001: 35–60) points out that we can distinguish between analyses of power which understand power as domination (power over) and those which understand it as the 'expression of collective autonomy' (power to). Lukes also considers this distinction, but only (like Weber) to reject power to, as a capacity or ability, in favour of an exclusive focus on power over, as relationship, because the former is 'out of line with the central meanings of "power" as traditionally understood within the concerns that have always centrally preoccupied students of power' (Lukes 2005: 34). Stewart's distinction is very similar to that made by Poggi between power to act and power to act upon (Poggi 2001) and the distinction made in recent radical political theory between constituted power and constituent power (Hardt and Negri 2001; Raunig 2007a). Stewart treats his distinction as though it refers to two ways of analysing power, but the political theory tradition uses it in a mutually inclusive sense to indicate two relations of power, even two kinds of forms of power (see table 2.2).

The distinction between constituent and constituted power derives from the analysis of the French Revolution by Abbé Sieyès, who pointed out that, if the political is the foundational, constitutive act, then, unlike the constituted power that operates on that already established basis, constituent power or political action per se, as contrasted to politics within a constituted framework, can never be legitimate purely on its own terms. Having deposed the constituted power of the king in a constituent act, the French Revolution had to invent for itself a new source of legitimation when it acted within its own framework, referring its constituted power to a concept of the people, elevated to sacral status, as substitute for the authority in

Table 2.2   Distinctions between constituent and constituted power

Constitutive (or constituent) power	Constituted power
Power to	Power over
To act	To act upon
Agency	Structure
Civil society	State

religion or natural law that had previously legitimated the absolute authority of kingship (Arendt 1965: 161–4).

We can see clearly enough that constituted power today is exemplified in the presidential power of a USA that 'won the Cold War' and has unchallenged military superiority across the world. But what is constituent power? Logically, constituent power (power to) should precede constituted power (power over) – one can only hold power over once some prior agency has already brought that power into existence.

It is, however, rare to see constituent power *disestablish* constituted power. The mechanisms are obscure, since many revolutions are carefully engineered by a coherent actor which already claims to represent a source of legitimacy. An example is the Leninist party that seized power in Russia in October 1917 as representative of the proletariat in the world-historical role accorded to it in the Marxist model of history, and therefore already a constituted power, able to substitute its own hierarchical structure for that of the tsarist state. Lenin's own argument that power was seized by the proletariat, as constituent power, is controverted by the almost immediate Bolshevik concern with retaining power, just as the French Revolution shifted from its constituent moment into the struggle against counter-revolution and the institution of the Terror. Revolution, at least as the seizure of sovereignty, seems to contain within it a de facto movement from constituent to constituted power, regardless of the intentions of revolutionaries.

The question of whether constituent power demands spontaneity has exercised revolutionary thought across the political spectrum and continues to problematize contemporary radical political thought and radical politics. The anti-neo-liberal globalization project declares its objective in the slogan 'another world is possible', but which world, who decides, and the mechanisms by which such questions can even be addressed bedevil attempts to establish frameworks for the co-ordination of local and spontaneous actions. This tendency to sovereign domination may be avoided in theory by elevating constituent power to a normative ideal, as Negri does, but it produces the problem for political practice of how to co-ordinate action strategically without a central decision-making function – i.e. without establishing a constituted power with a claim to normative authority.

Constituent power may have its effect in unexpected ways, in simply suspending participation in the performance of constituted power. The fall of Nicolae Ceauşescu, dictator of Romania, in 1989 followed the model of Hans Christian Andersen's fairytale of the emperor's new clothes. In the context of the other Eastern European revolutions, a crowd compliantly assembled as an audience for the dictator to address with a speech which was intended to legitimate his repression of protests disintegrated into heckling and mockery, and within twenty-four hours the regime that had ruled Romania for over thirty years was gone. Ceauşescu's fall also indicates that the distinction between these two facets of power often simply looks like that between the state (constituted power) and civil society (constituent power), in which command of the state, its 'power over', is always dependent on at least the passive compliance if not the active will of civil society.

Constituent power, power to, in modern society seems to be a property of civil society, though that concept lacks critical insights into social disparities of power, formations of identities and inequalities. Constituted power not only exists in the state, but is also distributed through the structure of wider society, so theories of constituent power must address the political in a much wider sense than the formal institutions of state, though the state is constituted power in its most concrete form.

3

From Identity Politics to the Politics of Representation

The subject of the political has shifted perhaps most self-evidently in the emergence of social identity as a focus for and source of political action. The modern politics of distribution were always a politics of identity, in the sense that they were the outcome of struggle between social classes and were organized around parties representing class interests, but this simple reductive comparison seems to miss the distinctiveness of our era, since medieval peasant rebellions were in this sense equally about social identity, as were the struggles between the plebs and the aristocracy of ancient Rome. To restore analytical distinction, we need to trace ruptures rather than continuities; the politics of plural social identity have replaced rather than developed from the singular class-based politics of modernity.

Class has not disappeared, and is still politically significant, but in a different way, as one subjective identification alongside and in inter-relation with other identifications rather than as an objective ascription that could act as a master signifier for the analysis of politics as the articulation of class interests (Skeggs 1997; Devine et al. 2004). Understanding class as simply one contingent identification among others enables us to realize how it is as much an effect of political activity and organization as it is a pre-existing relation that produces politics by articulating its collective interests in ideology and party. Interests are also shaped by and formed around the context and the action. Rather than emanating from a pre-existing collective, they arise in the course of action that is constitutive of its own subject. This formulation was developed in the analysis of the emergence of the English working class in the early industrial revolution by E. P. Thompson (1970).

Conceptualizing social identity

A common-sense approach to social identity would see it as already there in social experience, but that neglects the way in which our experience of social reality is always mediated by concepts that are part of our shared social understanding – concepts subject to contention and redefinition. In particular, our categories of social identity are open to and are shaped by representation, both political representation and cultural representation, which increasingly involves the media. This contingency shows how critical sociological enquiry cannot simply accept any social identity category as given, but needs to look at its construction and representation in popular and official discourses.

This is not entirely a new approach – Max Weber's work on status and group formation (1978) suggests that the markers around which identities are formed are contingent, so that groups become identified by incidental markers which form a common point around which individuals with convergent interests in a particular aspect of life organize to maximize their 'life-chances'. These markers could be as diverse as consumption patterns, skin colour, educational qualifications, or anything else by which people can distinguish themselves from others. Weber sees society on the model of a market, in which there is ongoing competition for scarce resources and opportunities for life. His analysis begins from a methodological individualism which sees each of us as pursuing our own self-interests, though he differs from liberal economists by setting that interest pursuit in the context of our human drive to create meaning, which can make the pursuit of distinction quite irrational in terms of objective interests. Mid-twentieth-century sociology assimilated Weber's reflections on status to the sociology of social stratification, a structural model which reduced the role of action to the pursuit of structurally determined interests, but today his work can be seen to provide the potential for a sociological analysis of the politics of social identity, which sees identity as an effect of action and organization rather than structurally given.

It may be worthwhile differentiating a sociological conceptualization of social identity from other social scientific, analytical understandings. Weber has already given us a sense in which we can differentiate social from political identity, or, rather, social identity from the way in which political identity is understood by political scientists as an identification with a political institution, as in nationalist identifications with the state. Weber offered a sociological analysis of the politics of social identity as something that is not simply given but is also constructed in the course of social action. This is also political action, because it is producing identities around which competition for power may be organized. Weber's approach took account of the emergence of class politics in modernity by seeing that development as an indicator of a wider opening of the political beyond the parameters of the existing public institution of the state, without ascribing any particular significance to class as source and subject of the political. Class politics already politicized the social in the sense that it was grounded in the contractual relations between individuals, rather than in the relation of individuals to the state. In this sense, it is sometimes seen as the death or end of disinterested public politics, in which the political concerned individuals only in their identity as citizens or political subjects without particular interests (Arendt 1965; Sennett 1976).

The concept of social identity is also used in psychology, but the psychological literature tends to be anti-sociological. Psychological social identity theory is based on the experimental abstraction of individuals from social context, creating situations that were the model for the globally adapted TV programme *Big Brother*. The capacity of social identity theory to explain how people actually interact in society is severely limited by this experimental grounding, which quite deliberately attempts to exclude all the factors that mediate our social experience, creating a supposedly socially neutral environment in which to study interaction, so that variables can be introduced in a controlled way. The problem for such experiments is that we carry society within us, as habitus and disposition, and it exists outside us as context, in the form of categories of social identity that exist as Durkheimian social facts, independent of our subjective self-identity.

A social identity can be imposed on people; for instance, in Germany from 1933 many people from assimilated Jewish families were unaware of that identity until the Nazi regime used the bureaucratic apparatus of the state to register the population using racial classification. So social identity is not unique to an individual; it is something that is shared with others. But it is not entirely separate from self-identity either, because individuals can identify themselves with a social identity. As Mouffe puts it, collective identities 'are in fact the result of processes of identification and [as such] . . . they can never be completely fixed' (Mouffe 2005: 18). Social identity is not an essential, natural quality, but a social classification that can be imposed on or claimed by individuals and groups and that is thus open to contention, negotiation and revaluation, and that is subject to power. Social identity is inherently political, yet its formation largely escapes the scope of political sociology attuned to social structures and political institutions. Here, we are already talking about a process of identification that entails a degree of agency, something actively imposed or actively claimed (Calhoun 1994).

For sociologists, it is important to recognize that a social identity is more than simply a label, and more than simply a contingent relation to others. It is a social category that applies not to a specific individual but to a group, and is not merely a neutral label but carries with it a range of emotive, practical and moral connotations imputed to individuals assigned to that category. In this sense, a social identity is conceptual, a bundle of associated meanings and implicit qualities. As Erving Goffman puts it:

> Society establishes the means of categorizing persons and the complement of attributes felt to be ordinary and natural for members of these categories. When a stranger comes into our midst, first appearances are likely to enable us to anticipate his category and attributes, his 'social identity'. (Goffman 1963: 11–12)

Goffman argues that social identity is a better term for sociological analysis than status because it also involves personal attributes such as 'honesty', as well as structural ones such as 'occupation', but his definition and analysis tend to neglect the extent to which this relates social identity to power, in the sense both of the power to define and of the power to produce new identities in contention – i.e. both constituted and constitutive power.

Those imputed attributes produce social expectations of what is socially expected of people in a particular category. In so far as we identify ourselves in such terms, a social identity produces our expectations of what we can achieve and of how we will be treated by others. In order to function like this, social identities have to be socially recognized and indicated in a code that is accepted by everyone, or at least by those with the power to define others. We cannot make up a social identity and expect others to treat us accordingly, like a rough sleeper requesting service in a Michelin-starred restaurant, and, if we attribute an identity to others, that imposition has to be social and forceful.

But the attributes of social identity are not fixed, and are not given in the individual themselves. They change over time and according to the sets of relations in a particular situation. For instance, the attributes associated with the social identity of 'woman' changed over the course of the twentieth century. As an example of how they are relational, think of the very different social identities that might be imputed to a male Loyalist Protestant from Belfast – in Northern Ireland an 'Ulsterman', with distinct and separate stereotypical attributes from a Catholic, but in England simply 'Irish', or even (derogatorily) 'Paddy', indistinct from a Catholic Republican and ascribed stereotypical attributes in striking contrast to those pertaining to the same individual in Northern Ireland.

In the case of Jews in Nazi Germany, imputed attributes were explicitly and starkly imposed, using the force of the state to back up the ideological differentiation and definition of 'the Jew' by legislating a series of increasingly severe social exclusions. This official exclusion of those identified as Jews from civil society enabled the Nazis to engineer their concentration in acutely under-resourced and overcrowded camps and ghettoes, conditions in which the ideologically imputed attributes appeared to be true, or naturalistic, before enacting the bureaucratic programme of mass killing devised at the 1942 Wannsee Conference. In other instances, the definition and imposition of identity can be more subtle, and less severe, though still stigmatizing, borne on wider discourses that do not have any formal political authority and that may not even appear to be ideological in the narrow sense. Racism, sexism, disablism, ageism, homophobia, and so on can thus be studied as variants on a common social process, even while acknowledging that each has its own particular forms and may be mediated to different effective outcomes over historical times and across cultural and social settings.

The social identity of women, for instance, is constructed across a very wide discursive field, including medicine, advertising, childcare, architecture, pornography, fashion – all of these imply for women particular psychological characteristics, a particular moral status in society and particular physical capacities. But because these constructions of womanhood require social recognition in order to be effective, they can be acted back upon, and changed. The social identity of women, and indeed any social identity, is therefore political. It can be imposed, but it can also be claimed, reclaimed and renegotiated, so social or cultural identity can never be considered as simply given; it has to be seen as a political effect.

Social identity can be differentiated from personal or self-identity, but these analytical categories cannot be separated out entirely. Social identity is *shared* by a group of people, but it is also something that individuals identify themselves *as*, as well as a category that others identify them *by*. There is an interplay also between the individual and the collective, in which the social dimension exists only in so far as common meanings are shared and implemented by individuals in social practice. In order to be effective, social identity has to operate as a social code, so a claim or an imposition of social identity has to achieve social recognition, and when it does it becomes enormously powerful, because it informs our expectations of others and of ourselves. Cultural representations are powerful in this sense, because they present to wider society certain connotations of identity, as well as their simple 'realist' function of depiction.

We like to think that the term 'identity' can be split into social and self-identity, society and the individual, external and internal life, objective and subjective conditions, effects as structure and agency, and encoded in ideology or experience, but such tabulations can be reductive and misleading. We are not only ascribed identities but may also identify with the imposed label, in processes that may be mediated by institutions and practices such as those described in labelling theory (Becker [1963] 1997). Identification (whether imposed or claimed) is not neutral, but carries all sorts of subjective connotations. The distinctions here are thus analytical rather than actual, but they reflect the dichotomized experience of the world that some theorists have argued is peculiar to Western society, where the legacy of Cartesian philosophy has been worked into everyday life and culture.

Sociology is largely formed around attempts to reconcile these apparently naturalistic dichotomies by theorizing how they relate to each other and finding some way to overcome the dichotomy, either by declaring one or the other side illusory, or by trying to theorize some mediation between the two sides. Functionalist and interactionist sociology both used the concept of role. Functionalist sociologists saw role specialization or performance as functional in terms of a macro-social system in which all aspects of life were (or could be) co-ordinated – each individual performing their allotted role for the greater good of the whole, which in turn enabled them to live a contented and satisfying life. Interactionist sociology saw role performance as the ongoing micro-social reproduction of social order. There was no macro-social structure or system, only the ongoing performance of scripted roles by social actors.

The concept of roles enabled sociologists to see how an individual in modern society could have multiple social identities and plural status beyond the singular concept of the essential, naturalistic subject, enabling us to see how roles could differ across societies and cultures. Social constructionism developed out of these sociologies, which produced accounts of social life that challenged the idea of naturalistic social identities and attributes intrinsic to individuals and categories of individuals (essentialism). Social constructionism shows how commonplace social identities become constructed. However, the concept of role fails to take account of discourses which ascribe differing values to different roles, neglecting power in the Foucauldian sense. Nor does it enable us to recognize political contention of those roles. Even within its own terms, role theory ascribes unitary identity, and thus overlooks the individual, personal cost of normative social demands, such as the fragmentation of self in multiple role performance. Above all, it does not enable us to explain how society could change. At best, role theory produces a model of 'shallow constructionism', of the socialization of diverse individuals into functionally given roles. It produces what Linda Nicholson calls a 'coat-rack' model of identity (Nicholson and Seidman 1995), in which the basic form to be filled out is always there, and just the particular content varies according to the social practices and discourse of each society.

More radical social constructionism challenges the very idea that social categories such as gender, ethnicity, sexuality (and even the person) exist independently of social processes. This approach reflects both the identity politics of the late twentieth century and the theoretical shift to post-structuralism (so it is at once both theoretical and a reflection of changing social practices). Identity politics subverts the conventional analytical distinctions between the personal, the political, the social and the cultural, as well as the modern separation of public and private, onto which modern politics was mapped with the effect that 'private' concerns (e.g. of identity and relations between social identity categories) were considered outside the scope of the political, and therefore not subject to question. Identity politics is often associated with the new social movements of the later twentieth century, but the reappearance of authority in these movements in the definition of their subject produced the reflexive critical response of post-structuralism. Post-structuralism breaks with older social theory which saw social structure as something extrinsic to and often determinant of identifications, politics and culture. In that old social theory, social structures (e.g. the way society divided into classes which stood in particular relation to one another) produced contending interests that were realized in social consciousness and social action, producing social identities which were privileged or oppressed by society in general. In contrast, post-structuralist approaches see the appearance of structures as merely an effect of active processes of differentiation and categorization, such as the social construction of identities.

Politics of identity in practice and theory

It is not coincidental that post-structuralism developed at around the same time as social and political movements which aimed to revalue (or reconstruct) social identities. The two are closely linked as part and parcel of the new political contentions of social order emerging after 1968. Post-structuralist theory challenges the claim to objectivity of the older mode of social science theorizing. It emerged out of struggles against authority within universities and academic disciplines and its leading theorists were engaged in practical as well as theoretical political activity. Much theoretical work on social identity (e.g. feminism, anti-racism, queer theory) was developed as theoretical intervention in ongoing political and cultural struggles to revalue social identities, and those working in this approach are reflexively aware that their theories are part of the discursive and political process of social construction of the identities they are analysing.

However, such awareness produces a tension between practical identity politics and the social theory of identity. Emancipation requires a subject, and that subject is most strongly and powerfully represented as essential – that is, as a pre-given category of identity that claims its rightful recognition alongside other legitimate social identities. Political organization and action, as well as the more traditional politics of making claims on the state, require the representation of social identity in the definite and fixed sense that is criticized by post-structuralist deconstruction of imposed identity categories. The emancipatory and the critical moments of social identity politics thus become contradictory.

The feminist theorist Diana Fuss articulated this in a question which resonates for all social identity politics: 'How do we reconcile the poststructuralist project to deconstruct identity with the [feminist] project to reclaim it?' (Fuss 1989: 70). Rather than treating this simply as a problem of theory and practice, sociology provides an overview of the dilemma by directing attention to the relations between the two. When we oppose essentialism and social constructionism, we neglect the interplay of theory and practice and the strategic field in which both operate. These are the 'politics of the politics' of social identity. However abstract the issue may appear, it has its effects in the real world in the playing out of the implications of social identification in the street, the workplace, the school, the law courts, the home, the bedroom, in which the freedom to construct and validate identities is always challenged by the need for recognition.

Some of those practical issues can be framed in terms of ethics. Once we see social identity as socially constructed, contingent, political, then we also see that any identity claim implies the identification *of* an Other. There will always be an excluded, and any construction of identity depends on its Other for its definition. Secondly, ethics arise in the requirement for recognition. Even collective self-identification is sustainable only in terms of more widely accepted categories. Social identity requires recognition *by* others, and so it has to be established on the terrain of recognizable terms. For instance, in modernity, collective identification as 'a people' can only effectively take the form of nationhood, which directs its aims towards the claim to sovereign statehood, and also implies that there will be an excluded who are not part of 'the people'. Similarly, at the level of national politics, the construction of a 'community' cannot but be exclusive and is used as a marker of boundaries of difference. We can conceive of difference only in terms of a self and an other which are equivalents, so that identification implies encounter with another rather than radical, incommensurable difference, a premise that has underpinned the use of community as a form to deal with cultural diversity within a national context, in terms of communities of sexuality, ethnicity, age, class, religion, bodily ableness, and so on.

However, such practices of the inclusive recognition of difference at the level of the state cement and reify distinctions which arise from society, and are thus subject to flux and reinterpretation outside the formal political representational process. Some critics of (for instance) multiculturalism argue that the state's recognition of difference undermines the concept of a universal identity in citizenship, but others maintain that it reifies difference, fixing and endorsing the very divisions it is intended to overcome, just as queer theory critiques gay rights for constructing norms of homosexuality that can be just as repressive as the exclusion it was originally intended to overcome. In all such cases, the core argument is that recognition renders difference into identity as a fixed category. This also means, of course, that recognition, or legitimacy in a political sense, comes to depend on the construction of identity in a normative and equivalent form, leaving no space for the emergence of new (e.g. hybrid) social identities or for radical difference that does not fit the legitimate parameters of identity recognition for citizenship inclusion.

Strategies and problematics of identity politics

The assertion of black identity in the USA in the 1960s exemplifies two ways in which people may seek to reclaim an identity by claiming new attributes for it, or socially revaluing it: against the acceptance of a stigmatized 'Jim Crow' social identity, the black civil rights movement developed two paths and models for itself – the model of universal citizenship and the path of political inclusion mapped out by Martin Luther King and the model of ethnic (national) community and political separatism mapped out by Malcolm X. Though the range of positions in the civil rights movement was much broader, these two can serve as ideal types for analytical purposes, corresponding to the alternative responses to stigmatization that had been identified by Erving Goffman (1963) at the micro-social level. In the context of a highly normative US society, Goffman argued that the stigmatized can accept and internalize the spoiled identity imposed on them by stigmatization processes, they can attempt to renegotiate that imposition in social interaction, or they may withdraw into 'communities of like' where the norms become their own, so that what is stigmatized 'outside' becomes valued within the community.

Goffman enables us to draw parallels with other identity struggles, such as those of disabled people, who have faced similar dilemmas and strategic options. The correspondence between Goffman's interactionist analysis and practical, large-scale political struggles also reminds us that micro- and macro-level sociological analysis are often simply two theoretical perspectives on the same problem and that the politics of social identity requires action in the micro- as well as a macro-social dimension – not merely public campaigns for the reform or replacement of policies and institutions, but the refusal or renegotiation of stigmatizing identification in everyday life, with the risk of violent reaction.

In King's model, black people demand accommodation in universal citizenship rights offered by the state, but, in Malcolm X's model, that concept of citizenship is seen as inherently white, so inclusion in citizenship rights requires the abandonment of claims for recognition of difference – black citizens could only ever be second class, on terms already established by a constitution written in times of slavery, with inherent implicit inequality. The same can be argued with regard to the specific cultural histories that have constituted supposedly universal citizenship as actually inherently, or normatively, male, bourgeois, heterosexual, able-bodied, and so on. This general argument was already articulated in Marx's critique of the constitution of the French Revolution and is implicit also in Foucault's critical analysis of the normalization processes intrinsic to a disciplinary society informed by the emancipatory human sciences of the Enlightenment. This assimilation/distinction question also pertains to particular identity groups, so in the gay movement there arose the question of whether lesbians form a sub-group of a common homosexual identity, and so on. The issue here is to do not only with the conflict between imposed and claimed identifications, but also with whether social identities can be considered as sub-groups of a broader category. The organizing category may be socially and politically contingent, as Weber had argued, so social identifications are always 'local' in a spatial, social, political, historical and cultural sense, rather than absolute.

This question of the context-specific nature of social identity engages with the tension between the deconstruction of imposed identities and the emancipatory (re)claiming of identities. We can show how race was a discursive construction of the eighteenth to the twentieth centuries, underpinned by biological theory that has been disproven by subsequent scientific research, especially with the mapping of the human genome. We can similarly show how supposedly universal citizenship normatively assumes particular cultural characteristics, and how it was from the outset imbued with racialized assumptions. But we can also deconstruct the category under which racial discrimination is contested; 'ethnicity' also has a history, and that history is colonialist, an idea of cultural difference that was imposed upon the peoples colonized by Europeans from the seventeenth century onwards. The idea of 'black people' as a unitary category was originally a white strategy of representation in which the conceptual construction of a category of 'black-skinned' people was a convenient way of demarcating a pool of bodies that could be enslaved from those which couldn't.

We can relate theory and practice by tracing the shifting meanings of the concept of ethnicity in the UK. Originally coined as an alternative to the concept of race, ethnicity and cultural identification became seen as a means of active resistance, the source of solidarity and shared experience which enabled minorities to articulate their own identity and talk back against their oppressors, to engage as a community in critical discourse directed against a discriminating society that still expected assimilation on its terms. There was an assumption in this phase, Hall (1992) points out, of a common identity given in the experience of racial oppression, as subjects of an imposed identity category. In the 1980s, ethnicity came to be seen as the source of a new, 'cultural' racism that abandoned the discourse of race for the grounds of culture which had been set up in the earlier phases of anti-racist struggle as an emancipatory means of inclusive differentiation, an alternative to assimilation. Anti-racism came to be seen as a failure because, in place of racial discrimination, it had established an 'ethnic absolutism' which played to prejudices and disenfranchised those who refused its normative identifications. The critical response was an attempt to separate the ethnic and the cultural, pointing out that the experience of mobilization against oppression had shown how communities of the oppressed were not static and could not refer to tradition as their basis of identity (Gilroy 1992).

The argument thus emerged that differences were constructed rather than given, and that political and cultural activity did not give expression to pre-existing social identities but produced new identifications. Critical studies thus shifted their focus from structures, ideology and cultural communities to culture and social identity as something being continuously produced, and thus as fluid and changeable.

Recent critical attention has focused on the local production of 'racisms' in a global context, in the guise of 'neighbourhood nationalism', antagonisms that are highly localized and context-specific, even if they refer rhetorically to wider debates (Back 1996). Race may be a 'zombie category', but Beck's metaphor (2002) should perhaps not be understood simply as a dismissal; it indicates also the danger of such categories for reactive and unreflective mobilization. To argue that all social identity is the outcome of political organization or cultural representation, rather than the expression of given social interests, does not necessarily imply that such formations are sociologically or politically insignificant. Most recently of all, the newly emergent postcolonial or global 'hybrid' cultural identities have been supplemented by the zombie figure of a 'white British working class' reconstructed as another minority in the image of a nation, assembled like Frankenstein's monster out of nostalgia for industrial society, supposedly oppressed by its de-recognition in multiculturalism, stigmatized in its own cultural practices by middle-class consumption norms, economically abandoned in the context of post-industrialization and presumed to be politically disenfranchised by the European Union. However, despite its nationalist identification, this phenomenon seems intensively localized, by industry, geography, aspiration and attainment.

Similar trajectories can be traced in the practices and processes of other identity politics, though they do not map onto the same timeline, suggesting this is a process rather than simply a reflection of background conditions. However, comparative studies would also have to recognize that those background conditions are experienced differently by different identity formations and, because social identities are cross-cutting, are never always the same for all fractions of any given identity formation. Furthermore, social identities, unlike the ideological ascriptions of interest of a class-based political sociology, overlap; they are held in plurality rather than exclusively, making recognition of internal, divisive differences unavoidable. Awareness of difference therefore tends towards fragmentation rather than the unitary identification required for political representation, producing further frustration with modern political forms of representation and a resort to culture rather than politics as an alternative medium for the expression and playing out of identity issues – particularly as the media become increasingly a source of social norms and expectations – and thus offers a means through which social change can be effected. Such shifts in political practice, moreover, are informed by changing understandings and analysis of power, which has shifted from the variation and development of understandings of power as power over to understandings of power in a discursive and social sense, as the power of social norms and expectations.

From the politics of identity to the politics of representation

These developments have been theorized by Stuart Hall (1991, 1992, 1997) as the emergence since the 1970s of a politics of representation, in which struggles in culture have problematized and opened to active contention what once seemed to be the most straightforward and fundamental premise of politics as a practice. From the Marxist tradition, Hall has argued that we should define 'ideology' in the widest sense, to mean any kind of representation of the world or of identities. With the Centre for Contemporary Cultural Studies in the 1970s and 1980s, Hall developed a Gramscian approach to cultural analysis which interpreted the artefacts and forms of youth subcultures in the widest sense, relating them critically to power and authority both sociologically and semiotically. The term 'ideology' used like this is sometimes superseded by Foucault's concept of discourse, which indicates a way of thinking, a set of ideas and concepts, often associated not with a class but with a particular domain of expertise. Hall thus synthesizes three sources – the analysis of language (and indeed of any 'texts', such as a subculture with its fashions, icons and bodily habitus) in terms of signs, the analysis of ideology, and the analysis of discourse – applying these to the cultural representation of identity (Hall 1991, 1997). We can follow his examination most closely through its application to the changing politics of black cultural identity in Britain since the 1960s, from a politics of opposition to racism and resistance against assimilation to a politics of representation which problematizes the very subject of emancipation that was originally to be liberated from oppression, opening the possibility of the production of new identities and new cultural formations.

If we look at struggles around racism, identity or difference in terms of culture rather than just in terms of formal politics and institutions, then we see two phases in black cultural politics in Britain. These correspond to two ways in which we can think about representation. Firstly, we can think in terms of images, or any other cultural representation, as depictions of a reality that lies outside the image itself, so that what is represented is ontologically distinct and exists independently of the means of representation. A drawing is thus understood as a representation of an object that is distinct from, independent of, the drawing of itself. In this version, an image expresses reality, and is thus subject to normative criteria of evaluation in terms of its accuracy, its representativeness of a given reality.

However, we can also think of representation in terms of constituting the social reality of its subjects, so there is no 'real reality' outside of the representation. A drawing of a black woman in the public domain (e.g. the black servant in Manet's painting *Olympia*) inscribes a *social* body – the social identity of a black woman is thenceforth not entirely independent of this public representation. Her social identity is already inscribed because the representation and its connotations have entered into our shared social reality. In this version, the image constitutes a reality regardless of what is given, and is thus powerful, constitutive of social identity.

We can double these up in terms of political representation also, and thus we can see them both as developments of wider theory and as examples of the general observations of Mouffe on the changing relation between society and politics and how we can theorize them. In the first understanding of political representation, a given interest group is represented, its interests expressed by a party or an individual such as an MP. In the second, the party, individual or ideology presents a programme which generates a grouping. In the first, politics (or culture) expresses the social; in the second, politics (or culture) constitutes the social. In this sense, political representation *constitutes* community – the political representation of a community gives it a social reality. These relate also to David Owen's (2001) distinction between a political sociology of postmodernity and postmodern political sociology, in which political representation constitutes rather than merely represents or reflects interests, and also in Sartori and Lipset's earlier distinction between a sociology of politics, which studies politics as the reflection of society, and political sociology as such, which can extend to the interrelation between the social and the political (Lipset 1969).

Hall argues that the first phase of black cultural politics in Britain corresponds to the first sense of the concept of representation. The emergence of 'black' as blanket category for the political identification and self-identification of ethnic minorities signified a common experience of racism and marginalization in Britain in the 1970s. In this phase, 'black' functioned as an organizing category that produced a politics of resistance, unifying diverse groups and communities. In particular, this unitary category of identity enabled a critique of the way that all ethnic minorities were represented as Other in the contemporary dominant culture. In this construction of blackness, black people functioned as an object of representation against which 'British society' was defined. In literature and art, but also in education and sports (indeed, in any form of representation), black was objectified, fetishized and racialized in a way that fixed all other identities in relation to a normative white British identity, which, as a norm, was thus rarely represented as an identity category at all. Hall's work here relates closely to Edward Said's similarly theoretical synthesis in his development of a critique of Orientalism, the way in which 'Western' identity constituted itself and its hegemonic world-view through the representation of its Other in the Oriental of imperialist discourse, across cultural and political forms, in literature, visual arts, political theory, philosophy and anthropology, as well as in imperial administration and its explicit ideology (Said 1988; Pickering 2001).

The primary objective of black politics in this phase was thus to achieve self-representation, to influence or establish autonomy in the means of representation. Political representation took the form of internal caucuses and lobbies within existing forms of political organization, such as the 'black caucuses' in the British Labour Party of the 1980s, or even on a national scale, such as the civil rights movement in the USA, as articulated by Martin Luther King. However, this phase also had a second effect, constituting an identity that demanded fully autonomous and independent recognition rather than the assimilation of its interests into the majority, producing what is known as identity politics. In the USA, this was exemplified in the black separatism of Malcolm X.

However, Hall (1991) shows how such struggles for political representation were inseparable from the struggle for cultural representation. Struggles over both political and cultural representation sought to generate a counter-ideology of positive black identity. Cultural production also functions as political action, not just in the sense of 'getting a message across' but also as a way of reinvesting meanings, constituting a community and providing a locus in which processes of identity reformation take place. Black identity becomes reconstituted in the process of mobilizing in cultural and political struggle against the way in which 'black' is represented in dominant culture and politics, constituting a subject of and for emancipatory political action. However, as Paul Gilroy (1992) also pointed out critically, in relation to this phase of black cultural politics, in his analysis of 'municipal anti-racism', it had the effect of producing fixed categories of identity which themselves become normative and even oppressive, and may further be subject to 'recuperation' by dominant cultural forces – particularly commercial capitalist institutions which market ethnic identity as a commodity, just as political parties can use arguments for categorical identity inclusions as a way of both constituting and appealing to interest groups among the electorate.

These critical observations of Hall and Gilroy anticipate the academic and institutional critique of multiculturalism, but the focus on political institutions and formal representation has produced politically recuperative arguments decrying multiculturalism's 'ghettoization' of ethnic minority cultures, its corrosive effects on national identity and the consequent 'neglect' of the white ('British') working class. In contrast, a focus on cultural representation and cultural production has produced realizations of new possibilities beyond the oppositional politics of identity.

Thus, instead of seeing identity politics as a dead-end, Hall explains how it has produced a politics of representation in which there is a shift towards the second sense of representation, with a recognition that 'black' is a politically and culturally constructed category. Hall's work has both reflected and informed developments in popular culture and the politics of ethnicity, and more widely of identity in general, changes which have taken place not only in Britain but through transnational networks and on a global scale. In the politics of representation, identity itself is understood as contingent, and cultural representation then becomes not merely an object of struggle but a political strategy for opening new possibilities of social life, as representation is liberated from opposition and from relations of Otherness. With this liberation of representation, difference appears as a diversity of historical, cultural and social experience. Hall's analysis of the cultural politics of representation suggests that the theoretical deconstruction of identity has found a practical form in radical cultural production which produces representations that undermine fixed identity categories and given social expectations.

When it is then no longer possible to represent identities as fixed categories, political organization and representation are compromised, as Diana Fuss observed in relation to feminism, but Hall argues that the cultural politics of representation presents an alternative field for political action. He contrasts this cultural politics to the formal, institutional politics of multiculturalism, suggesting that it has greater strategic emancipator capacity.

In response to the incompatible cultures represented by the new racism, which is grounded in cultural difference rather than biological notions of race, multiculturalism represents cultural communities as coexisting harmoniously, each respecting the integrity of the other in a politics of difference and recognition. In contrast, the new cultural politics of representation seeks to liberate its subject from the fixity of essentialist ethnicity (or any other identity category). Instead of culture itself, its subject is the producer of culture, enabling culture to be redeployed as a resource for social self-definition. Moreover, such cultural politics of representation are not a normative idealist project like multiculturalism, but are the actual practice of life in post-traditional and postmodern, globalized societies, as is indicated by the appearance of new, hybrid ethnicities. Again, we can extend the argument to explain the apparent breakdown of the old identity politics in other categories, such as gender and sexuality, where post-feminist and queer practices and theories have similarly problematized representation in formal political institutions while enabling novel developments in culture – not only in the arts, but in how people live their everyday lives (Gamson 1996).

However, the politics of representation are not unequivocally emancipatory. Solomos and Back (1994) argue that racism has not disappeared in the celebration of hybridity theorized by Hall. Rather, hybrid cultural identities produce hybrid racisms, and similar new forms of division and conflict have appeared in relation to other identity categories – for instance, in the apparent rise of violent attacks on disabled people, and in gender terms in the phenomenon of retrogressive or hyper-masculinity, with its misogynist implications.

These perhaps are mirrored by the rise of 'new nationalisms' under conditions of globalization (Evens Foundation 2002). I will leave consideration of alternative approaches to identity to the discussions of nationalism and citizenship, which will utilize the theoretical approaches set out in this chapter.

4

Sovereignty and the State

... the declaration of a state of emergency ... produced no perceptible shift in the desired direction, for, since the citizens of this country
were not in the healthy habit of demanding the proper enforcement of
the rights bestowed upon them by the constitution, it was only logical,
even natural, that they had failed even to notice that those rights had
been suspended. (Saramago 2007: 50)

In José Saramago's *Seeing*, a government that believes it is the
guardian of the state as an authority transcending all particular interests of society acts ruthlessly to restore the conditions of acquiescence
to its rule when the inhabitants of its capital city effectively refuse all
political domination by casting blank ballot papers in a general election. However, the city's populace never articulate their refusal and
thus deny the government any ideological marker that it could identify as its enemy, thereby frustrating its usual measures of restoring a
monopoly of domination by declaring a state of emergency administered by the ultimate power of the state in its police and armed forces.
There is no one to lock up, no homes to be identified for midnight
raids or demolition, no conspiracy to track, no oppositional ideal to
undermine. In short, there are no politics to the revolt, and thus no
political power in the situation.

Saramago's scenario is not an anarchist fantasy of the overthrow
of all hierarchical domination in favour of revolutionary self-rule,
whether communal or individual. Rather, the blank ballots represent
pure abstract democracy – the abolition of the political in the formal
sense that is usually contained within institutions and its substitution
by the politics of everyday life. In this novel the government reacts
by sabotaging society in order to create the conditions in which the

executive state can reassert legitimacy for its functions. Through this fiction, Saramago suggests that the state requires disorder and insecurity as its grounds of legitimacy. If these conditions are not present, the politics of the state would conjure their appearance.

Saramago's novelistic treatment gives ironic expression to recent developments in the critical theory of sovereignty and the state, principally developed by the Italian philosopher Giorgio Agamben (1998, 2000, 2005). Following a tradition of critical thinking that can be traced through Foucault and Arendt back to work in the interwar German Weimar republic, principally to Schmitt and Benjamin, Agamben argues that the core characteristic of the modern state from a purely political point of view – the attribute of sovereignty, the capacity to decide and to judge, unilaterally and singularly – derives from the continuous possibility within modern forms of rule of the declaration of the state of emergency, or exception, in which law is suspended by decree in order to secure the conditions upon which the law depends. Agamben's concept of sovereignty is not dependent on recognition by other states, but is understood as an intrinsic juridical quality.

This critical theoretical development has arisen at a time when security is popularly rearticulated as the essential precondition of political and social life and as a moral imperative for responsible government, albeit now in the normative context of a global security order. In terms of progressivist politics, that articulation indicates the reversal of apparent freedoms, but for a deeper critical theory it reveals the subterranean basis of modern society, the state and constituted power in the sovereignty of violence, exemplified for Agamben as the state of exception or emergency. Agamben's theoretical speculations have found resonance in the context of contemporary securitization – the process in which social and political issues become reconfigured as security issues – as a basis for critical analysis of the way in which executive power within the state has been relegitimized by emphasizing its function as provider of security. This is exemplified by the globalized anti-terrorist policy developments which have permeated through into domestic social control since 9/11, such as public order policing and the surveillance of citizen identity.

However, Agamben's account is exclusively juridical and formal. The behind-the-scenes debates among members of the executive government competing for power and influence in Saramago's novel, and in the attempts by the armed forces, the police and intelligence services to deal with the cognitive dissonance of their orders, regulations and lived experience of reality, all illustrate the inadequacy of reducing sovereignty to the declaration of the state of exception. Where Agamben comes closest to providing illustrative examples rather than abstractions, he identifies moments of general strike, the syndicalist moment of refusal of economic rather than political power, and neglects within this the politics of the organization that is assumed as the unitary state, as though the state apparatus comes into existence as a function of sovereignty. Not only is there, as Saramago shows us, a politics of power within executive decision-making, there is also within its elements a politics of definition which questions the purpose of those component functions, of whether they are performed for the unitary whole or as goods in themselves, in which case they have their own imperatives, their own ethics. The state of emergency is, as Paul Virilio (1986) has pointed out, not based purely on the executive exercise of sovereign power, but is the form of the military order of society, an ordering that remains latent throughout modern society, a continuous possibility or virtuality, in which the social becomes reconfigured in purely military terms.

The state and social theory

We can speak of the state form as a sociological reality independently of regimes and ideologies because the state has the same core essential functions, regardless of the political inclinations of governments who direct it at any given time and in any given place. Secessions and revolutions usually involve the formation of an embryonic state, and, while sovereignty may become divided, as Trotsky theorized in the course of the Russian Revolution, modern revolutions have historically produced either separate sovereign states (e.g. China and Taiwan) or the substitution of one state apparatus by another over the same territory. Even where there are abrupt discontinuities of regime, elements of the state apparatus, such as infrastructure (e.g. buildings, files, equipment), laws and even personnel, are pragmatically taken over to ensure continuity of administration of the state's functions. This is the case especially at the local level since, for political practice, administration in its broad sense, including schools, teachers, museums and staff, road networks and traffic police, law courts, tax officials, and customs and excise officers, is often considered ideologically neutral.

The sociological approach to the state retreads the development of sociology since Marx, for whom it concealed the real relations of power in society, and Weber, for whom 'a state is a human community that (successfully) claims the monopoly of the legitimate use of physical force within a given territory' (Weber 1946: 78). We can analyse this formulation into four capacities – administration, legitimation, monopolization of (legitimate) violence, and territorialization – though in the past three decades these capacities have become subject to the strains and challenges of postmodernization and globalization, which challenge the centrality of the state for political sociology.

However, the apparent reinvigoration of executive power through the state as the key unit of security points to its continuing relevance for political sociology, despite pronouncements that globalization processes would render it redundant – effectively another 'zombie category' (Beck 2002). Other approaches see the state as retaining and even increasing its importance (Weiss 1998; Hirst and Thompson 1999), though such arguments imply that in the process it becomes reconfigured as the agent of globalization processes (Sassen 2006).

These new approaches have cut across the political sociology of the state as it developed in the context both of the national state as the primary framework and medium for political action and of the state system as the network within which states were situated. Nineteenth-century philosophy of history provided a narrative for twentieth-century political sociology in which the state appeared as the *telos* or outcome of a long historical process. It seemed by the mid-twentieth century that postcolonial modernization processes were rendering the entire world into a patchwork of equivalent, mutually recognizable states which would eventually be integrated into a single system. The state thus appeared for sociologies of modernization as a necessity of history rather than as a contingency, an evaluation that was integral to the view of the state as a unitary entity rather than as a set of heterogeneous assets and practices, producing approaches that took the state for granted as the inevitable and even necessary form of modern political organization. At the same time, as I will discuss in the next chapter, globalization problematized the identity between citizenship, state and identity implicit in the modern formula of the nation-state.

By the 1970s, however, the state appeared to be losing its capacity to 'steer' complex society in the functional manner supposed by progressivist ideologies. Critiques of the limitations of the state appeared from numerous sources. Neo-liberalism on the right saw the growth of the state as constraining the necessary dynamic of the individual in modern culture and capitalism, as a source of amoral conduct and decline, with the assumption that the functions of the state were becoming bloated because public office was being used to advance the sectional self-interests of state employees. Neo-liberal policies of 'rolling back the state', however, turned out to be far more limited than ideologues had hoped, if not least because liberal regimes required an efficient state apparatus to implement and monitor their policies, often resulting in increases in state bureaucracy in the form of internal surveillance mechanisms.

On the left, the revolt against authority was theorized in relation to the state by Habermas's critical theory of the 'legitimation crisis' of technocracy (Habermas 1988), in which the science of administration had come to displace politics as a means of deciding how we should live, and was informed by Foucault's radical reconceptualization of power for the new social movements, which were developing alternative strategies of change that bypassed the state. Such critical perspectives have fed into a social reality in which the state seems of diminishing capacity and significance. In sociology, these theoretical and social developments produced the critique of 'methodological nationalism', which challenged the assumption that 'society' was demarcated by the territorial boundaries of the jurisdiction of the national state.

Daniel Chernilo (2007) has worked through classical social theory to develop an argument against the charge of 'methodological nationalism' that Beck and others have recently levelled against 'statist' sociology. However, he mistakes the object of that critique in two ways. The charge of methodological nationalism is not the same as ontological nationalism, which is the charge Chernilo addresses. Secondly, what we today call 'social theory' is largely an academic appropriation of work that was produced as political interventions in specific national contexts, in which politics was understood as bounded by the nation-state. Chernilo's attempt to defend social theory against the charge of methodological nationalism thus carries the heavy cost of reducing its political engagement to strictly academic parameters, so that work which was originally politically engaged is instead taken to address abstract, *a priori* and ahistorical concerns, a process of decontextualization that Chernilo anachronistically refers to as 'social theory's claim to universalism' (2007: 21), a claim that many of the theorists he enlists explicitly rejected.

Chernilo tends to elide the social theory of the state with the nation-state that has come to stand in for 'society' in mainstream sociology, but the concepts of nation and state can be separated analytically and historically; they are not intrinsically related, but have become the unitary object of political practice so long as politics operates with a particular understanding of power as power over, which is seen as concentrated in the modern state in its national form. We can think of the state as a permanent apparatus of administration consisting of officials who are paid salaries out of tax revenue, and who act within the law on behalf of what are seen as the interests of society as whole within a given territory. That society is politically represented by the government, including legislative and executive functions, whether democratically elected or autocratically appointed, but the state administration performs its functions regardless of government, ideology or political regime. 'State theory' accepts as given this conceptualization of the state as singular and unitary and considers it essential and central to social and political theory, so that theoretical developments can be reduced to their stance towards the state (Marinetto 2007).

The particular form of the state that had developed initially in Europe and which came to characterize political modernity appeared as the historical outcome of social and political development. However, we need to recognize that this process was global rather than merely European, including the effects of imperialism and anti-colonial resistance, of structural processes as well as structural factors endogenous to Europe (Arendt 1973; Said 1998). Over time, we can trace an accelerating development in the study of the state, from classical considerations of the nature of its institutional and sociological form, through analysis of the state in functional terms, to a focus on its development in the historical sociology of the state in the work of, for example, Giddens (1985), Mann (1986) and Tilly (1992), and which has most recently extended to its contemporary transformation in conditions of globalization (Gill 2003; Sassen 2006). More recent historical sociology has adopted a contingent perspective, enabling it to trace the gradual assemblage of technologies and forms that comprise the modern state.

The exceptional prerogatives of the state not only consist in the state of emergency but permeate throughout social and personal life, as the exception, in which rights are suspended and citizens become subject to the state as a result of social deviance, through categories which are continuously created by the systems of classification employed by the state in its social normalizing function. The state of exception, or emergency, extends to all of society the same suspension of rights usually applied to deviant minorities. The state can take away our children, our liberty and our wealth and demand from us our very lives, all without our explicit consent. We are born into and die in states, which record our birth and our death, our identity and our achievements, our biological development and reproduction, our economic and sometimes also our political activity, in the form of regulation, rights and entitlements, surveillance, international representation, and a range of other functions. However, attempts to explain the state through such capacities tend to founder on the normative nature of the claims made upon it, which have been intensively contested throughout the era of the politics of distribution, in which the state became the primary object of political action. Protest against neo-liberal 'privatization', for instance, takes as given the state's normative performance of certain functions, such as education, healthcare or infrastructural development, though those functions differ quite radically between different states, regardless of their respective capacity. The state therefore performs a limited function for the political, defining our horizons, so long as we consider only the binary choice of either state or private provision, mapping the public side of the public/private division onto a single, possibly outdated, institution, rather than considering radical alternatives. Hence the popular outrage in the USA against Barack Obama's proposals for healthcare system reform generated accusations of totalitarianism. While government has dealt with the crisis of the state's capacity to provide by resorting to privatization, conjuring a plurality of forms of market and joint market–state delivery, alternative forms of public provision are rarely considered.

In modernity, the state has come to appear as the only means by which manifestos for social life could be realized, but it also functions as a force which can shape its subjects (Durkheim 1992; Rose 1991). Such projects were most explicit and most self-evident under ideologically singular regimes but were also an inherent part of the democratic state project. This capacity of the state to shape its subjects inwardly enabled the politics of distribution to be manipulated by limiting the parameters and expectations of the political, so that the provision of services could be anticipated and planned strategically. It could employ means extending well beyond obvious propaganda, through the control of educational curricula, to inducements to particular kinds of behaviour via rewards such as family benefits, to policies which aimed to act upon the desires of the state's subjects in the more subtle ways analysed by Foucauldian studies of governmentality, where a multiplicity of agencies, beyond but including the state, are enrolled on a common programme of subjectification (Burchell et al. 1991; Barry et al. 1996).

Additionally, analysis in terms of functions and capacities is problematized by the critical recognition that the state as an apparatus of administration produces its own interests, not merely in the sense that public officials may come to act collectively through the state to advance their own interests, but also in the sense that administration, or bureaucracy, creates its own analytical framework for addressing the issues with which it is confronted, producing its own imperatives and dynamics. These were analysed by Max Weber in his work on bureaucracy as an 'ideal-typical' form (Weber 1978) and extended by the Frankfurt School critical theorists into a critique of the characteristic form of instrumental rationality which reduces political issues – to do with how we can live as a society – to technocractic problems for the state apparatus to solve (in particular, Adorno 2001). This approach has produced some of the most incisive sociological critique of the modern state form, as in Zygmunt Bauman's analysis of the Holocaust, which at its core simply points out that the genocide of millions was possible only through the rationalizing and depersonalizing apparatus of the modern state and was conditional on the particular kind of subjectivity that it produces (Bauman 1991).

Considering the state as a vehicle for the distribution of goods, and therefore as the object of contention of political action, sets it up unquestioningly as a concentration of the power of domination. It also has the effect of focusing attention on the state as it had developed by the nineteenth century. In so far as they consider the historical emergence of the modern state, such approaches are often couched within 'path-dependent' models of modernization theory, in which the state's development is seen as the outcome of progressive societal evolution, thus further fuelling the debate over its normative functions. In particular, those debates have drawn attention to the historical relation between the state and capitalist development, which has focused the attention of historical sociology on the West.

Historical sociology of the state

As an outcome of progressive social evolution, the development of the modern state is seen as the functionally necessary complement of economic development. However, in the context of globalization, scholars have begun to recognize the influence of the way that Europeans perceived (and frequently misunderstood) other political systems in comparison with their own, and of how the modern European state developed not in a merely European context but in interaction with other forms of political organization that they would come to dominate (Smith and Eisenstadt 2006). The modernist narrative is the most 'path dependent', since the particular form of the state at any given stage of development is defined normatively. This approach then directs developmental efforts to the governance of institutions, as in this view deviant forms would impede overall social development (Adams et al. 2005). In the Marxist variant of the modernization narrative of state formation, economic relations of production are ultimately always determinant, though the course of political struggle and the structural effects of political institutions can impede or distort that development. The modern state functions as an instrument of class domination, either directly through its 'special bodies of armed men', or indirectly through dominant ideology which delimits the scope of the agenda about the organization of society and tends to prioritize the processes of capitalism, so that the state becomes effectively an agency of capitalism, a role that is actually facilitated by its institutional independence and apparent neutrality.

While the modernization narrative tends to accept the state's neutrality as both normative and given, and Marxist analysis sees that apparent neutrality as ultimately functional for capital, Weber saw state neutrality as an effect of the relations of power that brought the state into being, premised upon the modern form of bureaucracy which enables 'the conceptual separation of "the state" as an abstract bearer of sovereign prerogatives and the creator of legal norms, from all personal "authorizations" of individuals . . . a conceptual separation of public and private' (Weber 1946: 239).

For Weber, bureaucracy in its 'ideal-type', or generic form, is dependent on formal rationality for the legitimacy of its administration, as legal-rational authority. Weber asserts that such authority is supported by a particular institutional structure, organized on a continuous basis, with tasks divided into clearly demarcated functions by written rules and staffed by a hierarchy organized in a career structure, whose work is all recorded in writing and governed by either technical or legal precepts, utilizing resources quite distinct from their private property and possessions. The duties of the officials are contractually demarcated, each with authority only within this limited sphere of competence. Bureaucratization has a 'levelling' effect because appointments within the career structure are based on technical qualifications and because the officials must conduct their duties 'without regard for persons' (Weber 1946: 196–240). Weber's bureaucracy is intended to be understood only as an ideal-type. In reality variations or alternatives to this form are widespread, but it functions as an ideal because it is the basis of the supposed neutrality of modern administration that is a necessary condition for universal political rights and of democracy, and is the most effective form for the implementation of political rule. At the same time it acts as a limit to them, since bureaucracy develops its own rules of operation extrinsic to the orders it is given, while its rationality and efficiency make it an indispensable requirement for the governance of modern society. In contrast to naive assumptions of the neutrality of administration and to unreflexive critical denunciations of bureaucracy as a constraint on freedom or as a distortion of social justice, Weber thus emphasizes the *ambivalent necessity* of bureaucracy, an analysis taken up more critically by Bauman (1991) and du Gay (2000).

Sociologically, one of the most significant features is that the state consists of a permanent formal and impersonal bureaucracy. Bureaucracy in itself does not constitute 'the state' in the sense of a unitary entity, but for modern politics the state has the capacity and aspires to function as such, despite its sociological reality as an assemblage of resources and practices in an imaginary unity, just as the nation is an 'imagined community' and the territory is an imagined geographical entity. This imagined unity is explored by Neocleous (2003), who points out that the nation-state is personified in the popular imagination as a discursive effect of its territorial and bio-political definition, as well as the permanence of the state apparatus.

In conceptualizing the state as a territorial power container, Giddens has attempted to grasp how this apparent singularity of the state arises from sociological conditions, and combines Weber's insights on bureaucracy with Foucault's analysis of disciplinary power. Giddens criticized Foucault's assertion that we live in a 'disciplinary society' where power is diffused throughout society, pointing out that the latter's examples of disciplinary power are not spread throughout society but are all spatially and juridically demarcated (Giddens 1985). Discipline needs a definite container to work within, such as a prison, an army, a school, a factory or, on a larger scale, the territorial nation-state: 'The modern nation-state becomes the pre-eminent form of power container, as a territorially bounded administrative unity' (ibid.: 13). Ironically, this has the effect of returning Foucault's analysis of power to state-centrism while also undermining Giddens's own attempt to escape the determinist implications of Foucault's ubiquitous conception of disciplinary power.

For Giddens, power is generated by the containment of resources, enabling a number of processes in which power is multiplied. The first of these is surveillance, which Foucault had already identified as producing expert knowledge from the close supervision of activities which defines its subjects. Secondly, in contrast to a commercial enterprise, where competition demands that every activity has to have some productive value, the state assembles a concentrated mass of individuals who are paid out of taxes and can thus be employed to undertake economically unproductive activities. Giddens notes a demarcation between external and internal forces of modern state sanction (i.e. the army and the police). Finally, the state as container enables the production of hegemonic ideology in the form of nationalism, exercising a dominance of ideas which construct perceptions of identity, society, history, and even of space and time. This is brought to bear through education, but also through what we conventionally understand as the media, through the state's regulatory control of all forms of representation, from popular culture to architecture and town planning, so that the state comes effectively to regulate the environment as the material context framing our social life.

Understanding the state as a container focuses attention on territoriality as the primary condition of the modern state. Historical sociologists such as Elias and Giddens have addressed this issue through their explorations of state-formation processes in Europe, and James C. Scott has extended it through a critical engagement with modernization processes to focus on the 'high modernist' moment in territorialization, when processes and perceptions that had developed over preceding centuries, largely through the symbolic representation of monarchical sovereignty in spectacular feats of landscaping and engineering (Mukerji 1997), became intensified by the concentration of resources available to the distinctively modern state (Scott 1998). As a consequence of Scott's analysis of 'statization' we become increasingly aware of the constructedness of the unity of the state, with territorialization being only a part of the process of construction rather than its definitive basis.

Scott discusses how territorial homogenization reduces distinct places to equivalents, but also how the state's attempts to 'map' its territory and population standardize everything it surveys: the creation of permanent last names (for population registers), the standardization of weights and measures, property holdings and legal practice, and language and accents in public life. Where sociologists hitherto had started from the given fact of the state and its functions, Scott shows how those already assume the state standardization of social life – the design of cities, the organization of transport, agricultural practices, even family life (the Chinese state policy of one-child families is simply a particular instance of regulation which has historically been exercised by regimes of all kinds under the rubric of eugenics). Scott's analysis thus ties in with Foucault's recognition that disciplinary power in modernity is supplemented by a 'bio-politics' of population (Foucault 1979).

> Early modern statecraft seemed devoted to rationalizing and standardizing what was social hieroglyph into a legible and administratively more convenient format. The social simplifications this introduced not only permitted a more finely tuned system of taxation and conscription but also greatly enhanced the capacity of the state [to make] quite discriminating interventions of every kind, such as public health measures, political surveillance, and poor relief. (Scott 1998: 3)

Like Foucault, Scott observes that such measures do not just measure, they construct – for instance, a map of taxable land tenures does not merely represent existing arrangements but can create a system out of diverse arrangements, assimilating all particulars to one single norm, a category of homogeneity, where before there were simply heterogeneous arrangements. We could say, in general terms, that Scott explores the vast range of ways in which the state reduces relationships between people to social relations. In this sense, the state produces the conditions for commodification by codifying and sanctioning the homogenization necessary for exchange. Giddens and Scott, then, both point out that the state functions as a kind of enormous Panopticon, in Foucault's sense, collecting data and producing norms, identities, deviances and projections of social development, and, as a result of those effects, also fears, passions, hopes and expectations.

The territorialization of space is not merely a bureaucratic function but also a characteristic effect of military order, so the processes Scott and Giddens describe can be seen as well as part of a process of military domination of society by the forces of 'legitimate' violence that make up the state. The body of the state is, originally, the bodies of the male citizens who defend the political community, and the territorial perception that Scott ascribes to the state is originally a military-strategic vision (Virilio 1986, 1989). Weber saw the bureaucracy of the state, like that of the large corporation, as modelled on the administration of the forces of violence, utilizing the techniques of discipline developed by modern military formations since the military revolution of the sixteenth and seventeenth centuries. The Renaissance recovery of mass military discipline in structured forms produced a singular, universal model of military organization that was emulated across Europe because of its unprecedented success. Modern bureaucracy had developed in parallel through a similar dynamic, in which it became adopted because of its extraordinary efficiency. Weber's analysis of the military and administrative aspects of the state in *Economy and Society* are closely entwined, a dual focus that has been followed by subsequent historical sociologists, in addition to their more explicit critical engagement with Marxist historical materialism, relating these forms to the development of modern capitalism.

The non-Marxist historical sociology of the state combined the focus of Weber's analysis of its administrative-bureaucratic and military aspects with the core problem for Marxism of relating economic domination to political power in the state (Tilly 1992; Mann 1986; Giddens 1985). However, these concerns direct historical sociology towards the institutions and forms of military and administrative power, with relatively little attention to the imperatives of legal-rationality or military knowledge. Organization is considered structurally, enabling it to be related to formations and processes of capital accumulation but neglecting internal developmental tendencies. Historical sociology thus tends to produce a narrative of the contingent development of structural capacities of the state which does not question its status in modernity as a concentration of power and as the object of political contention, but rather begins from those conditions as the given outcome of a process that is to be traced backwards through historical time.

The historical sociology of Norbert Elias takes the most long-term view of state formation (Elias 2000; Fletcher 1997), but the Eliasian account differs from others because it does not see the outcome of the process of state formation as accomplished or secured. Elias draws a link between the long-term historical centralization of political power, and especially the concentration of the means of violence from around the year AD 1000 through to the seventeenth century, and the emergence of a pacified modern subjectivity that is predisposed to recoil from violence in everyday life. Not only violence, but all the passions and impulses of the body have become subject to greater self-control in correlation with the centralizing concentration of authority and force in increasingly large units of political administration. However, Elias is careful to avoid the implication that society becomes pacified as a direct consequence of the development of the state's capacity for repression; modern people tend to avoid violence because it has become dysfunctional, not because they are more scared of punitive sanctions. The phenomenon in which Elias is interested is not repression but self-control, and the correlation is between internal and external pacification, of the psyche and of society (Elias 2000; Elias and Dunning 2008). He was not explaining the repression of an innate human tendency to violence, but rather treated violence as both effect and affect produced by the social and political conditions in which human subjectivity was socialized and through which societies and cultures were shaped over the long term (Elias 1997).

The scale on which Elias worked has provided theorists of the international state system with some interesting insights because it allows for long-term comparison within a developmental framework underpinned by sociological explanation (Kapteyn 2004). Beginning from a fragmentary mosaic of highly localized domination in Europe at the end of the first millennium AD (each knight within their own castle as ultimate secular authority over their village, a structure reproduced through primogeniture), there ensued a process of often violent competitive elimination through which the scope of this singular authority was enlarged, eventually resulting in one single authority dominating a large, integrated territory, in which it held a monopoly of violence.

The Civilizing Process (2000) traces the relationship between the centralization of authority and subjective pacification only through aristocratic channels, as strategies of violent competition are gradually supplanted among the courtiers by the mastery of cultural means and self-control. These in turn become habitual, displacing the earlier predisposition to violence, so that loss of self-control ceases to be a source of gratification and becomes a source of shame, emulated by aspiring factions and classes as the currency of status differentiation in the context of centralized and concentrated power that passes from the monarch to the modern state. In *The Germans* (1997), Elias shows how this process of cultural emulation can have perverse effects, producing rather than dispelling a violence which is all the more devastating because of its concentration in the state and the absence of a subjective limit to its use in the sense of the immediate gratification that had been effected by the functionality of violence in early medieval conditions of chronic uncertainty. Modern, state-endorsed violence can be relatively unlimited because it is dispassionate, as in the Terror of the French Revolution, the violence of fascism and the Holocaust, or the terrorist violence of factions such as the middle-class terrorists of the Baader–Meinhof group in 1970s Germany. However, for the unilinear Eliasian model of state formation, there can only be reversals or advances of the civilizing process. Elias scholars debate whether such instances of the breakdown of conditions of modern social pacificity can be best understood as de- or dys-civilizing processes – that is, whether they represent reversals or misdirections of the civilizing process. For long-term development, the perspective suggests that the next stage of the centralization of power in regional institutions, with their own elites and emergent cultures, is already emerging – for instance, in the shape of the EU. The limit extent of the macro-dimension of the civilizing process would be reached with the emergence of one singular sovereignty (Kapteyn 2004).

Elias's account largely escapes the model of power in state formation as the crude accumulation of resources that ultimately characterizes the accounts of Mann and Giddens. However, it is problematic because Elias neglects other sources of authority, such as religion, and his account depends implicitly on the under-theorized 'lengthening chains of dependency' in medieval trading patterns, which subsequent historical research has shown to have been less progressive than the theory seems to require, with extensive long-range trading breaking down at several points over his timespan and reconstructing itself each time from scratch rather than resuming previous patterns (Sassen 2006).

The same basic narrative of progressive state formation has been elaborated and explained in different ways by other historical sociologists. Charles Tilly's approach begins by suspending our preconceptions about legitimated power in an almost libertarian sociological argument equating the protection function of the state, which legitimates its fiscal and military monopoly, with a gangster protection racket. Fundamentally, Tilly (1992) argues, there is no effective sociological distinction between the taxing state and the extorting racketeer. He points out that most states can be traced back to such beginnings, though it is not necessary to do so in order to uphold the sociological equation. Furthermore, just as gangsters fight turf wars and develop greater capacities (or perish) in the process, so war makes states and states make war – in other words, warfare is at the core of the functions of the modern state because of its historical development and the fundamental, historically grounded basis of its relations to its subjects through violence. Ultimately, the state is simply the most effective form of protection racket.

Tilly argues like Elias that, in medieval Europe, there was a plurality of actors who possessed the means of coercion and of warfare (nobles who still had the right to wage war legitimately, but also nomadic discharged solders in roving bands, on land and sea, and locally based entrepreneurs of violence such as the Mafiosi). In addition, he notes the competitors to the centralized state as a mode of political organization, especially the hugely powerful city-states of the Renaissance. But throughout Western Europe, from the twelfth through to the nineteenth century, these competitors were gradually eliminated. Janice Thomson (1996) has shown that even relatively developed states made use of privatized forces up until the nineteenth century. More recently, the US state most notably has adjusted to its post-Cold War role as global enforcer of new norms of international order by utilizing private security companies to supplement its military forces. In parallel, while the long-term absence of an effectively functioning state in Somalia has produced a reappearance of piracy, warlordism has been prevalent for some prolonged periods of time in some areas, such as Afghanistan, and even appeared for a short time during the Bosnian wars of the 1990s in the former Yugoslavia.

Although this phenomenon is highly localized in one sense, it is also a global phenomenon – for instance, as the pirates' incursion into international shipping lanes leads to the development of procedures for ransom negotiations between global enterprises and the pirates who take ships and crew hostage, thus, in the absence of a sovereign authority, endowing piracy with rudimentary if tacit legitimation as a rational commercial exchange governed by emergent rules. This double-edged undercutting of the effective state monopoly of legitimate violence perhaps suggests that globalization is today reconfiguring the relationship between society and organized violence, from an exclusiveness under the modern state to a new social economy of violence in which the state monopoly yields or is challenged by a plurality of actors, some of whom do not aspire to establish a state form at all.

The organization of force was not the only factor in the emergence of the modern state. Tilly traces a historically specific functional correspondence between the state and emergent capitalism, which gives the modern state its particular form. He suggests three paths of state formation – coercion-intensive, capital-intensive and capitalized-coercion – each combining the military–state–capital nexus with different weighting (Tilly 1992: 30). In the last, most balanced, mode, Tilly describes a process in which capital accumulation and the accumulation of the means of coercion through fiscal revenues were not contradictory but mutually beneficial, and thus mutually reinforcing. The result produced the predominance of the modern state as the primary form of political organization on a global scale. In his historical sociology of the state, Tilly, like Elias, also saw the future as uncertain and the state as relatively precarious, and he too noted that its primary risk, in 1992, seemed to be the military–civil balance, at least in those parts of the world where the hopes and assumptions of modernization theory were most strongly invested, where the supposedly neutral and socially transcendent state form was still in undecided balance.

Further variants on this story are told by Poggi (1978) and Spruyt (1994), but, even as they seek to escape the structural determinism of modernization theory which saw the state as the necessary outcome of a teleological process of evolution, such explanations neglect the role of ideas and the historical evidence of those engaged in and commenting on such struggles in the process of state formation itself. In particular, the emergence of the concept of sovereignty as a model for a new kind of authority, replacing medieval kingship in early modern Europe, cannot be ignored, especially since that same concept underpinned the subsequent order between states that is today undergoing radical reconfiguration in globalization.

The state problematized

The perspective of the historical sociology of the state reflects the state today as the primary form of political organization for the entire planet. Despite predictions of its demise, its form seems to be ever more territorially extensive as claims are advanced to absorb in the territory of states all remaining 'global commons' (those geographical areas, such as the Arctic, which were hitherto outside the jurisdiction of any particular national authority and subject only to tacit agreements in international law). As well as this quantitative extension, the form of the state seems paradoxically intensified rather than diluted as an effect of globalization, with increasingly high standards of regulatory control of areas such as finance and trade now expected as a condition for membership of the international community of states that today underwrites sovereignty.

And yet the state is clearly not what it was. For in the early part of the twentieth century every state aimed to minimize its dependence on other states to guarantee its capacity to realize and maintain sovereignty (recognition by other states of the ultimate authority within a given territory) and maximize autonomy (the actual capacity to act independently of any external interests). At an extreme, that meant an aim of economic autarky (national self-sufficiency). Autarky today would clearly mean, at least in relative terms, severe austerity, if not actual impoverishment. North Korea is perhaps the only remaining example in 2010 of a state aspiring to independence from all outside links. The depth, extent and temporal irreversibility of globalization is illustrated in responses to the global financial crisis of 2008–9, against which even national resources such as the much vaunted energy independence of states such as Norway have provided no security, while state-level attempts to 'refinancialize' national economic activity flounder, even in the world's greatest economy, the USA. Economy today is no longer national, but global, inextricably interconnected on a world scale that now forms a distinct layer of activity and institutions that cannot be contained any longer under the term 'international', but need another term, such as transnational or global.

The emergence of international political institutions and practices has proceeded in parallel with that development (Beck 2007: 47–56), and Habermas (2001) has argued that this emergent system is already beginning to produce new norms, most notably the ethical principles of human rights which provide the basis for the substitution of nationalist identifications with the state by some form of postnational identification such as cosmopolitanism. Hirst (1997), however, pointed out that such developments remain dependent on the notion of the sovereign state, since the treaties establishing the institutions that develop the procedures from which new norms emerge are constituted only by agreement of the signatory states. Those norms are increasingly becoming used as conditions for recognition of statehood at the global level (Clark 2001). Even the USA under Bush was compelled as a requirement of legitimacy for its power to seek international coalitions or consensus for the invasions of Afghanistan and Iraq.

This example illustrates the significance of the question raised by Hirst, of whether the global is predicated on the national or vice versa, or which proceeds 'on licence' of the other. Hirst concedes that, in the context of this question, the status of the state has become fundamentally reconfigured as the primary *agent* of global order and regulation, its autonomy and even in extreme cases its sovereignty dependent to an increasing extent on its fulfilment of normative requirements developed at a level above that of its representative political function. Eliasians have thus seen this development as analogous to the transformation of the aristocracy of medieval Europe from quasi-independent feudal lords to the status of tax-collectors and magistrates, whose function was determined at court or in parliament. Sassen has pointed out that we cannot measure globalization in terms of conventional political science, as many of its processes bypass the institutions of both the national and the global, producing features such as the transnational social movements that contest globalist neo-liberalism, the formation of diasporic networks, and the development of translocal links between households across borders and continents (Sassen 2006).

It seems clear that the state is being transformed by globalization, gaining new functions as the agent of the process, while losing some of its old capacities. The question is, what exactly is the sovereign state of modernity turning into? This question matters for two reasons. Firstly, because the state continues to affect each of us in our social and personal lives, shaping those lives by both delimiting and enabling how we can live (and in some instances whether we live or die), and that effect is today more global than it has ever been before. Ironically, it is in the context of globalization that the state has finally become not merely the norm for modern political organization but, to the greatest extent ever, a lived reality for most people on earth. The state has become the normal form of political organization governing human social life. The few exceptions, areas where the state does not appear to function, such as Somalia or the Congo, are considered aberrant, and even there we assume the absence of the state to be temporary because, following Weber, we assume that, without the medium of the state, domination would be naked and unsustainable.

The second reason lies in the effects for the global order that is emerging from the system of states that has constituted the world since the break-up of the European colonial empires of the nineteenth and early twentieth centuries. Global order may be a function of the actions of nation-states, but if the form common to those states, upon which their interaction depends, is altered in that process, then the consequences could foreseeably undo not only the globalizing process but also the primacy of the state as a form of social and political organization. We thus need to ask what the state is becoming in itself, but also what the effect of that transformation may be for an order that is not yet even established or formed in discernible outline, and that remains for now only a promise or potentiality.

Rather than seeking to grasp the essence of the state, following historical sociology, we can thus begin to list its characteristics as a sociological formation, as an organization or assemblage, as it exists as a common form for modern societies, independently of types of regimes or ideologies of government. It is this particular form that has become globally extensive today. Even for Weber, however, the state was not a unity but a set of practices (Lassman 2000: 85). We can then begin to understand sovereignty in different ways, as an effect of particular practices rather than as an essential political relation which simply appears on the political horizon in early modernity and seems inevitable and necessary. The essential conception of sovereignty confines us to thinking about global order as either a reordering of the international order of the states-system or a consolidation of sovereignty in regional and even global power, but understanding sovereignty as an effect of practices enables us to analyse the emergence of an entirely different global order beyond conceptions of sovereignty raised to a global level.

State-systemic sovereignty

As well as establishing the international norm of non-interference by states in the internal affairs of other states, the principle of sovereignty as mutual recognition played a part in the convergence of states towards a common form, so they faced one another as clearly recognizable equivalents regardless of disparities in resources, pressuring alternative, unrecognizable forms out of the system. The international system can thus be treated as a kind of society in the simplest sense, with actors, interactions and a structure that produces real inequalities beneath the surface appearance of formal equality as sovereign states. It can be seen either as functional, exerting its own influence over its parts and even spontaneously evolving towards increasing integration, or as conflictual, a set of relations within which states each pursue their own interests. In conflict, this means that states can either pursue strategies of direct confrontation or attempt to undermine the recognition of their opponents in the international system.

The primary attribute of the modern state in international terms is its sovereignty, as the ultimate overarching authority within a given territory, but this ascribes to states a unity that they may not in fact possess. It treats what is in fact a heterogeneous set of institutions, practices and relations as a unitary entity. In short, it reifies and even personifies the state (Neocleous 2003). Political sociology has to unpack this assemblage, and even the attribute of sovereignty itself, rather than simply accepting it as an effect of a contract between states in the international agreements that formalize its mutual recognition, beginning with the Treaty of Westphalia. Sociology has conventionally been reluctant to discuss sovereignty as such, seeing this juridical concept as a conventional expression for the constructed effect of internal power relations and political practices characteristic of the modern state form, but such internalist accounts of sovereignty neglect its external condition, the mutual recognition of sovereign states. These relations of mutual recognition between sovereign states are usually seen as constituting a system or an order, which is the field of the discipline of international relations. However, treating states per se as actors, as the equivalent of social agents within such as system, reifies the contingently assembled character of 'the state' that is revealed by sociological analysis. Faced with the need to theorize transformation in the international system, or even its metamorphosis into a global order in which processes and relations at a transnational level may bypass national institutions, international relations theory has recently looked towards historical sociology for accounts of the modern state's emergence and development which might inform the analysis of current transformations by providing models that are not founded on the assumed existence of the state itself as a singular unit (Hobden 1998; Hobden and Hobson 2001). Similarly, sociology must now take account of sovereignty, not as a given but as a constituted quality that has real effects, in the process of the emergence of a new global order from the international system.

This approach is taken by Sassen (2006), who argues that tracing the development of globalization through global institutions ('endogenization') will be limited to description, unable to account for the appearance and authority of the institutions on which it focuses. Such 'endogenous' analysis of globalization mistakes indicators, in particular the emergence of transnational institutions such as the International Monetary Fund, for the phenomenon itself. Rather, Sassen argues that globalization in large part takes place 'inside the national'. She sees globalization as the reorientation and reassemblage of elements that previously made up the national and international order of the state and the states-system. The core of her argument is thus similar to that of Hirst, that the state and its sovereignty, rather than disappearing, are being reconfigured in globalization. This argument stands independently of the problems of methodology and ontology of her analysis, to 'take transhistorical components present in almost all societies and examine how they become assembled into different historical formations . . . today particular elements of TAR [territory, authority, rights] are being reassembled into novel global configurations' (Sassen 2006: 4). Sassen accepts that other categories could be substituted for those she has identified, and it is questionable whether these elements need to be seen as 'transhistorical' at all. In the process of global securitization that was accelerated by 9/11, in different political systems around the world, the power of presidential office and cabinet government generally has grown, as prerogative executive capacities increasingly become a conditional norm of an emergent global system (Neocleous 2008).

Hirst (1997) argues against endogeneity in the historical account of the emergence of sovereignty from recognition processes rather than as an effect of internal structural tendencies of state and society. In early modern Europe, most states did not have an effective monopoly of violence or absolute authority within their borders, and legitimate authority was divided between political and religious sources. Although sovereignty can be seen as an invention of legal scholars engaged in writing secular legitimations for absolutist rule to substitute for the idea of kingship as God-given, which could no longer be sustained after the Reformation (Krasner 2001), Hirst advances a sociological explanation for the conventional dating of the appearance of state sovereignty in diplomatic treaties of the seventeenth century.

The Reformation divided religious allegiance between rival authorities that cut across domains of political allegiance, producing divisions that were often theorized constitutionally in terms of established power and the common will, in which Quentin Skinner sees the origin of modern political ideology (Skinner 1978). In seventeenth-century Europe, the Treaty of Westphalia effectively ended the Wars of Religion by establishing the principle of non-intervention, effectively the beginning of the system of mutual recognition of sovereignty. Hirst points out that Westphalia did not of itself create the states-system and that the system did not emerge out of internal structural developments within states. Rather, it laid the foundational condition for both by effectively 'reducing international religious conflict below a crucial threshold', which enabled 'states to gain control of their societies' so that 'the emergence of the sovereign state and the system of states went together' (Hirst 1997: 219, 226). However, the political authority required for the treaty to work depended for its legitimacy on the popular contention of religious and secular authority.

Sovereignty can thus be understood as comprised of both authority and allegiance, command and obedience, the moments of constituted and constitutive power (Negri 2008). In structural terms, as contention of legitimate domination became opened from the time of resistance to absolutist monarchy, first under the rubric of religious affiliation and subsequently in the name of the common will, constituted power was posited in the apparatus of the state and constitutive power in 'the people' – a republican model corresponding to the movements of resistance and revolt through early modern European history, which had grounded resistance by positing the origins of power, as legitimate domination, in an 'ancient constitution' (Skinner 1978).

The act of constitution, however, engenders a force that then stands out against the power that constituted it even in the name of that original power. In modern versions, the power to decide for constituted, executive power is often justified as necessary to ensure security, whether of property, the individual person or, more amorphously, the public. However, the protector of the people constructed in this is but another version of the formula that Hobbes used in his theory of sovereignty in *Leviathan* ([1651] 1968), where all subjects implicitly consent to the establishment of a power over them in order to protect them from their own fear of the threat that each poses to the other. For Hobbes, there is no need for a constitutive moment, since it is rational that all should seek this situation, so that legitimation is already implicit in the universally individual faculty of reason itself. Though some have argued that globalization has produced an American empire, or at least failing aspirations to global hegemony, Joxe (2002) has used Hobbes as a critical counterpoint against what he analyses as the US military-capitalist policy of an 'empire of disorder' that promotes instability as a means of global control, enabling the USA to evade commitment to the routine maintenance functions of a global Hobbesian sovereign.

Sovereignty, power and war

Synthesizing Marx, Foucault, Deleuze and Guattari, and the republican tradition of political thought, Michael Hardt and Antonio Negri have attempted to theorize a novel form or mode of sovereignty – empire – emergent in the conditions of postmodernization and globalization (Hardt and Negri 2000). By empire, they mean neither American empire nor national sovereignty writ large. They dismiss what they call the 'substantialist' notion of sovereignty as the possession of a capacity and right for absolute domination, pointing out that sovereignty is always an object of contention between rival sources of constituted power and also that, rather than absolute domination, there is in reality a continually ongoing struggle for hegemony in which command depends on obedience. In the early twenty-first century, sovereignty is ebbing away from national states towards 'a new imperial power'.

Hitherto, sovereignty was always limited by requirements for mutual recognition in the states-system, but the new 'empire' has no outside. However, it is 'limited internally by the relationship between ruler and the ruled' (Negri 2008: 50), which means that its social constitution is immediately on the surface, immediately political, rather than mediated, subsumed and diffused within the container of the political nation-state, which shapes politics into particular institutional forms and delimits the parameters of the political agenda. As the constitutional becomes the social, so the social also becomes the constitutional, and the tension between constituted and constituent power, between ruler and ruled, between emergent institutions of global political domination and emergent processes of global social life, map onto each other. The new process, moreover, is no longer mediated by a politics of distribution within a container, or even of recognition within national culture and political citizenship, but by war.

Hardt and Negri's (2000) implication of an apocalyptic era of confrontation between the political and the tyrannical seems to follow a narrative of the republic as constitution rather than of the state as institution. They write at a very high level of abstraction while aspiring to inform concrete contemporary struggles, and their work is highly controversial, not least in its attempt to theorize the subject of revolt, or resistance, the constituent power which they call 'multitude'. The concept is grounded both in a political philosophical tradition from the early modern philosopher Spinoza and in a reworking of Marxist political economy, which theorizes 'social production' as everyday life and reconceptualizes the Marxist category of labour as 'cognitive labour'. Despite theoretical difficulties, their work has found considerable resonance in the globalized new social movements and the related revival of radical reimaginings of how we could live emerging from the global anti-capitalist and ecological movements.

However, the condition of those struggles is very different to those of the popular and class struggles of modernity. The limiting condition of the national container also reworks the operations of constituted power into a new form of sovereignty, which for Hardt and Negri radically reconfigures struggle itself. Sovereignty had already been transformed by the Cold War, in which it could no longer represent the aspirations of a people or an imagined national community, but now 'every war is a civil war' and sovereignty tends to become 'useless domination' because it can never succeed, can never become absolute, but must, in order to attempt to fulfil itself, mount a continuous 'police action' against the ruled and maintain eternal vigilance against the potentiality of the constitutive power on which it depends (Negri 2008: 57).

Far from undermining the legitimacy of an emergent structure of constituted power, however, war without end, even against its own subjects, could not only provide a focus and a demand for new global institutions and resources of control but also, ironically, secure the popular allegiance required as the other dimension of the command–obedience nexus. Koselleck (1988) argued that the perception of the state as neutral dated first from its function in promising order in contrast to the chaos and terror of the Wars of Religion. In the twentieth century, the postwar welfare consensus in which the state again appeared as the neutral administration of distribution was similarly predicated upon the historical experience of the consequences of societies given over to unbridled competition for resources, both internally in the class struggle and internationally between nation-states. In those historical instances, real and imaginary threats are not differentiated in the presentation of the institutional political promise of security, just as today 'security' conflates rivals in the constituted power of international crime syndicates or drugs gangs with the immanent constitutive power of those who challenge authority or even simply attempt to live beyond the control of political institutions (Toscano 2009).

The observation that fear provides a new source of legitimation today is extensive, from criminology to political theory, and is the core of the thesis of securitization to which I will return in chapter 8, but it also raises questions about recent changes in the condition of political consent and the persisting appeal of the promise of security in the framework of the nation-state, which, however much it is a 'zombie category' in an objective, analytical sense, still provides the lens through which most people experience not only domination, but also the hopes and fears that it produces.

5

Citizens, Nations and Nationalisms

We are born, and at that moment, it is as if we had signed a pact for the rest of our life, but a day may come when we will ask ourselves, Who signed this on my behalf? (Saramago 2007: 269)

Saramago's *Seeing* questions the notion of citizenship as subjection, but also its relation to political participation. In effect, the only citizens in his novel are the secret policemen sent by the government to destabilize everyday life in the city by disseminating misinformation. They turn against their superiors when they come to understand that their orders are intended to secure power for its own sake rather than to save the state, which proves merely an ideal to be deployed and dispensed with as required. The populace of the city refused their consent to constituted power by casting blank ballot papers in elections, but the novel illustrates the contradiction of that spontaneous refusal of power, since it is not organized; any conspiracy would immediately provide the government executive with the opponent they require to resume their game of politics in which they hold the trump card in their role as protector of citizens. It is always contentious whether citizenship is the subjection to, or the constitution of, authority. Stewart formulates these as, respectively, state citizenship and democratic citizenship (Stewart 2001: 187).

These distinctions roughly map onto differing comparative concepts of citizenship as it has developed from the monarchical and republican traditions in political thought, and further onto particular historical developments, in which the German and English developments embedded a passive and the Roman and French an active conception (Turner 1992).

Citizenship and social citizenship

However, contemporary English-language discussion of citizenship has been dominated by the model of social citizenship formulated by T. H. Marshall (Stewart 2001; Nash 2000; Isin and Turner 2002, 2008). Marshall's formulation was couched in terms of progressive political development, as the fulfilment of the promise of liberal Enlightenment in which private inequalities of access to goods would not constrain individual members of society from realizing their full potential for contribution to the public good, an aim to be accomplished through state management to equalize the distribution of opportunity.

Setting this discourse in historical context, Margaret Somers (2005) writes of how the 1990s saw 'an explosion of interest in citizenship' around Marshall's concept. She explains how Marshall's formulation elided the liberal conception of natural rights, which pertained to individuals in the private sphere, with the republican conception of citizenship as civic virtue, an exclusively public and political concept. Marshall developed his formulation through a progressivist account that traced the development of citizenship through three stages, in which, in early modernity, civil rights (such as rights against the monarch or state) developed and were institutionalized in law, political rights (from then on into the nineteenth century) were institutionalized in parliament and the franchise, and social rights (developed in the twentieth century) were embedded in the welfare state. Marshall's reformulation of the ancient concept of citizenship thus embedded it in subjection to a national state, but a state that was normatively defined by the discourse of modernist progressivism as a vehicle for social justice, which demands both state (passive) and democratic (active) citizenship.

Though the Marshallian approach situates sociological commentary securely within an academic paradigm, the concept on which it is founded has been unravelling almost since its inception as an ideal aspiration for modernizing progressive societies in the context of the postwar welfare state. Marshall's model was intended as a normative standard by which to evaluate the progress of the welfare state project and thus seems to lack validity as a reference point for sociological discourse that must acknowledge and offer theoretical explanations for the transformation of political contexts and concepts.

Marshall's formulation was distinctly related to Britain but has wider purchase, because it was grounded in the particular background conditions of the development of the welfare state in Western

Europe after the end of the Second World War. Marshall was writing at a point when membership of a political community with entitlements and responsibilities, conceptualized as citizenship, became a medium for the articulation of the politics of distribution, an effective institutional means for political moderation of the social question and thus a settlement of modern class struggle, which became reduced to technical problems concerning the delivery of equality of opportunity. The concept of social citizenship has served less effectively as a medium for a politics of recognition of multiple social identities which came to complicate those demands. Looking back, in historical context, the political functionality of the Marshallian concept appears relatively short-lived, but to explain its increasing irrelevance in terms of the rolling back of the state by neo-liberal forces in the 1980s is inadequate. Bauman has argued that the neo-liberal dismantling of the state institutions supporting the concept of social citizenship was possible because the concept itself had already become hollowed out, losing its original meaning (Bauman 2004: 42–7).

As Hirst observes, the crisis of citizenship is linked to changing social background conditions, in particular, the shift from mass society to an individualizing society, a shift effected not so much in the political as in the economic dimension, but on the side of consumption rather than production, in which individualized consumer expectations no longer correspond to the universalist, impersonal forms of delivery of the entitlements and demands of social citizenship (Hirst 1997: 6–7). This can be explained as a consequence of the effects of the postwar settlement itself, in which class aspirations found expression in consumer desires (Crook et al. 1992: 118–19). Similarly, the struggle for egalitarianism became mediated by technocratic management of the social system through policy development, detached from its origins in class, and was thus transformed from a source of collective discontent with the effects of social structure into a source of individual discontent with the very bureaucratic forms that underpinned egalitarian progress (Rancière 1995; Crouch 2004; Hirst 1997).

In political terms, the revolts of 1968 and after rejected the constraint of political struggle by the limit concepts of citizenship and the state, problematizing those institutions as the means of delivery of rights, inclusion and entitlements. Variations on the theme of citizenship (multicultural, ecological, etc.) have failed to reinstate it as a key object for political action by constitutive forces. Designed to mediate the politics of distribution, the universalist concept of citizenship has instead encountered first a politics that has demanded recognition of particular identities and particular needs for self-realization and then a politics of representation, as theorized by Hall, in which, regardless of content, the very relevance of national citizenship is contended.

Most recently, the precedence of the Marshallian model has finally been ceded under the impact of globalization. New critical perspectives begin by recognizing that the territorial framework of the nation-state may no longer provide a membership adequate for the subjects who require representation, an argument that derives from the 'globalization from below' perspective of cosmopolitanism (Isin and Turner 2008). Cosmopolitan citizenship will be discussed in a later chapter, but to do so effectively we need to consider citizenship in a wider context rather than simply in its most recent form.

The 'universality' of Marshall's formulation was exclusive in a number of senses. It required a distinction between 'citizens' and non-citizens that appeared straightforward in an imperial national-container context, but became problematized as that container became less insulated in political, population and cultural terms. It also implied a normative subject, not only in terms of nationality but also in terms of social identity. The disparity between his historical account and the emancipation of women implies that the model for social rights was the male citizen (Pateman 1988; Walby 1994). It assumed the subject of mass society, that everyone would have the same ambitions, the same range of needs, and thus needed the same opportunities, implicitly excluding or pathologizing difference, not only of gender but of other social identities also. Universalist citizenship functioned as a form of discursive authority, as delimiting and normalizing, in effect producing second-class citizens of those who could not measure up to the norms implicit in its construction of the subject of the state as the culturally homogeneous, male breadwinner head of a nuclear family (Lister 2003, 2008). In the context of challenges to the forms of authority of mass industrial society and the resulting shift from the politics of distribution to politics of recognition, universalist citizenship seemed to preclude the recognition of particularity that was necessary for it to succeed in its own idealist, inclusive terms. Eventually, with a politics of representation which challenges imposed identifications, and in the context of globalization eroding the container form of the nation-state so that citizenship no longer maps onto population, the very concept of citizenship itself comes into question, producing projects which attempt to map citizenship onto forms of authority other than the state, in proposals of transnational, postnational and cosmopolitan citizenship, where the same representational problems are carried over into the wider context.

Globalization challenges the link between citizenship and the territorial nation-state, but the concept also comes under challenge from social change and from attempts to live differently, since the protector function, and the welfare model in particular, embeds normative assumptions of their subjects regarding, for instance, permanent residence, paid employment, biological and mental health, sexuality, literacy, and so on. Attempts to live outside these parameters can be pathologized, invoking intervention by the state to normalize 'deviant' individuals. These limits of citizenship were revealed by the rise in the late twentieth century of new social movements, for instance of travellers, the unemployed, survivors of psychiatric treatment, prostitutes, linguistic and religious minorities – categories of resistance that were given by normative classifications of subjects by the state, intensifying under twentieth-century social welfare regimes: 'the classification of socially problematic individuals into precise categories, each requiring its own distinct form of intervention' (Miller and Rose 2008: 102–3).

It is thus questionable whether the discourse of human rights offers a very different approach, effectively enabling us to dispense with citizenship, but reproducing some of its inherent normative limitations of citizenship when the discourse is elaborated beyond the security of bare life that itself displaces the political as constitutive act, positing instead a pre-political subject of sovereign power as the condition of political action.

Citizenship as a strategy of government

While it has been assumed that citizenship can include different social identities by special disclaimers and inclusive legislation, this inevitably has the paradoxical effect of undermining universalism, establishing 'special' categories within citizenship which appear especially privileged in a way that all too easily becomes a source of prejudice and discrimination. This strategy also depends on the ideal of an adequately resourced and voluntarily interventionist state to ensure that legislation on such matters as equal opportunities and disabled access is realized in practice. But intervention is beyond the scope of a state bound by the limits of law only to defend individual rights, rather than to address emergent structural inequalities that may be increased as an unintentional consequence of the very

legislation intended to ameliorate them – such as when the requirement of maternity pay or disabled toilet facilities produces negative
discrimination in employment against women and the disabled. The
cumulative effect of such failure is to devalue the legitimacy of the
concept of social citizenship as a political medium. The strategy is
ultimately akin to that of assimilationism in 'race relations', and has
invoked radical critiques along the same lines of asserting the value
of other identities as 'different but equal' which produced the forces
expressed in the alternative citizenship policies of multiculturalism.

If the strategy above operates within social citizenship but exposes
its limitations, the strategy of multiculturalism quite deliberately sets
out to substitute criteria of difference or diversity for the underlying
criteria of sameness behind social citizenship. The policy has become
best known in relation to minority difference in cultural heritage,
'race' or ethnicity or religious community, but theorists have speculated how the same approach could be applied to gender (Young
1990) and other categories. Multiculturalism is a response to and
a demand of the assertion of social identities that were repressed,
stigmatized or ignored under the universalist model of citizenship.
However, it does not abandon the project of universalism, but
demands that respect for group difference is accorded the same entitlement of equality as provided for other opportunities. In a context
where some cultures are unequally valued or recognized, multiculturalism extends the principles of citizenship to accommodate rights
of equal recognition of culture, just as the addition of social rights in
Marshall's formulation provided for rights of equal opportunity in a
context of inequality in access to opportunity (Modood 2008).

Social rights, however, were never accorded to groups, only to
individuals. The resolution of the social question in the context of
the welfare state was accomplished by rendering the issue into the
context of liberalism, acknowledging only the individual as bearer of
rights. In a sense, multiculturalism can thus be seen as a governmental, post-ideological strategy to defuse the tensions of identity politics
and its potential to constitute new identities, aiming to keep those
struggles within institutionally demarcated limits but producing the
problem of what counts as culture for recognition.

With its celebration of hitherto repressed identities and provision
of inclusive identifications for citizens within the state, multiculturalism has produced an internal reorientation of British and other
national identities, in which even attempts to recover a monopoly of
the concept – as in the ideology of the far right – simply result in the
construction of a further 'minority', which is self-evidently just as

imaginary as any other identification, though none the less emotively powerful for all that. However, from the point of view of the politics of representation, multiculturalism institutionalizes the representational practices of resistance, enlists activists to governance and, in fixing identities, provides given categories of identification, rendering the constitutive power of identity politics, with its openness to critical deconstruction, into constituted power. The effect is to stifle innovation, channelling identity representation into familiar, stereotyped forms, while relegitimizing traditional and state authority.

From within the discourse of citizenship, multiculturalism's effect of fixing cultural identity is potentially disastrous because it institutionalizes and endorses social divisions, producing resentment and alienation in relations between its culturally given communities. Indeed, this aspect of multiculturalism appears effectively to endorse a perspective of irreducible difference, in common with ultra-nationalism and cultural racism. For citizenship theorists, this multiculturalist policy has thus become seen as reproducing and even intensifying the very prejudices and antagonisms it was designed to address, with some responses returning to the discourse of assimilation and others turning to the logic of separatism.

Buruma (2006) points out how multiculturalism is particularly vulnerable to critique where it has apparently endorsed intolerance embedded in cultural forms, producing reactions such as the Pim Fortuyn phenomenon in the Netherlands in 2002 or the deliberate provocation undertaken by Danish newspapers in 2005, publishing satirical cartoons of the Muslim Prophet Muhammad. Modood (2008) maps out courses for Islamic identification within the context of social prejudice that became intensified and specific after 9/11 which again echo those of Goffman's strategic options for the stigmatized – to internalize subordination, to hide that identity, to retreat into a community of like. These may include the development of a separatist ideology that in turn devalues the stigmatizing society, or the assertion of a positive Islamic identity that demands equal recognition within existing parameters of representation and interaction (Goffman 1969). Goffman is very aware of the risk of violence involved in the last course of action, but perhaps less so of the risk of the development of alternative values within self-enclosure that allows external prejudice to go unchallenged.

Multiculturalism seems to have succeeded best where it has been deployed as a conscious governmental strategy. In Northern Ireland, it is embedded in the Good Friday Agreement of the peace process between previously warring communities, providing the conceptual medium through which communities with apparently irreconcilable values can recognize cultural distinction as the basis of their authority as political actors, enabling them to engage in the 'game' of politics without loss of the source of cohesion that both holds those communities together internally and keeps them apart from each other. Strategic deployment of the discursive medium of multiculturalism within the peace process has provided the subjective grounds for engagement in politics where cultural differentiation and representation was already being used more or less consciously as a resource to secure the solidarity and cohesiveness of 'communities'. This discreet governmental strategy, designed to reshape perceptions of self and other and thus to act upon 'the conduct of conduct', appears cynical in terms of the normative presuppositions of the discourse of citizenship, but corresponds precisely to the analysis of governmentality.

Miller and Rose (2008) have traced and theorized the deployment by constituted power of new political strategies of governance through citizenship, emergent in response to the post-'68 crisis of the state–citizen relation. Governmentality perspectives displace social citizenship from the centre of the focus of the study of rule and subjection. In the new scenario, the tax-payer becomes treated as a customer of state services. This strategy reconstructs the state–citizen relation on the model of the consumer by enrolling agencies of expertise beyond the state. In this analysis of the practice of politics, government seeks to act more directly upon its subjects, by shaping subjectivity itself through a wide range of sources rather than operating only through the state (Barry et al. 1996).

Citizenship is also eclipsed to some extent in new political strategies of government through community. For Miller and Rose, the concept of the social per se is embedded in the project for which Marshallian citizenship was both symbol and objective. 'The practices that assembled the social certainly entailed "identification projects": programmes of mass schooling, of public housing, of public broadcasting, of social insurance, and so forth, had at their heart an image of the socially identified citizen, the person who, above all, understood themselves to be a member of a single integrated national society' (Miller and Rose 2008: 91). The discourse of community substitutes for social identification with the distant artifice of the national state, the apparently closer, more direct and more natural 'matrices of affinity'. Multiculturalism resituates the concept of citizenship in the identity category of community rather than society, governing through our allegiance to pre-existing (e.g. cultural or identity) communities, but in so doing it 'transforms them, invests them with new values, affiliates them to expertise and reconfigures relations of exclusion' (ibid.: 93).

Whether government operates through investment in consumption or in community, it changes citizenship from a relatively passive identification with the rights and obligations bequeathed by collective membership of a national society to an active pursuit of individual fulfilment through identification with culture and consumption (Miller and Rose 2008: 82). Even here, however, the sovereign still asserts itself in relation to those who refuse or otherwise attempt to live outside the parameters of governmental strategy, such as squatters or street protesters, who are subject instead of government to the state of exception and subsequently to disciplinary techniques of individualization and normalization.

The social/antisocial distinction focuses on behaviour and subjectivity rather than on relations. This distinction is a governmental strategy, but it is also a sovereign function of marginalization, creating zones of non-subjects in the governmental sense. Miller and Rose note that the formulation of an 'underclass' in the USA in the 1970s seemed to indicate a change in social categories from quantitative variation to a qualitative distinction. Whether discussed in terms of 'exclusion' or culpability, by social reformists or liberals, those who are marginalized become the object of specialist expertise in normalizing practice in which individuals are resituated in an active (and supplicant) relation to the community of inclusion, rather than addressed as a unitary social problem (Miller and Rose 2008: 104–5). This fragmentation of hitherto social problems as a function of the increasing specialization of interventionary disciplines shows how we can trace across these piecemeal policies, and the proliferation of agencies and expertise, general strategies of governmentalization which substitute new technologies and principles of ethical subjectivation and enterprise in place of the unitary social logic and regulatory mechanisms of welfare regimes.

The Foucauldian suspension of 'the social' as an effect of discursive practices and political strategies is an outcome of the same processes behind the critique of 'methodological nationalism' in the social sciences. Where Miller and Rose trace these limitations in terms of operations of government, other commentators have traced them in terms of the wider context of the national. However, in a wider historical and theoretical perspective, membership of a national community is not reducible to a passive relation to the state.

The concept of the nation

Ulrich Beck's dismissal of the 'zombie categories' of outmoded concepts in social science have probably been most contentiously debated in relation to the nation-state, where they have become complicated by the debate to conceptualize and theorize globalization. Despite changes in those background conditions, Beck's choice of metaphor undermines his own dismissal of the category of the nation: the zombie is characterized by its tendency, even though dead, to get up and walk and to wreak more havoc than the living, since it cannot be killed. It is animated not by reason, but by magic. Among those who believe in such spirits, curses really are powerful, and the zombie of the national is similarly real in so far as people act as though it is. Nationalism under conditions of globalization may be objectively empty, and it is certainly irrational, but it may still be able to animate the derelict corpse of the nation and to make it even more dangerous than it was as part of an organic nation-states system.

In the nineteenth century, nationalism promised a political expression of collective identity by identifying the state with its subject people as an organic unity coming to collective consciousness of itself in the state. It seemed clear that nationalism provided complex societies with a source of solidarity, motivation and secure belonging in a rapidly changing world, but in the first half of the twentieth century its trajectory propelled millions into death, destroyed entire cities, and motivated hatred and mass murder on an unprecedented scale. Organically conceived-of nations confronted one another on the field of total war, mobilizing their entire economies and populations in attempts to destroy those of others, while also turning inward to perceive deviance and otherness within the body of the nation in pathological terms, producing the clinically detached campaigns of extermination of the Holocaust.

We are accustomed to think of the state as a person, in the legacy of that nineteenth-century idea of the nation-state as an organic unity of people, territory, personality type, collective psychology, even as a community of fate, with a destiny to be fulfilled. This legacy in turn mapped onto the juridical, person-like legal status of the state as the Westphalian European states-system developed into an international order covering almost the entire globe. If the state appears as a person, it is because international order is based on the mutual recognition of states as sovereign, person-like entities. This mutual recognition constructs a system which began historically in the early modern era of absolutist regimes, when the body of the sovereign was considered as the source of sovereign authority, mediated by ritual and symbolism and, over time, by the administrative state apparatus that developed out of the extended royal household. The sovereign in the state was postulated by the concept of sovereignty as the ultimate power and the source of all liberties, so that the existence of subjects or citizens was confirmation of the legitimacy of that sovereign authority.

But parallel to this, in the republican tradition, the emphasis is very much on the sovereign state as representative of the sum of all the bodies that make it up, the people (Canovan 2005). In this tradition, Rousseau ([1755] 1973) reversed the common argument for the legitimacy of monarchical authority, arguing that if there is a sovereign it is only by virtue of the general will, so the quality of sovereignty resides always in the people in their constituent power rather than in the constituted power of the state. In this perspective, collective identification actively constitutes the political community, rather than passively identifying individuals with a pre-existing order and receiving the rights and obligations of that subjection, as in Miller and Rose's account. Rousseau opens for us a wider historical and theoretical perspective, in which membership of a national community is not reducible to a passive relation to the state.

In republican thought, the collective 'people', not the state, thus displaced the body of the monarch and appropriated the concept of sovereignty, which was now filled by the new imaginary entity. In this substitution of people for monarch, the sanctity of kingship also carried over, such that 'the people' took on a sacral quality, endowing executive authority for the protection of the popular will, however measured, as a moral duty of the highest order. It also meant that to die for one's country (i.e. the representation of the defence of a collective people) became a sacrificial passage into an exalted state of secular grace, a subject for ritual commemoration in which the nation would reaffirm itself through this commemorative representation.

This collective persona forms the basic template for modern nationalism, which developed through the republican, rather than the absolutist, concept of sovereignty and does not really appear until the nineteenth century, as an extensive reflex of the French Revolution. Patriotism had a longer history (for example, Machiavelli's identification with his city-state of Florence) as an identification with a particular state as a *political* entity, on the model of the ancient *polis*, an identification which transcended other political divisions as citizens provided their bodies in defence of their state as a political act. Only with the development of bio-politics as an outcome of practices of the eighteenth and nineteenth centuries, in the intensification of the state container's Panoptical function, do we get the emergence of nationalism as an assumption that the collective persona – the people – is a biological entity, in which the citizen's body is presupposed to be a given possession of the nation-state, such that its usage in war is a pre-political, even natural function.

Even today these two traditions, of nationalism and patriotism, are in tension, both in social reality and in sociological theory. We can differentiate between civic nationalism (or patriotism) and ethnic nationalism. Ethnic and civic nationalism are not politically exclusive and often coexist as sources of motivation and identity in the same state. For instance, US civic nationalists put the constitution at the core of their sense of collective identity, but US 'ethnic' nationalists range from adherents of racial biology, such as the Aryan Nation, through to those who hold that the basis of national identity is primarily cultural rather than political, and who therefore ascribe more importance to factors such as Christian religion than to the constitution, which they may subject to religious interpretation.

The distinction between civic and ethnic nationalism focuses on the identification itself, but Smith (1999, 2001) points out that different frameworks of analysis indicate different views of nationalism within sociology. There are two main approaches in the sociology of nationalism: that of the *modernists*, who view nations as political constructions, with both ethnic and civic nationalism as a source of identity arising from specific features of modern societies; and that of the *ethnicists*, who see nations as much longer-term cultural formations, though not necessarily as biologically distinct populations in the way that ethnic nationalists themselves tend to understand their collective identity. In a Durkheimian sociological approach, identification occurs through symbolic mediation in which even secular forms come to be treated as sociologically equivalent to sacred forms, in what is analysed as 'civil religion' (Durkheim 1992; Bellah 1967). In contrast to the ethnicist approach, this enables us to grasp the intensity common to all forms of nationalism without needing to ascribe an empirical reality to 'the people', which appears rather as a social fact in the Durkheimian sense – as real in so far as people act as though it is real. Smith (1995, 1999, 2004) has attempted to integrate these perspectives in his 'ethno-symbolist' approach to nationalism, which enables him both to trace long-term historical lineages of identification in culture and representation and to draw out the modernity of nationalisms.

Historical contextualization reveals shifting assessments of nationalism in sociological theory and in public perceptions. From the outset, modern nationalism was a paradoxical, contradictory phenomenon, originating in the European Enlightenment but with its basis in the Romanticism of resistance to Napoleonic imperialism, privileging irrational passions and feelings such as those of belonging, or of spiritual unity with a typical from of landscape, as a source of essential human identity. Nationalism is also a product of modernity, but traces an ancient lineage for its identification and claims legitimacy from tradition. It is an almost universal correlate of modernity, elevating the particular over the universal. Nationalism is contextual and ambivalent, providing a source of identity that may motivate resistance to oppression but that is itself also oppressive, often in actual practice, and always in its conceptual exclusivity. It has provided a secular motivational framework for the political realization of social justice but has also (like religion) generated genocide, and these two faces of nationalism have coexisted without effective contradiction because the identification of the social with the national can discursively and performatively exclude almost any category from the political rights of citizenship and the protection of the law.

Nationalism has appeared to have undergone a revival since the end of the Cold War in 1989, as if the ebb of grand-narrative universalist ideologies left a vacuum that was filled by other, local and minor, particular narratives of identity and emancipation as immediately available ideology, promoted by elites who used it with ruthless instrumentality to secure their own power even at the cost of state fragmentation and genocidal 'ethnic cleansing' (Kaldor 2006). Sociologists disagree, however, whether those particular identities were a latent reality that had been repressed under the old regime's universalist ideology, or whether they were an old illusion rekindled by opportunist leadership elites.

Of the sociological approaches to nationalism, the 'perennial' or ethno-symbolic approach argues for the former explanation. This approach implies that nationalism is inevitable, a facet of human social life with which we must come to terms rather than try to repress. However, this view had become unacceptable in the wake of the Second World War, which was seen as a consequence of nationalism unbridled by the constraints of the nation-state system. In the second half of the twentieth century, internationalism was popularly proposed as a more positive framework for human progress, supported by the ideology of modernization that projected the ultimate evolutionary development of an integrated universal nation-state. However, internationalism failed adequately to mediate the collapse of the ideological polarization of the Cold War, plunging Eastern and Central Europe back into fragmentary nationalisms.

The work of Anthony Smith has been singularly influential in propagating and developing the ethno-nationalist perspective in which the 'new nationalisms' figure as the reassertion of latent social reality. Smith (1998) argues that we can recognize nationalism as socially and culturally grounded, rather than as a purely political phenomenon, without accepting the biological claims of much ethnic nationalism. For him, nations are not 'natural' in the sense that they represent biological genetic populations, but they do represent historically long-term cultural identifications, which he refers to as *ethnie*, sustained and reproduced by myths, symbols and communication (primarily language). The ethnicist perspective enables us to understand the logic of cultural ethnic politics and even the cultural racism identified by Hall, but does not preclude a politics of human rights or even internationalism on the basis of that understanding. However, when qualified to avoid essentialism, ethnicist theories seem to add little to what we already knew – that culture provides a resource which political actors can draw upon both strategically and tactically. Alternatively, the modernist perspective sees these phenomena as a response to the sense of ontological insecurity produced by the erosion of modernist certainties in the context of globalization.

The archetypal case for arguments between the two approaches is the case of Jewish or Israeli nationalism. Smith argues that a common Jewish identity can be traced over the long term in the form of cultural practice (primarily religion), language forms and marriage customs (in fact, the observance of religious laws), which carried through the centuries an aspiration to return to the land of Israel. In modern times, that aspiration took on political form in Zionism. It is significant that Zionism was originally a secular movement but has become religious also, suggesting for Smith that it expresses something more deeply embedded than a modern political reflex. Modernists, however, point to the fact that Zionism appeared only in the nineteenth century, dissociating both Zionism and today's Israeli nationalism from Jewish cultural identity, and can trace many of the long-term cultural claims of Zionism to the modern political project (Pappe 2006). The argument is passionate and politically loaded in this case, but so it is in others, too.

Marxist analyses provide a way of bringing modernist and ethnicist perspectives together by recognizing that nationalism has some subjective reality in popular perceptions through cultural formations, but comprises a strategic resource for elite leadership, and by functioning as both a form of false consciousness and a unifying ideology for societies. However, Marxist theories of nationalism can be seen in historical and theoretical context as another form of modernization theory, just as Marxism itself can be understood as a radical variant of the state-centric response to the social question of modernity. The mainstream Marxist approach is framed by Lenin's work on nationalism, which acknowledges the subjective dimension of nationalism as a source of identity that must be accommodated internally by the state in the form of citizenship and externally as the right of all nations to self-determination, but sees it as ultimately subject to social and political conditions. Lenin ([1922] 1964) thus recognized how nationalism was at once a social reality, as an ideology, but also a fantastic effect of the social organization of capitalist economic production into national blocks.

Marxist writers on nationalism generally have reproduced Lenin's clear acknowledgement of *ethnie* as an ideological formation of modern capitalism, so that late Marxist writers such as Hobsbawm (1990) can thus be included with sociologists such as Ernest Gellner (1983, 1997) in the modernist approach. Hobsbawm's study, written under the impact of the nationalist revivals in Eastern Europe after 1989, emphasizes nationalism as ideology, as a programmatic project through which people seek to construct a sense of purpose for collective life, while Gellner, though recognizing its emotive force, analyses nationalism as an effect of modern social organization. For both these approaches, the nation is contingent, and it is therefore likely that globalization will produce something different, some other form in which the functions attributed to nationalism will be invested. These conclusions, however, perhaps neglect what both authors have in their different ways emphasized – the independence of nationalist identification, as an imaginary, from 'real' factors.

From ideology to imaginary

The modernist perspective is today dominated by Benedict Anderson's *Imagined Communities* (1983). Anderson's work was written as a reflection on the anti-colonial national liberation movements of the 1940s to 1970s, and hence it focuses primarily on nationalism as an emancipatory rather than an oppressive force, but acknowledges also how this is changed by the shift from constitutive to constituted power in the establishment of postcolonial regimes. Critically departing from the Leninist formulation of nationalism as ideology,

Anderson's focus on the imaginariness of nationalism has been the greatest influence drawn from his contribution, but reducing his analysis solely to the concept of the imaginary neglects the sociological conditions that he identifies for the development of nationalism, and so overlooks how these have been undercut by social change on a global scale since the 1980s, rendering nationalism anachronistic and unviable as a long-term identification, even as it persists as ideology and imaginary. Despite the erosion of the background conditions for nationalism, it persist today as a 'zombie' identification, functioning as an instrumental (and perhaps knowing) self-delusion, a fantasy enjoyment (Žižek 2004).

Anderson discusses three cultural 'roots' (or conditions) of modern nationalism. The first is a particular sense of community, the sense in which the nation inherited the salvationist and utopian functions of religion, taking up this role in the rationalized form of nationalism as a symbolic medium for grand-narrative political ideologies which themselves substituted for religious dogma. The second is the concept of embodied sovereignty, carried over from the association in medieval thought of 'the body politic' with the body of the king, which rendered the people sacrosanct. And the third is the transformation of temporality from messianic religious time, in which past and future are always simultaneously present, into a narrative historical time that is qualitatively identical with industrial working time, which the German critical theorist Walter Benjamin (1973) called '"homogeneous, empty time", in which simultaneity is . . . measured by clock and calendar' (Anderson 1983: 30).

Other factors that Anderson notes as conditions of nation-state formation, whether early modern or of the twentieth century, are the fragmentation of older (imperial and religious) unities – a pattern which fits the break-up of the Soviet bloc – the development of print media in vernacular languages, the creation of a public sphere and a diverse civil society, and the emergence, however demographically small, of an intelligentsia – an intellectual elite who act as ideological entrepreneurs. Anderson's personification of the subject, this 'historically clocked, imagined community', is the figure of the newspaper reader, engaged in a daily ritual of hierarchical communication, 'observing exact replicas of his own paper being consumed by his subway, barbershop, or residential neighbours . . . continually reassured that the imagined world is visibly rooted in everyday life' (Anderson 1983: 38). But as the circulation of newspapers drops, other sources of information such as the internet present events and issues in different contexts, disembedded from or unconstrained by the parameters of the national state, their consumption privatized rather than in the public domain. The anachronism of this figure vividly reveals the contemporary sociological status of the modern concept of the nation and nationalism as untrammelled fantasy, free from the conditions that Anderson traced.

This effect of this new context on the nation and nationalism can be explored through the new nationalisms that appeared after the break-up of the Union of Soviet Socialist Republics, a unity that perhaps could be better understood as an empire, particularly given the way that Russian imperial hegemony operated even more extensively through a gradation of less directly controlled states (the Eastern bloc, or Warsaw Pact countries) on its European periphery. The out-break of the new nationalisms was accompanied by violence in many (but not all) cases and was popularly interpreted by some observers as the revival of ancient identities (and hatreds) after repression, as though these populations are possessed by a historical 'thing' that had survived imperial suppression 'underground', beneath appear-ances that turned out to be no more than the trappings and artefac-tual constructions of socialist political ideology.

However, there is evidence that new nationalisms did not become a constitutive force spontaneously, but were fostered either by exist-ing elites as a substitute source of legitimation (hence many 'new nationalists' of the 1980s were ex-officials of the previous com-munist regimes) or by new elites, ideological entrepreneurs from the intelligentsia. These modernist explanations thus argue that the new nationalisms were the outcome of rational calculation by elites who ideologically manipulated the popular masses (Kaldor 2006). While this approach assumes that the masses are puppets of ideol-ogy, an alternative scenario can be sketched in which nationalism developed through a hegemonic process, where it simply became difficult for dissenters to extract themselves from the spectacle pre-sented by activists who assumed a real or symbolic position of lead-ership of civic events, for instance, placing themselves at the head of marches, appropriating monuments and ceremonies of collective remembrance, festivals, etc., as expressions of the national identity that their movement claims explicitly to embody, thus appropriat-ing everyday and civic life to their particular nationalist project. This strategy works through the symbolic representation of the nation or people to substitute one nationalism (e.g. the ethnic) for another, such as the civic, appropriating the spectacle for the articulation of a particular meaning – exclusive nationalism – with its intensity of demarcation reaching discursively deep into the body, in the concept of bloodlines, stereotypical body practices, traditional diet, and so on, promising closure, completion and the immediate psychological gratifications of a sense of self-certainty in an increasingly uncertain world (Kaufman 2001).

Seen in this sense, national celebrations and indeed any other form of representation are not given in meaning but are sites of political contention through cultural media. Critical hegemonic analysis argues that all political concepts can be contested, since their meaning is not embedded in but only mediated or articulated through texts, ceremonies and symbols. So, for instance, the content of national identity is not fixed but actually provides a site open to political contention (Laclau 1994). Through such media, radically alternative interpretations and projects can be articulated, in contrast to the delimited scope for political contention where social issues are reduced to technical delivery and procedural implementation in the politics of distribution and its institutionalization in electoralism, social citizenship and the welfare state. Those institutions have been ineffective media for the conduct of the politics of identity and representation, and thus the exercise of democratic citizenship has shifted not only in terms of its agenda but also in terms of the media through which it is pursued, away from institutional politics and into cultural and other mediations of the politics of representation (Trend 1995).

If new nationalisms are considered as a different category of phenomena, we are then able to reconsider 'existing' nationalisms as having also undergone a sociological shift in content as a consequence of their recontextualization in globalization, postmodernity and securitization. The outer appearance and form remain the same, but the way that nationalism motivates and structures political action (i.e. its relation to its subjects) has changed in ways that reach deep into its core and thus alter the meaning and the effects that it has in the world.

We can see the new nationalisms as a reflection of new social forces (postmodernity) and new conditions (globalization) in a number of ways. In this new context, new nationalisms provide differentiation. Firstly, they establish self-value against the 'levelling' effect of economic globalization, providing at least the illusion of security in the form of the sovereign nation-state as protector (Bauman 2004: 56). Secondly, in the context of capitalist globalization and continuity of the commodification process, the reduction of ethnicity to style becomes marketable (e.g. crafts, tourism, food, fashion, film) (Featherstone 1990).

In the new context, the assertion of nationhood also functions as normalization and as legitimation of claims to recognition in the global order. Thus, nationhood is a condition of entry to supra-national organizations (e.g. the EU, NATO) and represents a break with the modern past in which identity was defined by political ideology (e.g. communism, fascism), so that the performance of nationalism functions to emphasize distinct cultural identity as the basis of a claim to international status in a global political context which treats states as interchangeable agents. This can be seen most clearly in the symbolic dimension of international sports events and representations of national identity in florid and extravagant displays of conspicuous consumption of 'traditional' cultural forms at international political forums, where nationalism becomes an almost cynical self-representation for instrumental purposes.

On a darker note, this scenario sets up what we could call a performative economy of violence, in which the degree of transgression against hitherto accepted norms (such as the taboo against violence) in relation to an 'other' is an index of its effectiveness in creating a community 'of misdeed' – the closer the previous attachment and the more violent the differentiation, the greater the cohesion resulting from a shared need among perpetrators and bystanders to secure a particular protector in national sovereignty (Bauman 2004: 57–8). The violent assertions of Serbian, Croatian, Hutu, Hindi and Dayak national identities over the past two decades seem to fit this pattern, for example.

National identity as 'real' fantasy

Laclau's (1994) post-Marxist discourse analysis does not in itself explain the force of nationalism, but we can make use of the psychoanalytic concepts of denial and projection, given that nationalism presupposes a common thinking which grips and constitutes a collective in the same way that strong emotions affect us individually, sweeping us up, so that we become, for a moment, totally filled by rage, fear, grief, love or some other overwhelming emotion that makes us temporarily 'forget' our fragmented, indecisive, polyvocal self of competing and contradictory imperatives and desires. That affective collectivity is formed or constituted in part by projecting onto some 'other' whatever it is that we do not want to admit about ourselves, such as our duplicity, our aggression, our desperation, our incapacity to control our desires or our sense of our own animality. It is projected through an act of collective imagination, establishing a fantasy for collective identification, a process that does not even require an actual other, since the scapegoat is as fictitious an identification as the self or nation that is being imagined. Slavoj Žižek observed during the Balkan wars that this process was taking place not only in the Balkans but also in the representation of those conflicts in the West – critiques of projection onto the other must include a reflexive look at our own 'critical' projections, for instance, onto the 'new nationalisms' (Žižek 1992).

In the condition of globalization, in which long-standing certainties of identity are suddenly revealed not only as unrealistic but as having always been fantastical, fantastic identities become the norm, the global 'real'; so, 'while we recognize it as fantastic, we have no option but to act as though the imaginary were real' (Žižek 2006). Additionally, there is a pleasure of indulgence in fantasy identification, a sense of wholeness, and also of being absolved of responsibility for our actions because we imagine we are fulfilling deep, innate drives.

Nationalism seemed to be linked to the era of the nation-state, but it may be surviving and thriving in the context of globalization independently of the sovereign nation-state itself, as a free-floating discourse of identification, precisely because of its contradictions rather than despite them. Rather than depending on data or evidence, nationalism was always about interpretation, and, with the populist proliferation of information, that has ceased to be a closed social practice in which only experts could claim legitimate knowledge. Secondly there has been a radical democratization of access to cultural production and representation via those new media, in contrast to the one-way communication of the print technology on which Anderson focused. Changes in the public sphere appear to have re-opened spaces of debate that had been closed by the monopolization of media under public institutions and private corporations.

Thirdly, the disintegration of ideology makes nationalism a very different phenomenon from the nationalism of the nineteenth and the mid-twentieth centuries. Nationalism then functioned as a kind of false consciousness, but today, with the ubiquity of new communications technology and the universal access to information and to diverse viewpoints and perspectives, it is implausible to suggest that adherents of nationalism are innocently ignorant dupes of ideology. Today, nationalists know full well what they do in conjuring identifications of self and other out of a conjecture, but they do it anyway, in an enlightened false consciousness that is fully aware of its own self-deception. Nationalism provides a source of pleasure, of indulgence, as well as self-justification for what are really more venal motives.

A further factor is globalization – in an age of indeterminacy, nationalism can be understood as increasing because it provides a sense of ontological security (that is, it gives people a sense that they have something they need), but it has also become necessary. As globalization turns out to consist not of a smooth plane, in which all difference is eliminated in a liberal fantasy, but of deeply scored or striated space, composed of series of agents all performing the same functions in the (uni)form of national states which are thus politically indistinguishable, so national identification in a cultural sense, stressing the differentiation of 'peoples', actually becomes more necessary for global operations than it was in the time of the Westphalian inter-state system, when nation-states could be differentiated by different sovereign policies.

Finally, national identity has become commodifiable, a market as well as a political asset. The performance of culture in tourism is well known and has been analysed as both enabling the maintenance and recovery of traditions and reconfiguring those traditions, emptying them out, disembedding them from everyday life, and effectively alienating them from their producers as a product of labour under capitalism. Such performance then becomes economically reconfigured – culture itself becomes labour, with the capacity that the producer can recover their self-creation by taking back control over the process. The process is not limited to tourism but extends into production, too; and, since culture adds value, the process spreads to non-national, corporate enterprises, which invent their own distinctive culture to be performed by their employees, once again and further reducing the national state and its differentiation to parity with other agents of the globalization process. National identity may thus appear as analogous to a brand (Featherstone 1990).

In Saramago's novel *Seeing*, the city's collective refusal of political domination does not lead to the collapse of everyday life. Indeed, even the councillors continue to conduct their work under an ethos of public service, while privacy and private life similarly continue uninterrupted. This speculative fiction suggests that there are other ways of conceiving, or imagining, the relation of the public to the private, of the individual to society and to the state, than through the institutional conventions of citizenship and nation-state.

6

Civil Society and the Public Sphere

The scenario explored in fiction by Saramago (2007) bears some resemblance to the strategies pursued by the Czechoslovak dissident movement after the Russian repression of attempts to reform the political order from above (albeit driven by popular initiatives and support) in 1968. In response to the subsequent repression of even cultural expressions of resistance to the hegemony of the party, the dissident intellectual Vaclav Havel wrote a document that later circulated as a kind of unofficial manifesto through the loose networks of dissidence across Central Europe. In 'The Power of the Powerless', Havel points out that the legitimacy of totalitarian regimes is constructed out of minor, everyday, routine acts of acquiescence which construct the spectacle of legitimation as a panorama of signs with an ambiguous function, at once intimidatory and legitimatory, which 'reminds people where they are living and what is expected of them' (Havel [1978] 1985), so that routine acts of everyday life play a part in the reproduction of compliance and command.

Under such conditions, dissent becomes an internal relation to self, a refusal of the given meaning, a refusal to adjust to this norm, and where possible a refusal of those acts that 'make everyone an instrument of a mutual totality'. The very reaction of the authorities to such refusals, even those that are not political in any conventional sense, reveals 'the power of the powerless'. Through the associations of the 'independent life of society', 'a more coherent and visible initiative may emerge from this wide and anonymous hinterland, an initiative that transcends "merely" individual revolt' (Havel [1978] 1985), leading to the development of parallel social structures of private and non-political association that do not aim to overthrow the existing order, but that provide society with at least minimal cohesion and space for debate and speculation and constitute a latent basis for social reconstruction and even political opposition at some time in the future.

The power of the powerless in 'apolitical politics'

Havel's 'apolitical politics' is defined by a strategic refusal to participate in the political game in conditions where participation only legitimizes the existing regime (Havel 1988). This mode of political action in the Soviet bloc between 1968 and 1989 extended the scope of the political, to encompass not only the politics of representation but even everyday life. It developed separately and largely in isolation from parallel post-'68 developments elsewhere, and thus from other sources of ideas, but was articulated through the concept of civil society. There is some controversy whether this formulation was initiated by Western commentators and then adopted by Eastern European dissident intellectuals such as Havel, or whether the indigenous political traditions of Central Europe provided the source for this conceptualization of 'the independent life of society' (Havel [1978] 1985; Tismaneanu 1999). Whatever the case, the concept of civil society provided an alternative to the limitations of thinking political action through the concept of citizenship.

Active citizenship, which was not an available mode of activity under totalitarianism, has to remain essentially uncodified if it is not to become state citizenship, which illustrates the limits of the concept of citizenship per se in failing to encompass the constitutive aspect of power and right, or capacity. An alternative way of bringing together the social and the political, the public and the private, outside of the state is offered by the concept of civil society, which may stand in for constitutive power more effectively than some other formulations for a social agent of political change.

Histories of the concept of civil society

It is not usual to attempt to investigate civil society sociologically or to measure it empirically in the way that sociologists have investigated social class. As the articulation of a project, a resistance or refusal, opposition or alternative, civil society remains a normative concept. Its development as a concept is, however, tied to social and political relations. The concept of civil society is potentially all-inclusive, but implies the condition of civility for participation, distinct from a mob, as the term indicates both self-discipline and a shared code of conduct and underlying values. The concept is not defined in a fixed way but usually indicates some moral force, because 'civil society' relates to the source of public opinion, to a supposedly reasoning and well-behaved society that engages in reasoned debate about the common good.

Marx's critique of civil society points out that it posits an ideal of universal equality without regard for actually existing inequalities, as though public debate can be equal even if there is disparity in the level of material resources available to different individuals and groups. Subsequent feminist intensifications of this critique have argued that the concept not only entails an unrealistic assumption of equality but also assumes homogeneity of the subject of civil society, and is therefore inherently exclusive, since some individuals and groups will be unable to comply with the conditions for participation regardless of the distribution of resources. While feminists argue that this often excludes women, other social identities may also be inadvertently passed over, such as the deaf who do not use spoken language, or those who simply cannot access public discourse because the means to do so ignore their particular embodiment (for instance, wheelchair users). Feminists point out that classical civil society of the eighteenth century actually excluded women, slaves, children, paupers, prisoners, etc. (Pateman 1988). However, the concept enables us to think more precisely than just talking about 'society' or the social, because it indicates a network of voluntary association that constitutes public opinion and that can have a real force.

In social and political thought up the eighteenth century, to be a citizen was to be a member of civil society, and 'civil society' and 'the state' were interchangeable terms (Keane 1988a: 36). During the European Renaissance, civic humanism provided state and subjects alike with reasoned secular guidance for conduct in the emergent public domain. However, over the seventeenth and eighteenth centuries, civil society came to be thought of as distinct from the state, a change in concept that Keane traces to the Anglo-American context, principally in the work of Adam Ferguson and Thomas Paine.

The concept is sometimes misused as interchangeable with community, but in fact was intended to denote a form of *association* distinct from community, a web or network of intersecting elective or voluntary solidarity characteristic of modern society, in contrast to traditional community (Heelas et al. 1995). The original term was revolutionary in its implications, because the 'civil' part was intended to differentiate this potentially all-inclusive concept from the more exclusive notion of 'society', as the network of the aristocracy.

Ferguson's developmental account draws a model of an emergent integrated state-society that would tend towards despotism were it not for independent social associations (Keane 1988a: 41–4). Thomas Paine added to these a natural rights element which established civil society in the associational sense as an index for the legitimacy of states, but also made it an expression of human need which produces emotive social solidarity, reducing the role of the state to that of guardian. The naturalistic account was jettisoned by Hegel, for whom civil society was the outcome of historical transformation, appearing only as bourgeois society. Divided against itself (individual against individual, class against class), civil society is unable to overcome its particularity and so requires the sovereign state for its political order.

Keane (1988a) points out that, contrary to the property-centred account that Marx and Engels developed from Hegel, in the nineteenth and twentieth centuries civil society came to be seen as a refuge from and a site of resistance to unbridled state sovereignty, or despotism. Through the course of this development of the concept, in assuming a characteristic self-organization and a quality of civility and mutual respect in the interaction of its members, civil society came to figure as a moral counterpart to citizenship. While the normative and evolutionary dimensions underpinning the concept of social citizenship had introduced a moral register for the politics of the welfare state, the concept of civil society did the same for politics beyond welfare citizenship, so that the 'we/they' framework of the oppositional politics of distribution is displaced by a 'good–evil' axis (Mouffe 2005: 75).

The effect has been to reify the concept of civil society as a 'good' against the state as a 'bad' (Foucault 1988: 167–8), a simplism that, at least initially after 1989, rendered post-communist societies, where civil society was necessarily relatively weak and (as Havel projected) embryonic, without a source of resistance to the particularities of private, propertied interests described by Hegel, whether those arrived from outside or developed from within in the privatization of the state property. Ray has analytically differentiated the concept of civil society used in Eastern and Central Europe in the 1970s and 1980s from the development of the concept in social and political thought from the Enlightenment. In Eastern Europe, civil society functioned as a 'harbinger of a new type of society', to describe how 'a democratic polity is embedded in dense networks of civil associations' (Ray 2001).

Eastern European participants and theorists such as Mastnak and Havel (Keane 1988b) have argued that the concept was in fact reinvented among dissident networks before 1989 as a normative category and a focus for discussion, and was only subsequently 'reimported' into the West as an analytical concept by which these revolts were retrospectively explained from outside. The argument has significant theoretical implications, since it questions whether civil society is something that pre-exists the dissent it thus supposedly produced as its expression, as in the Western version, or whether it was an effect constituted in political discourse, as in the Eastern version.

In the articulation of dissidence, the concept of civil society functions as the subject of constitutive power. The crucial question for contemporary political sociology is whether the normative presuppositions of the concept of civil society enable us adequately to theorize the capacity for experimentation and the production of ideas and practices about new ways to live demanded by a postmodernizing, globalizing society under pressure from the recuperative forces of securitization. Hirst (1997: 161), following Koselleck, points out how civil society took on a positive moral and emancipatory role in early modernity only in relation to the emergence of absolutist monarchy in the seventeenth century. Civil society offers to substitute harmony for the pursuit of a particular sovereign interest through the state, and so also offers harmonious international relations. However, it can only offer this in its character as constitutive power, in contrast to the constituted power confronting it. The civil society of dissidence that was created in resistance to the communist regimes failed to provide a source of solidarity for the subsequent post-Soviet societies because its constitutive role was over once the old regime fell (ibid.: 172).

Hirst argues that what was needed in post-Soviet society was the rapid creation of parties that could provide institutional expression of the plural interests of an actually divided civil society rather than the idealist maintenance of the illusion of a homogeneous civil society that had sustained the resistance to communist hegemony, a move towards his own advocacy of associational democracy through the democratization of society and the pluralization of the state. However, Hirst's associationalism depends on precisely the kind of stable social relations and identities that are rapidly becoming 'fluid' under conditions of postmodernization and globalization, and we can similarly question whether civil society, with its focus on associations rather than networks and its assumption of a bounded community, could be similarly problematized. In subsequent chapters I will address, as an alternative to resurgent nationalisms and identity politics, the idea of 'global civil society', which has been propounded as an empirical reality (Keane 2003) and posited as the normative, projected grounding for 'cosmopolitan' democracy in global politics (Archibugi 2003).

Critiques of the concept of civil society

While Hirst's critique of the claims of homogeneity derives from recognition of plural interest groups, Tester has also pursued a critique of the concept of civil society on the grounds of its 'reduction of all individuals to some homogenous quality shared by all' (Tester 1992: 129). This analysis seems aimed at an Arendtian understanding of civil society as composed of humans with universal capacities for action, which is conceived primarily in terms of speech, betraying the exclusiveness inherent in such qualifications (Arendt 1958). Tester argues that it is difficult to reconcile this with the grounding of the claims made for the inherently democratic quality of civil society. Schmitt had made a similar observation about democracy requiring the elimination of heterogeneity, an observation that could equally be applied to the concept of citizenship as it became exposed by feminist and multicultural critiques. However, such reflections do not take us as far as Hegel had already done in analysing these phenomena in the general terms of particularity and universality.

Discussions of how civil society could provide the basis for political life, or simply for democracy, thus eventually return to the question of the conditions of civil society itself. This can be clearly illustrated through a debate implicit in the discussions among radical democrats in the West in the wake of the events of 1989. Michael Walzer (1992) argued that civil society could be thought of as the condition for all other identifications proposed for 'the good life', ideologically encoded identifications with citizenship (social reformism), creative labour (Marx), the market (liberalism) or the nation as bearer of tradition (conservatism). He argued that, unlike these institutional identifications, civil society does not make normative demands, but he does so only by naturalizing the concept as the condition (sociability) of all other social identifications. Thus, civil society articulates the social and the political, but the social becomes reduced to the natural, as given sociability. In implicit reply, McClure (in the same volume) reminds us that the social is itself contentious: 'its multiple identities are themselves not given, but contingently constructed and reconstructed through the reiteration of cultural codes and through participation in social practices through which these codes are enacted in daily life' (McClure 1992: 123). McClure's response suggests that, rather than looking to the institution of citizenship as the vehicle for the ongoing project of a truly political life, or democracy (Mouffe 1992: 238), we could look instead to everyday life (Vaneigem 1979), a proposal that will be followed up in chapter 7.

Foucault's comments on civil society as it was being used to theorize the Polish Solidarity movement against communism, in contrast, argue that we need to retain a historical understanding of civil society, which may no longer be a relevant concept to theorize constitutive power (Foucault 1988: 167–8). In the eighteenth century, civil society faced the absolutist state, either in practice or in theory, and was thus imagined as a relatively coherent and unitary entity, but that homogeneity consisted in its relation to the state. Where new social movements direct their attention away from the state and towards power operating in other modalities, on other registers, beyond the state, a new source of ethical legitimation and solidarity is required across those disparate movements. For some, this demands a new conceptualization of the subject of resistance and of constitutive power that is not limited by the normative and structural constraints of civil society, such as 'multitude' (Negri 2008). The conditions for the emergence of this new subject are problematic, so it is worth looking at the conditions of civil society.

The public sphere

In Saramago's novel *Seeing*, civil society never articulates itself, though the author is clear that something more coherent than individual self-interest, but less institutional than a secret conspiracy, binds people together after the delegitimation and withdrawal of the state executive. Everyday life, even the functions of public service, continues, mundanely and banally, but as the life of a given, bounded community that apparently does not aspire to be or to become anything else. In that sense, Saramago's city refuses not only the state, and its citizenship, but also eschews the political in a way that Eastern European dissidents did not, even if their associational discourse eventually failed to sustain itself as the basis for a new polity. Saramago's vision is universally apolitical, not apolitical in the dissidents' particular sense, which enabled an alternative political discourse. Its only representative, the councillor with whom the government retains contact, simply withdraws from politics rather than speaking on behalf of the city, disengaging from the game but not entering another. However, government machinations proceed not only through the activities of their secret agents in the city but also through the manipulation of a gullible press, eager for scandal and engaged in intense competition.

One of the ways in which civil society can be understood as political in Havel's sense is through its role in producing meaning, in interpretation and representation, the work of the media. The emergence of civil society and of democracy is traced in tandem with the emergence of a mediated public sphere in early modernity, most notably in the work of Habermas ([1962] 1989), who argued that the democratic functions of the public sphere were undermined by the exploitation of private (in contrast to public) interests much as Saramago suggests in his novel, which could be about both the travails of politics in our era and the failure of alternatives, as a kind of double tragedy.

However, we also need to recognize that the means of representation and interpretation, of making social meaning, in our society have changed in multiple ways in the past thirty years – in scope (from national to global), in access (new technologies progressively democratizing the means of broadcasting and communication) and in relation (from one-way flows to the almost universal ability to interact discursively via the internet). Those same developments, however, have not been matched by an extension of the normative criteria that Habermas identified as indicators of the democratizing function of media, but rather have contracted, so that new media and information and communication technologies seem to invoke not social solidarity, but division, not individual sociability, independence and confidence, but isolation, dependence and insecurity, not democracy, but authoritarianism.

The politics of representation are played out not only in the media but also in self-presentation in everyday life, and take on an increasing importance in a society which some observers argue is characterized by the ubiquity of images constituting ideology, or identity (Debord [1967] 1992; Kellner 1994; Best and Kellner 1997). Such concerns raise the issue of the political effects of the mass media and questions of who controls it that have been the subject of sociological theorizing since the mid-twentieth century (Adorno and Horkheimer [1947] 1997). Against such negatively critical analysis, Habermas developed the concept of the public sphere to think through the positive potentialities of a common discourse of representation and interpretation. He traced the emergence of the public sphere in a comparative historical sociology of developments within civil society in eighteenth-century Europe. More recently, the concept of the public sphere is used in debates on the significance of mass media and ICT.

Civil society refers to a *public* domain that is not part of the state, and the public sphere can be most readily understood as the space between civil society and the state. That 'space' can be anywhere – discussions in the street, in newspapers, on radio, TV or the internet (especially blogs, email discussion lists, etc.) – anywhere that communication is public rather than private but that is still not part of the state (so email discussion lists could be part of the public sphere, but not chat rooms, which can be confined to private, intimate exchanges). Like civil society, the public sphere is at once social and political: 'a realm of our social life in which something approaching public opinion can be formed . . . A portion of the public sphere comes into being in every conversation in which private citizens assemble to form a public body' (Habermas [1962] 1989: 102–3). So the public sphere is a space which transforms private into public opinion, when arguments are presented on their own merits rather than on the authority of the speaker. Rather than authority being vested in an office or title, legitimation in the public sphere depends on the conditions of participation: 'authority is vested in the public sphere itself' (Eickelman and Salvatore 2002: 96).

Habermas's work on the public sphere effectively reversed the pessimism of critical theory, which had argued that modern societies were becoming 'totally administered societies' in which 'public opinion' was reduced to the sum of mass individual consumer choices manipulated through advertising and marketing, extending to politics through pre-packaged choices presented as both rational and desirable because they were designed by technical experts. The political thus became displaced by the institutional games and agendas of professional politicians, in which parties competed for the allegiance of voters like corn flake manufacturers competing for consumers.

Habermas's central work, *The Structural Transformation of the Public Sphere* ([1962] 1989), traced the development of this technocratic turn in modern politics but came to rather more hopeful conclusions than his predecessors in critical theory. Habermas concluded that, although the public sphere was distorted and deformed by power and capital in modern society, it retained the potential to develop independently of those state and corporate interests.

The historical sociology of the public sphere

Habermas traces the development of the public sphere out of the feudal Middle Ages, in which there was no public and no private domain, only a distinction between the state (embodied in the sovereign and his household) and subjects. In that era, only the state/sovereign could make use of means of mass communication or spectacle. However, the development of commerce in the late Middle Ages produced trade newsletters that circulated among merchants, reporting on harvests and markets around Europe, new taxes, the comparison of weights and measures in different places, outbreaks of war or banditry in particular locations, opportunities to tender for state contracts, and so on. Thus, 'Traffic in news developed alongside traffic in commodities' (Habermas [1962] 1989: 16).

The story Habermas tells from there is much like Tilly's, as the state and capital began their symbiotic but fraught relationship. The patrimonial state became the bureaucratic state, with greater independence from the monarch's personal assets, while the king became the crown, increasingly dependent on revenues from taxes and duties, and increasingly depersonalized a permanent bureaucracy that survived royal death and succession. The term 'public' came to refer to matters to do with this emergent depersonalized state (as we use it today, when the 'public sector' means the state sector). Rather than being financed out of the assets of the king and authorized by his bodily presence, in Europe by the eighteenth century the state was a bureaucratic structure dependent on tax revenues, its authority dependent on law and military power rather than tradition. It began to use the press that had developed out of the merchants' newsletters as a medium for proclaiming (we could say *publicizing*) taxes, duties, regulations, etc. As the state supervised economic activity and provided the conditions that underpinned and enabled the market to operate, so that function became an issue of discussion and debate. So now the state confronted the economic sphere upon which it had become dependent. 'Public authority was consolidated into a palpable object confronting those who were merely subject to it and who at first were only negatively defined by it . . . Civil society came into existence as the corollary of a depersonalized state authority' (Habermas [1962] 1989: 18). This argument is very clearly distinct from the naturalistic explanation of civil society propounded by Walzer after the classical theorists, and is closer to Foucault's observations.

So the interdependency of state and civil society produced a state that needed to use civil means of communication to get its message across and a civil society that began to have things to say about how the state performed its (public) functions.

> Because, on the one hand, the society now confronting the state clearly separated a private domain from public authority and . . . on the other hand, it had turned the production of life into something transcending the confines of private domestic authority and becoming a zone of public interest, that zone of administrative contact now became critical . . . in the sense that it provoked the critical judgement of a public making use of its reason. (Habermas [1962] 1989: 24)

Thus, publicity became more than reporting the actions of the sovereign monarch, news more than private matters circulating among individuals, and the means of communication that had developed to circulate commercial news became rapidly more developed in technology and shifted from reportage to discourse, in the sense of reasoned argument and discussion. At the same time, civil society as the association of private individuals produced a capacity for commentary on matters deemed of 'public' significance, rather than merely important to its participants as private individuals.

Especially in England, Habermas argues, the press became a medium not just for economic reporting and state pronouncements but for critical opinion pieces, opening a space between civil society and the state – a public sphere – that was far wider than the press itself. At this time, newspapers were not only read by individuals, but were read aloud in 'public', in the expectation of generating expressions of solidarity of opinion. Habermas points out particularly the coffee-houses that proliferated in England, of which by 1810 there were 3,000 in London, each with its core of regulars. Habermas argues that these were essentially democratic because everyone entered on an equal basis, though we need to retain sight of the limitations of this historical analysis as the basis for a general conceptual and analytical formulation, since women, and workmen, were barred from the coffee-houses. The question is whether this oversight of identity (and Habermas undertook this work before the development of identity politics challenged such implicit normative assumptions) carries over into current uses of the concept of the public sphere, whether it is inherent in the structural parameters of the concept itself.

In France, there were *salons* and, in Germany, *Tischgesellschaften*, often organized by women, who were thus not entirely excluded from this original public sphere. From these specifics, Habermas analyses common characteristics from which he extrapolates conditions for the development of democracy, and it is here, rather than in the historical specificity of the original forms, that we would need to identify assumptions as identity exclusions.

Firstly, these institutions provided conditions of 'social intercourse that, far from presupposing equality of status, disregarded status altogether' (Habermas [1962] 1989: 36). It was not social hierarchy in office or economic standing, but the better argument that carried the day, with the result that these conditions produced a common public interest in equality for discursive purposes as the basis for the validation of any argument. Secondly, the matters of 'common concern' were not merely economic and political but also cultural – the public sphere was from the start concerned with representation in cultural as well as political forms, and cultural discussions often provided a milieu in which powerful collective identities (such as national identities) were shaped. Also, out of this milieu came the modern concept of art as something separate from the reproduction of life. Artists in the public sphere were deemed to represent something 'higher', to represent society to itself, and were thus elevated to the status of seer.

Thirdly, in principle, the public sphere was inclusive: 'it could never close itself off entirely and become consolidated as a clique', because then the discussion (discourse in a Habermasian sense) would no longer be public, its concerns would no longer be general, applicable to all – 'everyone had to be able to participate' (Habermas [1962] 1989: 37). Fourthly, Habermas points out that the discourse of the public sphere was very different to that of community, the previous frame for discussing matters of common concern. In the public sphere, each spoke as an individual. This makes the concept of the public sphere very different to the notion of community that is often counterposed to the state today, where solidarity is based on homogeneity and speaks with 'one voice'. The public sphere, in contrast, is grounded in a plurality of voices that may not be particularly harmonious. Public opinion can be a polyphony, but any co-ordination emerges, rather than being orchestrated by given expectations, and thus it may equally be discordant, difficult, indeterminate and confusing.

Though Stewart (2001) argues that Habermas idealizes the public sphere as a source of consensus, this is not necessary for the public sphere to function, as Habermas claims, since its most important effect is not to produce consensus on issues but to embed democracy in implicit principles of widespread social practice (Habermas [1962] 1989: 250). The problem Habermas's study invokes is a different one:

in setting up the public sphere as a condition of active democracy, he establishes normative conditions that are both historically and structurally contingent, and questionably inclusive. Habermas focused on these particular and exclusively bourgeois institutions, but other social institutions and settings in the same period provided similar conditions within their parameters of membership, producing a plurality of competing 'publics', each with its own frame of 'universal' interest (Fraser 1992; Stewart 2001). However, if each public sphere simply represented the standpoint of a particular interest group, then the universalist public sphere as Habermas describes it was actually a fiction, an imaginary, like the state, the nation and civil society. This would liberate the concept from the structural conditions that Habermas traces, so we could then say that 'the public sphere' is always contingent, continually re-emerging, an immanent effect of civil society and the state, and perhaps something that can be produced as a strategy of constitutive power. This would bring it closer to the networks of discourse that Havel envisaged as arising from his 'apolitical politics' of 'parallel associations', outside the structures of domination, where each is committed to living the truth, even at the expense of the pursuit of their particular interests. I will discuss below how this has been seen by some of the proponents of the new social conditions made possible by new communications technologies.

The eclipse of the public sphere

The public sphere enabled reason to emerge from opinion as a critical authority on the exercise of social and political power, but became simply an organ for the production of 'public opinion' as an object shaped to correspond to the spectacular presentation of particular programmes of private interest (Habermas [1962] 1989: 236). Habermas argues that the democratizing effect of the public sphere was undermined by structural changes, but since it is actually the source of some of those changes it is difficult to see how he supposes it is sustainable enough to provide the criteria necessary for normative underpinnings of democracy.

Firstly, the public sphere succumbs to democratic overextension without economic emancipation. Rational-critical debate was sustained by its emancipation from the conditions of reproduction of life since, although it had arisen from economic activity, public debate was possible because its participants had some degree of control over their own time. Habermas has acknowledged that restricting his

analysis to the bourgeoisie neglected historical evidence of a plebe-
ian public sphere of the eighteenth and early nineteenth centuries
(Linebaugh 1991). However, as the notion of the public became
extended to include the working classes, who were increasingly
subject to the introduction of clock time to regulate work (Thompson
1970), their part could be undertaken only in leisure time, making
public debate an appendage of work, in which labour reproduced
itself for exploitation. Secondly, the media were transformed by
commercialization. Most eighteenth-century journals, which printed
articles, essays and letters as public discussion, were run at a loss
by early newspaper proprietors, who saw themselves as providing
a forum for public expression rather than presenting a package of
opinions. However, commercial competition drove these out of
business, with the result that the press retreated from producing
public opinion for active engagement to producing private opinion
for passive consumption. Thirdly, group needs began to enter into
the discourse of the public sphere, so it ceased to be 'the medium
of public discussions of private persons' attempting to appeal to the
common interest, and became a mere platform for partisan groups to
make claims for themselves upon the state (for instance, the working
classes demanding support from the state to ease the effects of market
forces, or employers demanding lower taxes on profits). The public
sphere thus became a medium for the politics of distribution, excluding more radical speculative discussion of how we might live. Rather,
it was filled by ideology and the representation of party political
programmes and ultimately collapsed into a space which political
elites use for plebiscitary purposes, which Habermas refers to as the
'refeudalization' of politics.

Public spheres today?

Habermas himself has vacillated over whether the original conditions
of the public sphere could be re-created in the late twentieth and the
early twenty-first century. Various media have been touted as inau-
gurating conditions for a new public sphere, from raves to fanzines
to pirate and community radio to the internet, but none seem so far
to correspond to the conditions that Habermas ascribes to the public
sphere of the seventeenth and eighteenth centuries, which nevertheless he says provides us with many of the key ideals of modern democratic thought. Critics (Calhoun 1992) have taken issue with the
structural parameters of Habermas's analysis, but, if changes in the

organization of work and associated class recomposition undermined the public sphere of the nineteenth century, it is possible to see new conditions for such a sphere opening today with the spread of precarious employment, increased 'free time' and widespread ICT expertise as its new social conditions.

Fraser's (1992) critique reminds us that the public sphere even in Habermas's idealist definition, and much more in practice, was itself particular in its differentiation from the private sphere, yet the latter was not an apolitical or a pre-political space, as it was structured by relations of domination and subjection and suffused with the ideology of naturalized gender roles, which implicitly and inevitably structured and conditioned also the differentiation of the public domain and the 'universal' interests articulated in the public sphere. A public sphere demands the eschewal, the abnegation, of social identity, and the domain of political democracy would thus prove an unusable site in which to renegotiate difference, since it is a condition of its function that difference be ignored.

However, in contrast to postmodernist refusals of the public sphere on the grounds of its prerequisite claim for discourse to be framed as universal rather than particular, Kellner has argued that new technologies hold manifold potentials to function as mediums for the reconstruction of a public sphere, though they can equally be used to represent particularistic interests and even promote violently exclusive projects of racism and ultra-nationalism. Moreover, Kellner reminds us that the essential condition of a public sphere is not the medium, but the conduct of self (Kellner 1997). Technological innovations in communication currently develop at such a pace that it would be imprudent to comment on the 'latest', but we can observe a number of distinct changes to the social relations enabled by communications technology media in the past thirty years.

Most significantly, the media have ceased to form exclusively a one-way street. The initial change came with the proliferation of media, but dated from the time of radio broadcasting rather than from 'new' digital technologies. 'Pirate' radio was highly attractive to radical political thought in the 1970s, not least as a means of overcoming the scenario theorized by Horkheimer and Adorno, in which mediated popular culture, marketed commodity production and administered politics become a singular totality, with its promise to decommodify and de-bureaucratize media broadcasting. However, the subject of such radical broadcasting was often 'the community', a politically inert subject fixed in a given identity, the representation of which invokes exclusion and resistance to innovation. In contrast, the broadcast itself remained for Debord ([1967]1992) a medium of domination per se, and such attempts to reappropriate it simply a naive pseudo-radical reproduction of the relations of consumption that structured modern capitalist society (Debord's own films were monochrome, devoid of images).

Democratization of the broadcast media has more recently been outflanked by the aim of much contemporary technological development to enable interactivity. Such developments hold the radical potential to render representation superfluous, enabling direct democracy – or even to circumvent the medium of political institutions altogether – rather than simply the deliberative or discursive democratic participation of the public sphere. The internet provides a medium for direct action in the domain of representation itself, on Hall's model of the cultural production of mediated reality and the assemblage and presentation of social identity without reference to tradition or ideology, writing one's own code. Similarly, simulated environments, such as Second Life, offer the potential radically to reconfigure selfhood independently of social norms, a seductive prospect for the realization of individual life projects which could have indirect effects for wider society in the same way that religion functioned historically as a medium for the transformation of life conduct.

However, the public sphere should not be misunderstood as a medium in which each and every individual participates equally and simultaneously in a single forum, or as a medium in which each pursues their own self-interests. Habermas rather theorized how a multiplicity of sites of discourse produced a general social condition oriented towards objective public interest. The internet today consists of a multiplicity of sites which effectively function like a global public sphere, but it is unlikely to achieve the coherence of the public sphere of the Enlightenment, at least partly because of linguistic divisions between networks. The global space constituted by the internet is culturally as well as linguistically fragmentary compared to the bourgeois public spheres, which were predominantly nationally bounded, often a significant element in constituting nation out of linguistic and cultural commons, as Anderson (1983) suggests. However, the public sphere should not be understood as restricted to texts and speech, as its repertoire can be symbolic, as in Habermas's exploration of the cultural and aesthetic dimension of the bourgeois public sphere, which suggests that other 'events' and happenings, such as street demonstrations, graffiti, even shoe-throwing, can constitute participation and can transcend linguistic and cultural divisions.

The public sphere and social control

Such a range of potential media then suggests that Habermas inadequately theorized the issue of access, which qualifies the public sphere even in 'open societies' such as those he supposed. In addition to the restrictions implicit in assumptions of universal homogeneity (such as exclusion of wheelchair users from public buildings with stepped access), the privatization of much public space in the form of malls and closed streets, the requirements of most internet usage, identity papers, passports, etc., all codes, qualify the public sphere for all. Gilles Deleuze (1995) theorized that disciplinary societies of the kind Foucault used the Panopticon to analyse were being replaced by control societies, in which one set of freedoms and controls would be replaced by others. Control society would radically redefine the 'public', so that participation would become a qualified privilege, thus neutralizing the critical function that Habermas ascribed to the public sphere and that we automatically assume for protests. Instead, under conditions of control, such acts would be legitimatory in the same way that the many minor acts of acquiescence in the post-totalitarian society analysed by Havel legitimated the old communist regimes, regardless of the actor's intention.

The bourgeois public sphere also marked the development of new modes of public control through surveillance. Foucault's commentary on Bentham's Panopticon provides the best-known conceptual icon for the exercise of disciplinary power/knowledge in surveillance, but overusage has had a reductive effect on the reception of his analysis. Of perhaps greater significance for the practice of politics as the exercise of counter-power was the almost simultaneous development of the mobile, embodied state surveillance of *agents provocateurs*, infiltrators and informers, developing precisely where the public sphere and the origins of democracy flourished. In England this developed *against* the influence of the French Revolution in the repression of the Corresponding Societies and advocates of Tom Paine's *Rights of Man*, but in France in *defence* of the revolution, in the shift from constitutive to constituted power under the Jacobin Committee of Public Safety. Both sets of measures comprise a discourse of security, of anticipation and pre-emption of risk, and both foreclose politics in the sense of an openness to constitutive change while consolidating power that is already constituted.

Today, such agencies are multiplying and taking on new 'post-bureaucratic' administrative forms, while being deployed also in new governmental strategies. Deleuze's analysis of control society provides a conceptual framework for the analysis of contemporary processes of governmentalization and securitization. Deleuze (1995) argues that the normalization processes at the core of Foucault's analysis of disciplinary society are becoming supplemented or even replaced by control processes, so that a ceaseless requirement to produce codes of access for elementary interaction replaces the mass disciplinary regulation of modern, industrial society with new processes, operating at the level of the individual. This is particularly evident in relation to policing, a function that was characteristic of a normalizing, disciplinary society and is now yielding to new processes of 'intelligence-led security', where old police functions and military power, which were strictly separate in modern disciplinary society, come together in a new configuration of control. This is exemplified in the generation of databanks that no longer function as a representation of a mass to produce norms and deviations, as did the power/knowledge generated by disciplinary surveillance, but rather demand ceaseless imperative and unavoidable communication from the individual. Mass society operated by the terror of exclusion, of the norm, but in control society we all become suspects; we are all only nominally free 'on licence'.

In such a perspective, civil society and the public sphere become themselves part of the medium of control, requiring formal codification of the conditions of participation, such that surveillance becomes integrated with political activity in even the 'apolitical' sense intended by Havel. The next chapter will look at how politics has become organized beyond the formal institutions designed to contain it, how those have exploded the parameters of the political, but also, more critically, how they have interacted throughout their history with mechanisms of discipline and control.

7

Social Movements

In José Saramago's novel *Seeing*, the anti-government groundswell is expressed only through the blank ballots; there is no 'it' that could express itself. The groundswell does not articulate aims or demands, but remains mute; there is no collective personification as 'the people' or even any claim to representation in the form of a party. Saramago may be trying to tell us that something can be going on, political activity can be taking place, even in the absence of the signs that we conventionally identify as political. In the nineteenth and twentieth centuries, the politics of distribution were articulated in ideology and organizationally expressed in the form of the party, and we are used to seeing identity politics through the more amorphous but still tangible form of multiple organizations clustered around a single theme or objective. The term 'social movements' has been designed to conceptualize such phenomena, which continually extend the parameters of the political until the term loses its institutionally given definition and comes instead to refer to all contention of authority and to any action that effects change in society.

The concept of the social movement

Social movements can be defined loosely as the self-organization of part of civil society. They have no centre and are not an organizationally centred, or necessarily ideologically coherent, singular mode of expression, like a political party. Parties may emerge from social movements, and may aspire to substitute for them, subjecting the movement to their own organizational discipline as constituted power, but seem to subsume the wider movement entirely only when the party becomes identical with the state and can repress civil society. Social movements are generally understood as more visible than Saramago's fantasy of the blank ballots, which refuses to articulate itself, while social movements are polyphonic, or at least polyvocal. They form often around single issues or particular concerns, and vary in scale and extent, but have been the vehicle through which political activity has created sweeping change that has transformed societies around the world over the past thirty years. Much of the contemporary agenda of politics, on personal, local, national and global scales, derives not from ideologies, but from social movements.

Thus, apparently unlike Saramago's mute revolt, social movements are explicitly political, though they operate in areas of concern that are at least initially outside the agenda of formal politics – such as children's rights, women's suffrage, racial discrimination or climate change – but which today may quickly become incorporated into the post-ideological agenda of post-democratic party politics in the sense that Crouch (2004) described the current plebiscitary populism that has displaced the mass politics of modernity.

However, the study of social movements has become in sociology a distinct disciplinary sub-specialism and thus has become detached from the discourse of political sociology, with the effect that the latter often collapses back into the 'sociology of politics', focusing only on institutions. Where social movement theory has entered into a theory–practice relationship with radical politics aimed at social transformation, political sociology has tended to become a de facto, perhaps even unwitting, legitimation of political practice that has sought to recuperate the legitimate authority of institutions and offices under challenge since around 1968.

The concept of a social movement has been very widely applied, but attempts to differentiate analytically between their supporters, active participants and the institutional elements have foundered on the heterogeneity of the forms these movements assume, in favour of the looser understanding of them as comprised of networks of social interaction, involving organizations, groups or simply individuals. Networks provide both a means for mobilization of resources and a novel social context for the development of social identity and solidarity (Diani 1992).

Since social movements in the broad sense do not represent themselves, because no one can speak for them, they are rather inherently pluralist and are by virtue of their composition intrinsically engaged in a politics of representation, in the contention of what is represented as their subject, and how, which was throughout modernity largely obscured by the focus on the politics of distribution.

Social movements produce identifications that are diverse and fluid rather than singular. However, when movements crystallize in the form of political parties that claim to represent their aims and values in the formal political process, they become assimilated into the mainstream political game and tend to lose definition. For example, the European Green parties have lost distinctiveness because mainstream parties have simply adopted some of their concerns as policy, as part of the wider process in which those parties have largely abandoned ideology in the pursuit of populism. Rather than illustrating the persistence of ideological perspectives under new social conditions of postmodernization and globalization, the diffusion of ecologism across the conventional political spectrum shows that it is not immune from the tendency for ideology to fragment and lose coherence. The distinctiveness of green politics lies in its movement form, not in its party representation.

The aims of social movements can be much more specific than those of ideologically oriented formations, but, at the same time, the term 'movement' refers to something wider than a specific campaign. Social movements may produce a plurality of campaigns, sometimes co-ordinated, but at other times contradictory in their different tactics and ethics (e.g. the pro-life (anti-abortion) movement, or the labour movement of the nineteenth century). Social movements may also operate on any scale, from the personal to the global, aiming to change social identities and the norms or inequalities inherent in interpersonal relationships, or global trading patterns between consumers in the economically developed world and producers in underdeveloped localities. On a local scale, even people organizing to save allotments from development could be called a social movement, but would be more so if a larger trend to preserve the existence of allotments could be identified within which any particular campaign could be analytically (if not organizationally) assimilated. So the concept can be seen as applicable to both local and global scales. The form of the social movement also occurs across the ideological spectrum, from neo-Nazi skinheads on the extreme right to eco-anarchists on the far left, but social movements are always more broadly based than on narrow ideological adherence.

Secular social movements as we would recognize them today appeared in the context of the emergence of civil society around the seventeenth or eighteenth century, with objectives not only of changing state policy but also of making much deeper changes, in society itself and even in the individual's sense of self and other. Social movements of the eighteenth and nineteenth centuries, though, often defined their objectives in terms of citizen–state relations – i.e. in legal-political terms – campaigning for aims such as the universal male electoral franchise or for equal legal rights for women, including the right to inherit property and sue for divorce of marriage. These objectives were usually couched in the wider emancipatory discourse of the Enlightenment, claiming their legitimacy from the common aim of extending human freedom for self-realization, but were limited to demands upon the institutional, formal political and legal order, with the consequence that achievements of formal rights could coexist with extreme informal discrimination and hierarchies of power in the private domain.

More recent identity-based movements (e.g. movements based on gender, sexual, ethnic or disability identities) continue to operate on the same fundamental grounds of human emancipation – they seek to liberate a social identity that is perceived as stigmatized and oppressed by society. This identity basis is sometimes seen as characteristic of 'new' social movements, arising after 1968, which are supposedly distinguished by their shift of political objectives from social redistribution (of goods and opportunities) to social recognition (respect, inclusion, acknowledgement of difference), but critics such as Calhoun point out that older social movements were identity based also. For instance, the labour movement of the nineteenth and early twentieth centuries was not only about gaining equality under the state and equalizing the distribution of rights and goods (regulation of working hours and conditions, social insurance, equal access to education, etc.), it was also concerned with gaining respect, or recognition, for the working class (men), both from the state (as citizens) and from wider society as a whole (as 'respectable', or civil) (Calhoun 1993). Furthermore, the identity-basis argument for the distinctiveness of new social movements becomes strained when it is applied to the ecological movement, and requires a stereotypical and distorted view of 'green' activists as middle class and bohemian, which often does not correspond to reality.

Social movements in historical context, from 'old' to 'new'

Movements tend to be characterized by shared values rather than by an ideological framework aspiring to explanatory coherence. We can differentiate feminism, as a movement incorporating many different explanations of male domination while all sharing the same values of women's equality, from Marxism, as an ideology which, though fractured by internecine disagreements on particular points, strategies and tactics, shared a common singular coherent explanation of capitalism, as well as the values of social equality and justice which it shared with the wider labour movement.

The appearance of social movements, along with the emergence of a discernible civil society, corresponded also to the historical period when secular ideas begin to displace religion as the source for thinking about how people should live together. However, social movements (and also civil society) should not be conceptualized as exclusively secular or even as part of a process of secularization. Religion played a major part in early and modern social movements, and today religious fundamentalisms (Islamic, Christian, Hindu, Buddhist, Shinto, etc.) effectively become political by taking the form of social movements. Some new age religious movements have been analysed as themselves taking the form of social movements, such as Falun Gong in China, while others developed in large part out of social movements, as paganism has emerged from the same milieu as ecologism, but framing the same fundamental concerns in spiritual rather than scientific terms (McDonald 2006).

That same process of transformation of the values of a movement into a religious framework can also be seen working the other way around. Despite their appeal for legitimacy from divine authority rather than the authority of secular reason, modern religious fundamentalisms can be analysed as the reformulation of a religious perspective as an equivalent to a political ideology such as Marxism, liberalism or conservatism. They attempt to develop a 'totalizing' analysis of the world and human affairs. Following the classic studies of Durkheim and Weber, the theological element of fundamentalism can be seen as sociologically and politically irrelevant, except in so far as it informs responses to questions about how one should live in the world. For instance, suicide bombings are often explained by crude reference to the influence of theological beliefs, but this distorts the phenomenon and neglects valid comparisons with secular ideologies such as Marxism and liberalism, which have produced plenty of 'martyrs' who have given their lives for ideals such as equality, justice, freedom or progress. It is therefore unnecessary to uncover incentives, since suicide bombing cannot be reduced to individually interested calculative rationality; what is pertinent is the way that a belief system informs life conduct. In this sense, the phenomenon of fundamentalist martyrdom has more in common with the sociology of modern secular social movements than with the traditional theology of religious belief to which it is usually attributed.

Earlier forms of collective resistance to power from above, such as peasant rebellions in medieval and early modern Europe, usually legitimized their actions in terms of tradition (often claiming to restore lost liberties that had been illegitimately usurped by the contemporary power-holders) or by divine authority, which were of course exactly the same sources of legitimation to which power-holders laid claim. Foucault critically makes the point that modern social movements, up to the 1970s, similarly shared the same discourse as the power they opposed and lay claim to the same sources of legitimation, so that both liberal and Marxist ideologies legitimated their claims to power by reference to the Enlightenment project of human emancipation from constraints and illusions (Foucault 1979). Those modern social movements tended to see the state as a neutral form of organization, while education, medicine, science and so forth were considered to be progressive means that could be used to realize the ends of human emancipation. In so doing, however, they failed to extend their critique of existing power to the way that those discourses and institutions constructed the very subject they sought to liberate, with the result that every movement for emancipation reproduced the policing of processes of normalization – the only effect being that the boundaries were moved and the old norms were replaced with new.

In the same way that Foucault attacked these dominant discourses as forms of power because they foreclosed the political by pre-defining the subject they were supposed to liberate, so *new* social movements in the 1960s and 1970s began to resist the power of these institutions in practice (e.g. the gay and lesbian movement resisted not only popular prejudice but also the medical pathologization of homosexuality, while the disability rights movement developed a 'social model' of disability to counter the medicalization of bodily impairments, the anti-psychiatry and mental patients' movements resisted the medical pathologization of different ways of thinking, and the movement for home education resisted the institution of education in the form of the disciplinary school). The critique of knowledge as power was perhaps most extensively developed by the environmental movement, which argued that science itself was not neutral because the conception of science as an instrument with the sole aim of human emancipation neglected that humans were very much part of and subject to the environment as a whole. The application of science as an unquestioned instrument of human progress was seen by environmentalists to have actually produced a lot of the problems emerging by the 1970s, such as deforestation, desertification and global warming.

These new social movements then sought to develop explanations that did not reproduce the authority of the expert discourses they sought to resist, and in that sense represent a break with the older tradition of social movements. In order to accomplish this, they had to produce new political means or, in Charles Tilly's terms, new 'repertoires' of political action (Traugott 1994; Tilly 2004), because the old means or instruments of politics, such as political parties, newspapers, the technocratic state, militant organization, centralism, hierarchical command structures, and so on, were often seen as part of the problem. The critique of expert knowledge extended to conventional political forms and techniques. For the new social movements, the reform of subjectivity or selfhood of the activists themselves, through work on consciousness-raising and self-criticism, could come to substitute for external political objectives.

However, the distinctiveness of 'new' social movements after 1968 remains contentious. Charles Tilly sees, rather, a continuity between the social movements of modernity and those of today, tracing a long history through from medieval and early modern revolts as well as modern social movements (Tilly 1995, 2004). The latter, he argues, were a new political form created in the eighteenth century, from about 1750 onwards. Situating these movements historically, Tilly (2004) identifies distinctive features such as the disciplined street march (in contrast to the riot) that we now take for granted as part of the repertoire of social movement action. He says these new means utilized three distinct elements, new to politics from the eighteenth century.

Firstly, rather than the reactive rebellions typical of previous forms of resistance, social movements operated through 'a sustained public effort making claims on target authorities' (i.e. a campaign), focused on specific and clearly articulated objectives and requiring some degree of conformity by participants on these key demands, which were usually targeted at the state. Modern social movements thus tended to situate themselves in a national context. Secondly, Tilly argues they developed a distinct repertoire of political forms of action and organization, including 'special-purpose associations and coalitions, public meetings, processions, vigils, rallies, demos, petitions, statements to and in public media, pamphleteering' (Tilly 2004: 3–4). Today, we take these for granted as the tools of political action outside of the state, but since the mid-1960s this repertoire has been challenged on all number of counts: the street march, for instance, can be critiqued as 'macho' politics, an adoption of a military form with a predisposition to authoritarianism that was successfully exploited to the full by fascism. Modelled on the mobilization of a male working class exhibiting its power by a show of collective discipline in refusing its labour to capitalist production while suspending economic life by occupying the space of commodity circulation, and thus increasingly anachronistic, the street march under today's conditions can produce a sense of isolation and powerlessness as easily as solidarity and empowerment. It thus becomes part of the repertoire of control rather than of resistance, enabling the surveillance, selection and corralling of demonstrators as a kind of collective street arrest.

However, the street march became a conventional means of political action because it was effective not only instrumentally but also symbolically, in forms that remain recognizable across modernizing societies, in which the street, in addition to its economic traffic function, has a particular political resonance as public space. Above all, repertoires such as the street march provided a register through which social movements were able to legitimate themselves, primarily by displaying what Tilly (2004) calls WUNC: worthiness, unity, numbers and commitment. In this, they immediately differentiated themselves from figurations such as riots, rebellions and revolts, and thus implied grounding in reason rather than reaction, meeting the condition for an overwhelming collective contribution to the public sphere, conveying one message from a multitude of individual voices, articulated in a wide range of media. Social movements represented these attributes through features which recur in most street demonstrations: worthiness through sobriety and respectability; unity through props and practices such as badges, banners, costumes and chants; numbers by headcounts and petitions; and commitment through the practice of self-sacrifice, a show of steadfastness, and subscriptions which, even as merely token sums, still functioned symbolically to demonstrate the principle that all members contribute in some way. However, it is questionable whether these carry the same force today as they did in industrial society.

In his later work Tilly admits to the utility of the qualifier of 'new' social movements but argues that we should abandon attempts to find some sort of sociological key that would explain all social movements; we should instead simply focus on what they actually do. He also cautions us that, to retain any useful significance, the term has to refer to a particular kind of civil political organization, and cannot be applied simply to any group or anyone who tries to exert influence in politics or society at large. While initially stressing continuity, Tilly's later account thus allows for change and development of social movements over time, and even for the possibility that the form itself might disappear.

Tilly's historical analysis parallels the 'history-from-below' perspective that was developed by the Marxist historiography of Christopher Hill, E. P. Thompson, George Rudé, etc. Also, like theirs, his work opens onto the possibility that the identity represented in the politics of contention is socially constructed there, rather than political action representing a pre-existent identity group. In this sense, all social movements are performative in the sense that Judith Butler (1999) uses the term – they bring into social reality, or discursively and conceptually constitute, the subject they represent. Though it has been highly influential in social movement discourse, Butler's concept of performativity simply transposes into post-structuralist terms a sociological understanding of how social action creates social identity. This had already figured in interdisciplinary approaches to social movements such as E. P. Thompson's account of how the English industrial working class was not in fact constituted by economic relations of production, but emerged out of the transformation of struggle, and in particular out of a politics of representation that was only subsequently sidelined by questions of resource distribution (issues such as what kind of struggle they were engaged in when campaigning for higher wages, the 'moral economy', the moral status of the collective actors involved in these struggles). In this process, repertoires of collective action shifted from those of a status-based rural community to those more recognizable to us as forms of collective self-representation in an industrial society.

However, Tilly's earlier work was concerned with social movements as the expression of aggregates of individual interests, in which street demonstrations are understood as expressions of pre-existing interest groups, not in themselves new social forms or the source of new identitifications (Tilly 1978).

Social movements as resource mobilization

The resource mobilization (RM) framework of analysis similarly focuses on movements as the mobilization of resources to influence policy through political processes (Zald and McCarthy 1987). It is thus premised on the assumption that social movements are about the contention of established, constituted power. In this view, social movements seek to exert a power-from-below equivalent to power-from-above, by mobilizing resources that are more widely distributed in society than those concentrated in the state or in corporate capital. The RM approach has constructed complex analytical models for objective empirical research, but its focus on formal results rather than social effects overlooks the ways in which social movements since the 1960s have successfully reconstructed and revalued social identities (as with the black civil rights movement, the gay and lesbian movement and the women's movement). Although these social transformations are far more extensive in effect than any policy change, the resource mobilization perspective either reduces them to side-effects or considers them as pre-existent, arguing that the representation of identities as an expression of 'community' is just another resource that social movement elites or 'entrepreneurs' (Jenkins 1983) could call upon. Identity politics is thus seen as merely instrumental means for the pursuit of self-interest through collective representation.

In the RM model, there is no sense of constitutive power, merely quantitative variations in power distribution. Social movements thus mobilize the dispersed resources of a civil society that is considered as already a power, as already constituted, albeit in dispersal. Rather than focus on transformations, this model thus focuses on organization and tends to assume that social movements will tend towards a general form, the social movement organization, or SMO, an equivalent category to the party or the state. The resource mobilization approach thus retains a narrow concept of power and the political, as being about the power to control resources, make decisions and set the agenda, in common with Lukes, with whom this approach shares its underlying methodological individualism. Despite implicitly acknowledging civil society as a reservoir of resources, it assimilates the analysis of social movements to the analysis of all political action as ultimately about the contention of sovereign power, and thus fails to comprehend much of the activity of social movements as constitutive power, attempting to achieve widespread social change outside the medium of the state. Non-instrumental action is effectively dismissed by the RM perspective as a psychological function of expressive affect, rather than comprehending such aspects as effective in the sense of creating new identities and perspectives.

The RM or 'political process' approach sees social movements as a mobilization of resources in a political process that is ultimately oriented towards the state and towards decision-making in institutional forms. It developed out of 'objective' analyses, deliberately distanced from the subjectivity of activists, a viewpoint which originally perceived new social movements from a conservative functionalist perspective, as a danger to the constituted, established forms of politics that were seen as functional for democracy (Meyer 2001).

The resource mobilization approach has developed mainly in the USA, where it can be related to the particular, formal but pluralistic American approach to politics. Though they may create new repertoires of action and new modes of expression, in this approach new social movements are seen as always oriented towards the state, towards influencing policy (Meyer 2001), and represent social identities which pre-existed their mobilization, at least in the form of an aggregate of individual interests. In this ahistorical view, there is nothing particularly new about social movements after 1968, or 1989, or at any time.

Social movements as social creativity

Where Tilly and the resource mobilization approach see continuity, others have theorized a rupture, around 1968, between the modern social movements characteristic of industrial society and the new social movements. The 'American' RM model is challenged by the 'European' approach, which focuses much more on the meaning and effects of new social movements, adopting a much wider conception of the political to focus on the effect of movements in the construction of identities and cultural change. As Scott puts it, new social movements are 'distanced' from politics in the formal sense of institutional decision-making (Scott 1990).

Developing out of a focus on class and culture that was absent from US analysis, in the wake of the events of 1968, the European tradition developed the concept of 'new social movements' (NSM), distinct from the old by virtue of a number of factors, such as their tendency towards horizontal rather than hierarchical structure. In particular, it is characteristic of European analyses to engage with the subjective intentions of the movements themselves, producing a much greater focus on their aspirations to effect wider social and cultural change, beyond influencing specific policies (Hamel and Maheu 2001).

The NSM approach to the analysis of social movements, and social movements which aim to transform social identities (e.g. feminism), locate power not exclusively with the state but also (and more importantly) within culture and social relations of control, the 'background assumptions', culture or ideology that shapes and frames what is considered to be contestable in society (i.e. Lukes's third dimension of power). On that understanding, new social movements have developed novel modes of action which operate by changing culture rather than (or as well as) by attempting to set the political agenda and influence decision-making. The European tradition of social movement analysis developed out of engagement with theories generated by the movements themselves, focusing on the function of movements in the formation of identities and social processes of transformation, in contrast to the more objective American focus on movements in terms of resource mobilization.

Through attention to the way in which movements change the lives of participants, and through them may effect cultural change at the level of everyday life, such analysis has moved away from a strictly rationalized conception of action and tends towards acknowledgement of the personal, and even the affective experience of activism that has recently been advanced as characteristic of a new modality of action peculiar to 'global movements' (McDonald 2006). In the European analysis, the creative effects of new modes of political action (such as the production of new social identities or communities, new repertoires of action, new forms of organization, the politicization of issues or activities) tend to be considered as effective accomplishments in themselves rather than as effective only in terms of their instrumental relation to political processes, implying a very different concept of power to that of the RM approach.

New social movements themselves have made use of new ideas about power (wider concepts of ideology, discourse, representation, etc.), and the new modes of action that they have pioneered have also found responses in theoretical developments. Foucault's engagement was announced in celebrated lectures where he rigorously and explicitly rejects the model of sovereign power, referring to the new modes of political action of the emergent social movements of the 1970s. These lectures were quite explicitly intended as a guide for new ways of thinking which might enable resistance that did not mimic existing structures of power in its discourse, practice, organization, orientation and focus (Foucault 1980: 78–108). However, such close engagement with activism meant that new social movement theory retained a romantic association with 'resistance' to power-as-domination, an association that was disturbed and challenged by movements of the far right, which adopted many of the practices of the post-1968 movements but generated violent, exclusive identities, such as 'skinhead' subculture, with its close associations with the extreme right and celebration of violence.

Social movements and identity

Social movements have from the outset contested the parameters of the political, rather than simply operating within the given scope of politics. The social identity element of a social movement indicates a challenge to the naturalized status of the social order. Campaigns for political recognition of social inequalities, which began with the bourgeois revolutions against the aristocracy and the model of the natural body politic, continued through the labour movement of the nineteenth and twentieth centuries and the successive 'waves' of the women's movement, and extended in the late twentieth century to movements against racial discrimination, sexual normalization, and so forth. In this phase of social movements, social recognition and political representation appeared to be two sides of the same coin, mutually necessary. However, each successive movement called into question what the others left unchallenged, so that feminism, for instance, initially restricted its challenge to the formal legal and political status of women, but its 'second wave' from the 1960s came to question also the residual inequalities of the private sphere and the way that gender inequality was embedded in culture and ideology. In these phases, instrumental and expressive aspects of the movement (respectively, action to achieve rights and action as a celebration of identity) were unified, but attempts to renegotiate the social status of women also opened the question of the social construction of that identity. Once the idea of a universal subject of woman was challenged, issues of who could speak for whom and conflicts of interest across the standpoints produced by divergent social experience began to pull the movement apart, at least in the sense that it had operated until then, as was indicated by the abandonment of the title 'women's liberation movement'. That title had functioned as a way of providing a coherent object for struggle only as long as the movement operated with a model of identity as given, rather than as constructed.

As rifts opened in the women's movement, so did they also in the movement for the recognition of homosexuality as socially and politically legitimate difference. Many successes were initially gained by the gay and lesbian rights movement through their adoption of the egalitarian citizenship model of the civil rights movement. Gay men and lesbians achieved representation in the public sphere by laying claim to a given identity as a minority, which produced a quasi-ethnic, even tribal self-understanding in well-defined communities. Utilizing the civil rights notion of a minority, rights were gained by demonstrating similarity, implying that the minority subjects were in all respects like the majority, excepting differences that were individual and private and therefore should be protected, rather than stigmatized, by citizenship.

However, such normalization in the context of a universalist model of rights did not sit easily with the celebration of difference that motivated activism and self-representation (Nicholson and Seidman 1995; Fuss 1989; Gamson 1996). It was as if, in order to gain rights, minorities had to reduce the rainbow of difference to the grey of universal similarity. This tension between normalization and expression exposed the constructedness of identity, at odds with the essentialism required for admission to universality. By the 1990s, these tensions had surfaced in the lesbian and gay movement in the form of 'queer' theory and politics, which eschewed the given nature of gay identity assumed by the movement up to then in favour of political practice which presented and represented myriad hybrid identities instead of the singular subject which could both be campaigned for and celebrated expressively. Queer politics was aware of its continuous construction and deconstruction of sexual differences and corresponded to the rise of constructionism in social theory as an alternative to the essentialist and naturalist notions that had informed earlier formulations of identity. In the constructionist perspective, all identity categories are socio-historical effects, whether of intentional action or of structure, which require explanation rather than merely description. In this view, heterosexual and homosexual do not describe transhistorical cultural forms; even if sexual practices are the same from one society to another, the meaning given to such practices is culturally and historically specific (Seidman 1996). Furthermore, sexual practices come to indicate a fixed sexuality and type of person only where it is assumed that individuals must have one gender and one sexual orientation, which Foucault (1979) had argued was peculiar to modernity. To assert a positive identification of homosexual thus affirms the very system that oppresses and renders deviant differences in sexuality, just as asserting the singular identity of 'women' also obliterates differences among women (Mohanty 1988).

Diana Fuss (1989) explains how this approach takes up the Derridean concept of the supplement (that meanings are organized through difference). What appears to be explicitly outside a system of meaning as its Other is already implicitly inside it, a necessary supplement. Thus, homosexuality appears outside, deviant, but heterosexuality needs homosexuality for its definition, so homosexuality is always already implicit in the concept of heterosexuality. Following this lead, queer studies thus undertakes the critical deconstruction of cultural representation, looking at cultural forms and texts as constructions of sexual difference and identity. In sociology, the argument is that no facet of social life can be understood without a grasp of the sexual differences implicitly marked out in it, but as an ongoing process of construction, never completely and definitively fixed. The politics of identity and recognition thus become, at their most radical, the politics of representation, of the continuous performative construction and reconstruction of difference.

Queer politics explicitly adopts cultural forms rather than the frame of rights or citizenship of the politics of recognition, since the intention is not to represent a given subject, but to push and extend the boundaries of representation, often through deliberate transgression such as the queer subversion of gay kiss-ins, which used this conventional expression of intimacy as a means of presenting gay identity not as an equivalent of straight, but as a myriad of hybrid, 'queer' identities (Seidman 1996). Such politics does not declare itself, since to do so would fix identity, and its actions may thus appear oblique or even obscure from the outside, since, for its practitioners, instrumental effects are secondary to the immediate effects of performativity, aiming to impact directly in the experience of everyday life.

New social movements and the revolution of everyday life

Perhaps the most radical development of new social movement theory has come from the Italian theorist Alberto Melucci (1989, 1996a, 1996b), who has linked changes in the modality of politics and the parameters of the political effected by new social movements to changes in social conditions as a dialectical relation, rather than one being an expression or a cause of the other.

Melucci argues that identity becomes more central to new social movements as an effect of the increasing reflexivity of complex societies, referring to the way in which social institutions (both formal and informal) organize social action in such a way that it reproduces the subjects of that social organization. In complex societies such as those of the late twentieth and the twenty-first century, this produces both ever increasing control over every aspect of life (e.g. health, sexuality, spatial access, childrearing, even death) and increasing individual autonomy. In regulating our behaviour, institutional organizations put resources of knowledge and communication at our disposal because a complex social system depends on self-regulation, which requires the development of capacities for training and education, and the ability to transform oneself as an individual. Melucci argues that networks of social actors are able to use such resources in ways not intended by agents of control such as administrators and managers. Individuals in complex societies 'work on themselves' in interactive negotiation with others in everyday life through the language they use, their sexual practices, emotional management, dress, patterns of consumption, and so forth, and in the process make cultural innovations. Melucci argues that establishing the meaningfulness of these innovations in interaction constitutes a form of collective action which modifies the social order. Everyday life thus becomes a political theatre, in which given identities and practices become contested.

Social movements can thus be sustained in 'invisible submerged networks' which undertake experiments in everyday life, creating new experiences and forging new social identities. This institutionally invisible political action can effectively transform society without formal political or cultural representation, but through interpersonal networks, consumption networks and the use of public space, effectively changing social reality from within, simultaneously bypassing 'politics' and politicizing the everyday. Such a 'revolution of everyday life' has no articulation, no name, no explicit aim other than opening the possibilities of life itself (Vaneigem 1979).

For resource mobilization theorists, new social movements dissipate when some actors reach accommodation with the demands of the state, which sets requirements for recognition of political legitimacy that effectively enrol movement activists into the games of conventional politics and distance them from the grass roots, a process that had been formulated much earlier by Goffman (1963) in the 'professionalization' of group spokespersons as a function of their representation. This tendency can be seen increasingly from the early 1990s, through strategies of liberal 'governmentalization', in which the aim is no longer to control or stifle protest but to foster and enrol the movements' capacity for self-regulation, so that some aims, objectives and even activists can be assimilated into the agenda of mainstream politics without threatening the overall order of authority and legitimation upon which institutional politics depends. In the UK, this has been achieved largely through the quasi-governmental organization of the unitary Equality and Human Rights Commission, which replaced the earlier phase of professionalization of identity politics in the separate institutional bodies. The centralized commission provides legal representation for the few token cases that are deemed to have a high chance of success in law and refers other cases to local organizations, often similarly governmentalized through close association via funding by local government.

So if the radical fate of identity politics, and perhaps of social movements generally, is to self-destruct into fragmentary difference, the recuperative pole seems to lead to professionalization and governmentalization. However, Melucci suggests a rather different analysis, arguing that, even in the apparent absence of challenges to authority, social movements may not have been assimilated or dissipated but have simply shifted from a visible to a latent phase. He argues that approaches such as resource mobilization mistake the form of mobilization for the movement itself. Mobilization simply makes visible a hidden network of latent constitutive power, effecting social change without taking the form of power over. It occurs only where the everyday production of meaning in latent networks of actors comes into conflict with public policy, and otherwise the process remains invisible. Latency thus does not mean inactivity, rather: 'The potential for resistance or opposition is sewn into the very fabric of daily life [because] it is located in the molecular experience of individuals or groups who practice the alternative meanings of everyday life' (Melucci 1989: 71).

Such practice has little to do with politics in the formal, institutional sense. McDonald (2006) points out how, in a further shift since the late 1980s, movements have increasingly come to adopt 'direct action' that is neither instrumental nor expressive, but which temporarily enables an alternative social order of experience in protest events. Jordan's study *Activism!* (2002) distinguishes direct action from other instrumental attempts to effect change by its immediacy and its willingness to transgress given social norms and law. Jordan retains a distinction between activism and everyday life and thus sees change as actually effective only through the transformation of constitutive power into constituted authority, but his study extends much further than this instrumentalist perspective, to encompass cultural movements such as rave and to acknowledge how change often comes from the action itself. In this sense, what at first appears as the narcissistic self-indulgence of hedonism – for instance in the subculture of rave or even the network of virtual interactions of Second Life – is revealed as radically transformative in so far as it becomes the experience of its participants.

In the analysis of the politics of representation, pleasure-seeking practices are often reduced to an instrumental function as a challenge to codes, in much the same way that cultural theorists such as Hebdige (1979) read youth movements of the 1970s as encoded, implicit ideology. In contrast, McDonald's focus on the whole milieu of what has been called the 'movement of movements' (Mertes and Bello 2004) emergent around anti-globalization in the new millennium enables him to argue that: 'The forms of action . . . all involve a break from th[e] paradigm where groups are constituted through the act of representation. Rather than the "power to represent", we encounter other grammars of action . . . grammars of embodiment, as experience, as mode of presence and engagement with the world' (McDonald 2006: 37). The focus is on the immediate rather than on the future, and thus the global movements and modernities studied by McDonald are beyond ideology, oriented by 'an ethic of the present . . . committed to living differently now, as opposed to programmatic or linear attempts to shape the future' (ibid.: 64). McDonald points out that the 'new humanitarianism' of NGOs such as Médecins Sans Frontières shares in this ethos of immediacy, of urgency, and also affective qualities that increasingly characterize direct action protests since the 1980s.

The 'movement of movements' has developed novel modes of organization through networks, affinity groups and personalized relationships of affiliation which McDonald argues indicate 'a clear break with the paradigm of "identity correspondence" and "civic grammar"' characteristic of even new social movements when they are understood as constituting a group 'through the act of representation' (McDonald 2006: 86, 84–92). These momentary, molecular forms can thus be understood as new life experiences, even ways of living, rather than as instrumental representations of new possibilities.

Some approaches have often applied the term 'tribe' or 'neo-tribe', in contrast to the older concept of subculture, to conceptualize the fluidity of new movements, since, 'groupings which have traditionally been theorized as coherent subcultures are better understood as a series of temporary gatherings characterized by fluid boundaries and floating memberships' (Bennett 1999: 599). Bennett argues that the concept of tribe incorporates the affective, emotional dimension of the contemporary phenomenon of 'resistance' within global movements. As with other arguments for the special characteristics of 'new' social movements (Scott 1990), it can be claimed that social movements have always functioned on an emotional register; it is often the emotive elements that differentiated social movements from rationalizing, unemotive contemporary politics, as noted in Weber's (1948) rationalist critique of the 'ethics of conviction' of revolutionary movements of left and right in Germany after the end of the First

World War. However, it is not simply the existence of an affective and experiential quality that differentiates current, global movements from previous social movements, but rather the way that affect is experienced.

In the mass movements of the nineteenth and early twentieth centuries, affect was experienced as a collective, in which the personal was subsumed within the mass, not merely organizationally but subjectively, the mass providing the frame for experience, so that individual affect was collectively generated in mass participation. The repertoire of action identified by Tilly (2004) as characteristic of modern social movements functioned in large part through exposure of the aggregate body in mass marches, rallies and pickets. Unarmed demonstrations were a condition of the claim to membership of civil society and to citizenship, which demanded recognition of rule of law by excluded classes and groups such as workers and women, who assembled in face of the risk that they could be violently assaulted and even fired on by the forces of the state, producing a euphoric sense of solidarity and power. Durkheim ([1912] 1996) had analysed such effects as 'social effervescence' as a source of collective identity, a concept which was intended to be applied to a whole range of phenomena from 'primitive' aboriginal religious rites to 'modern' party rallies, football matches, and even the vicarious experience accessible through the consumption of mass media. In McDonald's scenario, the crucial distinction is that affect and experience are now not framed and constitutive of a collective identity, but rather consist in the social context of personalized relationships of affinity:

> through the affinity group, each person enters into a relationship with a concrete other (people you know and trust) as opposed to relating to a totality . . . The paradigm is closer to friendship in that each person recognizes the other as a person, as opposed to someone carrying out a function on behalf of a collectivity or organization . . . a friendship is not based on sharing a category: a friendship is an experience of the recognition of singularity. (McDonald 2006: 87)

Since the late 1980s, movements have increasingly adopted 'direct action', which inaugurates a new social order in protest events as a means of 'a "prefigurative" politics that sees no separation between means and ends . . . we want to be the change that we want to see in the world' (Harvie et al. 2005: 247). In the UK, the genealogy of this can be traced through the Greenham Common women's camp of the early 1980s, where protests against the use of the air base for anti-nuclear armaments fused 'counter-cultural' currents, 'new age' religion, radical feminism and a punk 'DIY' ethos, manifesting an alternative social order of fluid boundaries and a floating membership who came to experience themselves and the world in radically new ways as they passed through the camp. Subsequently, UK anti-roads protests, especially at Twyford Down and London's A40, constituted similar spaces of emancipation from determinant social and cultural structures, fusing further cultural politics from the 'new age travellers' and the UK rave and festival culture (McKay 1996).

While these convergences can be traced intellectually to such sources as classical anarchism or to the Situationist International (Plant 1992; Purkis and Bowen 1997), explicit ideological links are weak. Rather, it is personal experience that articulates the linkages. Thus, experience of protest on a global scale, especially around the G8 summits, has produced a renaissance in radical political theorizing by participants themselves (Jones et al. 2001). Looking at activism through interviews rather than its own theoretical discourse, McDonald (2006) understands the importance of experience in individualistic terms, assuming that individuals carry the 'memory' of activism from one event to the next, validating an individualizing methodology and thus tending to produce an unintentionally elitist picture of movements, in which significant persons rather than cultural practices or political discourse constitute innovations and maintain movements over time. Overall, MacDonald's conceptualization of 'experience movements' also tends to analyse activism as something sufficient unto itself and, while it may be that activism tends to take the route of direct self-realization through action that increasingly lacks external purpose, focusing on the creation and possibility of gradually extending what the anarchist philosopher Peter Lamborn Wilson has called 'Temporary Autonomous Zones' (Bey 2007), even such intrinsically oriented movements have to define themselves and are affected by their relation with other forces, principally those of control. In a control society, any escape attempt is inevitably a relation to entrapment, not pure flight, and thus returns the movement to instrumentality and strategic reason, as Jordan (2002) has noted in relation to the 'white overalls' factions of the anti-globalization movement.

This tactical innovation in the repertoire of street protest had developed in the years before the G8 summit at Genoa 2001. Activists wearing protective gear beneath white overalls would take the forefront of a street demonstration to push back against physical police blockades, with the aim of exposing the violence latent in social control while refusing it themselves. However, such tactics could be undone both by pre-emptive excessive police violence, as at Genoa, and by the method of concentrating, dividing and then corralling off demonstrators ('kettling'), immobilizing the demonstration for hours and reducing activists to mere embodiment, which produced eventual demoralization and a sense of futility.

Conclusion

The primarily formal practice of the old movements expanded into entirely new forms of 'politics', new ways of transforming society, by undertaking identity construction in everyday life and through cultural representation, all but abandoning traditional political demands. These new ways of creating social change proved extraordinarily successful in shifting social attitudes and opening up new ways to live. New politics based as much on cultural production and consumption, on everyday life, as on representation, seems to have had more success than the old strategies in achieving change. Formal political alignments have thus come to appear, and indeed effectively to function, as disempowering rather than empowering, prone to compromises, liabilities and assimilation to the interests of constituted power. But the mode of protest characteristic of the politics of distribution has become transformed via a politics of representation into a mode of direct emancipation. Such politics have come to appear as an end in themselves, the production of TAZs as moments of liberation and self-creation.

McDonald (2006) analyses the (personalized) memoirs of 'experience movements', pointing out that affective experience is grounded in a personalized conception of the body, which is celebrated as a source of authenticity and immediate experience, escaping all control. However, the focus on embodiment depoliticizes the body by reducing it to experience and sensation, neglecting its social reality, the sense in which our bodies are conduits for social forces which frame our experience of sensation and even shape the physical body itself. Attempts to ground 'experience movements' in the body thus appeal naively to a naturalistic body and its corollary, an ideology of romanticized 'resistance'. They also render 'experience movements' subject to control, which reduces activism to 'bare life' in the sense that the term is used by Giorgio Agamben (1998) to indicate the depoliticized, rightless, merely biological subject of sovereign power.

This has in turn produced new strategies of domination. Control thus addresses not the long-term strategic ends of instrumentally oriented movements, which are dealt with by governmentalization, but the immediacy of movements oriented towards experience and the creation of new ways of being. The effect is to circumscribe the sources of self-identification and possibilities of representation to those that are socially given and institutionally embedded and which legitimate authority that can be enrolled into strategic projects. New ways of living confront the control imperative as risks, ontological threats to security itself.

8

Risk and Securitization

In Saramago's novel *Seeing*, the conventional parameters of politics –
its restriction to party agendas, plebiscitary elections and circulations
of elites – are eventually restored not by the necessity of executive
political organization for everyday life, but by the covert deployment
of the forces of the state to produce a sense of insecurity which alone
relegitimates the imposition of executive power. The security agents
can be read as analogous to much wider strategies of 'securitization'
in the contemporary world, but have particular resonance with post-
9/11 contractions of civil liberties in the name of security.

Public order policing, the interface between security and protest,
as constitutive and constituted power, has shifted from a response to
breaches of law to the apprehension of potential transgression. Pre-
emptive 'kettling' – the containment of demonstrators within a tight
police cordon – polices the virtual, what might transpire, neutralizing
and using the concentration of bodies to gather intelligence rather
than breaking up the crowd. For liberal governmentality, the police
figure as experts in public order and so must be free to perform their
function, but, as a general approach, such piecemeal tactical innovations add up to a general strategic shift that now polices the parameters of the permissible, of legitimizable conduct, since, in the new
strategic frame, any action that breaks existing normative routine
parameters of behaviour – street assemblies, camps, even meetings
and networks of communication – becomes suspect (Hornqvist
2004). Pre-emptive police measures, particularly the closure of
public space and the use of arrest to prevent demonstrations, are
frequently denounced as erosions of civil liberties, but, rather than
providing an explanation, such denunciation in itself appeals to constituted power in authority to uphold liberties supposedly grounded

in some natural or traditional order, distinct from the act of protest itself.

To understand how this shift in public order has appeared, we need to refer to critical theories of social transformation. In Deleuze's terms of the control society (1995), social phenomena such as street protests are 'extra-dividual' scenarios. They will be suspect because participants are not required to produce a code to verify a given identity, but rather are creating social identity anew, collectively, for themselves, in situ. The political, in this sense, is inherently outside the parameters of control, which constrain the conduct of life to the given, the pre-political. What remains unexplained by the conceptual analysis of control society, or the confrontation between constitutive and constituted power, is the sociological question of why perceptions have shifted in this way. How is it that unanticipated behaviour or attempts to live differently have come to appear as dangerous? Why have we moved from a disciplinary society, in which experiments could still be tolerated, albeit as anomalies subject to social sanction, to a control society in which they cannot be socially negotiated and appear as an ontological threat to sovereign security?

This chapter deals with two concepts that have developed independently of each other, but which seem to address that same general phenomenon: the reframing of issues that would hitherto have been dealt with in the frames of the politics of distribution, recognition or representation, as issues of risk, or security. This phenomenon has provided a ready context for, but pre-dates and is much wider in extent than, the discourse of the 'war on terror' ensuing as a result of the 9/11 attacks on the World Trade Center. Firstly, Ulrich Beck's theorization of 'risk society', which was first fully articulated in 1986 in the context of the sociological discourse of modernity, addresses the question of what kind of society we live in. Secondly, Buzan, Waever and de Wilde produced their thesis of 'securitization' (1998), which was developed in the context of debates in international relations, a discipline confronted with the apparent undermining of its basic unit of international analysis in a similar way to the challenge to the analysis of society within a national frame posed by globalization for sociology.

I have used the term 'securitization' throughout this book to denote the general phenomenon theorized also in Beck's work on risk society because it indicates a process rather than a condition. The formulation of Buzan and his colleagues indicates that securitization is something that is done, while Beck's theorization lacks an explanation of the shift in perception which would provide a sociological equivalent to the political scientists' analysis of the process through which securitization is effected. Beck's analysis is surprisingly asociological, lacking the explanatory dimension that would have been supplied for earlier generations of theory, before postmodernization, by a grand narrative analysis of capitalist, modernizing or industrial society, each with its developmental logic. While risk society seems to pinpoint and link together sociologically significant aspects of our contemporary world, it lacks an explanation of how these arose, and of why perceptions changed from high modernist optimism in scientific development to risk society's fears of the indirect consequences of such development. The question cannot be resolved empirically, because unintended consequences of human action upon the environment (the characteristic of risk society on which current fears focus) have been apparent throughout human history.

Ulrich Beck

Beck's essential argument is that industrial, scientific, technocratic society, or 'first modernity', has succumbed to its own successes and their unintentional consequences or side-effects, producing a social transformation as great as that of the original industrial revolution. However, where that great transformation was produced by faith in progress through technological solutions to problems, aiming to utilize all resources maximally, the subsequent era (risk society) is based on an acute awareness of risks and loss of faith in progress. Beck synthesizes an entire tradition of German critical thinking in the development of his argument. The idea that modernity is sustained through instrumental reason, the imperative to use or exploit all resources, was first advanced by the Frankfurt School theorists Adorno and Horkheimer ([1947] 1997), and its effect of displacing ethics and politics was further followed up by Jürgen Habermas (1988). Habermas argued that the very success of systems-thinking in the political administration of modern society produces an escalation of demands beyond the capacity of the system, resulting in a generalized 'legitimation crisis', to which the 1968 revolt against authority and the neo-liberal reaction of the 1980s are responses.

Habermas's concept of the legitimation crisis of advanced industrial capitalist society is really the precursor of Beck's argument. Both identify a critical watershed in the fate of modern political systems around the late 1960s and early 1970s, when the modernist faith in both technological and technocratic systems-style solutions began to be called into question. The welfare state, corporatist capitalism and state socialism were all subject to similar critical tendencies, appearing inadequate to the very objectives that they set for themselves. So, also, did modern art and architecture, psychiatry and healthcare, employment arrangements and the division of labour, industry, agriculture, fisheries – in short, everything that mediated mankind's relations with nature and with itself.

Beck (1992) explains why this occurred as itself an outcome of modernity, which was based on the production and distribution of goods. With scarcity as the main regulatory mechanism for such a society, politics came to take the form of a struggle over the distribution of scarce goods (e.g. the distribution of access to higher education by social class, gender or ethnicity). Modern governmentality produced institutions and forms of knowledge to manage this distribution scientifically, such as expertise in the analysis and design of social policy, but it also developed specialist institutions in all sorts of other areas and issues, in the course of which politics became subordinate to techniques of administration.

This was an ironic outcome for the politics of progress of the Enlightenment and the industrial revolution, as the Frankfurt School had already recognized. The nineteenth-century Utopian thinker Saint-Simon had argued that, in a future egalitarian socialist society, the government of people would be replaced by the administration of things, a proposition taken up as a material objective by Marxism, but state socialism in the Eastern bloc countries had accomplished societies of total administration only by converting people into things. In the West, the corporate capitalism engineered by social democracy in postwar Europe claimed to provide an alternative path to egalitarianism and emancipation, but that very situation seemed intolerable in actuality. It offered not scope for self-realization but deep alienation, offset only by the superficial, manipulated satisfactions of consumerism with the functionally imperative foreclosure of possibilities for alternative ways of organizing social life, in which people similarly become objects of manipulation. Not only Marxism and liberalism, but all ideologies of modernity, all ideologies subscribing to faith in progress, were critically rendered ironic by this outcome.

Beck identifies the problem: that the institutions of industrial modernity were not designed to handle the flipside of the production of goods – the production of 'bads', of risks and hazards. This extended across the social domain. For instance, enlightened psychiatric treatment produced the 'risk' of institutionalization in back wards of long-stay mental hospitals, and then the subsequent 'magic bullet' of new medications enabled community treatment, but produced inadvertent prescription drug addiction.

We can find further examples of the phenomenon of reflexive realization of critical side-effects right across the social domain, but Beck concentrated initially on environmental issues. Energy production by exploiting the earth's reserves of coal had enabled most of the European states to achieve a degree of 'autonomy' in their strategic energy supplies in the first half of the twentieth century, though insecurity of resources had produced two world wars. After the second, a common market in coal became the precursor of the EU, resolving tension over energy resources. But domestic coal-burning produced smog, a dense mixture of fog and smoke that cloaked major cities by the mid-twentieth century. Unlike goods, this 'bad' could not be subject to a politics of distribution; smog affected everyone. Shifting domestic energy consumption away from coal-burning relieved smog but meant that national energy production had to be increased, often still using coal while searching for longer-term sources of energy, while reliance on gas has had the effect of using up local reserves and creating new tensions between gas sources and consumers, especially in the supply crisis in Eastern Europe in the winter of 2008–9. Beck identifies the problematization of energy as one of the first identifiable issues of 'risk society'.

From the early 1970s, a qualitative change appears to have taken place in societal perceptions as the 'bads' of modernity became at least as perceptible as the goods. The political institutions of modernity were not exempt and appeared not only as inadequate to resolving these issues but even as part of the problem. They operated within a paradigm in which society and nature were entirely separate and the aim was for society to control nature, but now nature in its transformed state, altered by human intervention (by exploitation or attempts at control), had become a problem outside of that paradigm; the new risks appeared out of 'socialized nature'.

Beck's analysis of risk society has a strong sense of cultural dynamics – the language of risk is always prone to diffuse out from any particular issue to others by metaphor or analogy, so that sensitivity to risk, or 'risk perception', becomes almost socially contagious, transforming issues across different spheres of social life, changing the communicative logic that enables social and political action, as communication becomes both more central to social life and more uncertain in risk society. Beck does not relate the shift in perception or consciousness to any other significant social transformation, and it thus remains sociologically unexplained. In contrast to the thesis of postmodernity, he argues that risk society neither replaces modernity nor ends the modernization process. He writes of 'second modernity' and 'reflexive modernization' (1998a, 1998b) and argues that we need to abandon some of the preconceptions or assumptions under-pinning earlier social theory, though in order to renew rather than to reject rational and scientific approaches to the problems of a society that can no longer be considered as separate from its now 'socialized' natural environment.

Risk society as a critical theory

Beck maintains a commitment to the interpretation of modernity as emancipation and to communicative action (i.e. reasoned public deliberation) as the political means through which human emancipa-tion must be pursued. He argues that social theory must repoliticize itself in order to continue to inform the emancipatory project, by which he means we must abandon attempts to use unilinear reason-ing to develop singular responses to social problems (Beck 1997). The new issues confronting risk society are simply not amenable to that kind of systems-thinking solution, because it will simply produce side-effects which will then confront us as problems of 'second nature'. So, where new social movement theory associated itself with new social movements and their anti-institutional politics, Beck's theory of risk society suggests that sociology or social theory needs to re-engage with institutional politics in order to inform, reform and guide them. In common with some social movement theorists, however, Beck seeks an engagement between sociology and politics, rather than sociology studying politics as though it were a distinct field or thing, somehow separate from theories about what it is and does.

Beck advocates what he calls 'reflexive modernization' in place of industrial or first modernization. Reflexive modernization would not reject technology and science because they may have unforeseeable adverse consequences, but would politicize that 'may have'. The task of the theory of risk society is thus to put technological developments on the political agenda for discussion and consideration, calling us to reflect as a society on exactly what it is that we want to achieve, and, more importantly, given the potential capacity of technologies of reproduction and of the need to reconfigure society to respond to climate change or even to eliminate its causes, to reflect on how we want to live and what we want to be.

Risk society needs a new approach to politics. Modern politics derived from the Enlightenment project to control the external world, to exploit what it understood as an external nature, 'out there' in the world, in order to develop society. Reflexive modernization helps us to develop politics which recognize that there is no 'out there' to social and environmental problems – the problems of risk society are effects of our own activity, social constructs. Beck illustrates the political consequences of this shift. He draws an opposition between class society (focused by the issue of scarcity) and risk society (focused on the issues of risk). For instance, water pollution was tackled in Europe in the nineteenth century as a public problem, but that had the effect of subordinating politics to technology, so that decisions were turned over to 'experts' (sanitary engineers, administrators) and pollution became depoliticized, as a merely technical and administrative issue which everyone left to the experts to deal with for society as a whole. This scenario pitted expert knowledge against external risk (which came from outside society). But in risk society we are all too aware that risks are not external to society and that expert knowledge can be part of the problem rather than the source of a solution. Even politics itself has become the province of experts, a set of affairs removed from everyday life, and which those who are not part of 'the political process' feel they cannot understand and so experience as threatening.

In modernity, we came to entrust politicians with the task of realizing democracy and liberty for us, just as we trusted the sanitary engineers to provide us with clean water. However, the functional success of this politics is its undoing, just as successful control of the external environment is the undoing of the monopoly of legitimate scientific knowledge. Scientific control of nature comes to be seen as part of the problem – the abstraction of water into supply reservoirs and pipes becomes a factor in drought as the leaking system diffuses water where it cannot easily be re-collected. As scientific control over nature becomes seen as part of the problem, it loses its monopoly on legitimate knowledge, which becomes plural, contentious and politicized. Expert politics similarly comes to be seen as part of the problem, appearing as an impediment to democracy and the individual rights that they set out to realize and protect.

Sub-politics and life politics

Beck (1997) argues that, in risk society, disillusion with institutional politics produces what he calls 'sub-politics', operating on a different level, outside the formal political process, with a very different agenda. Issues of consumption and lifestyle – what we eat, listen to, desire – all become issues in sub-politics, an agenda which originates from below as a reaction to the absence of relevant issues from the formal political agenda. They also take place in the context of de-traditionalization, and therefore in the context of individualization (which Beck has conceptualized as the disembedding of ways of life from traditional institutions and parameters) and globalization (the issues of sub-politics overspill the container or borders of formal, national political processes).

The social framework of sub-politics enables actors to make their own definitions of issues (so sub-politics is the politics of discourse) without relying on experts (whether scientists or spin doctors). The political agenda is no longer given by ideologies which address the distribution of resources and opportunities, of goods, which means that conventional political parties have to scramble to get back in touch by running focus groups and consultation exercises, and by making electoralist pronouncements in an attempt to regain control of the agenda. Making promises and invoking hopes they cannot meet has the unintended consequence of furthering disillusion with conventional politics, producing a spiral of delegitimation of formal political actors and institutions and disenchantment with the democratic electoral process, so that the procedures of celebrity-making through TV contests and phone-in voting appear relatively open by comparison. Against this trend, sub-politics is a positive sign of the revitalization of society, since it seems to be inherently democratic.

Beck's concepts of reflexive modernization and sub-politics are close to and informed by Giddens's concepts of reflexivity and life politics, which are also premised on the recognition that modernity has undergone a fundamental shift since the 1960s (Giddens 1991). Like Beck, Giddens sees this shift as a consequence of modernity itself rather than as a new era (Giddens 1990). Modernizing processes continue, but are more complicated, in late modernity. However, Giddens is concerned more with the subject of the new forms of social order, with the sociological conditions through which we come to define our sense of self, our self-identity (Giddens 1991).

For Giddens, key processes of change differentiate modern from pre-modern societies. Disembedding or de-traditionalization, where social relations become separated from traditional forms, occurs through the way in which abstract systems operate. Modernity is uniquely permeated by abstract systems, by symbolic tokens as abstractions of value (money, or credit cards), by the media, which disembed experience from place and time and intrude distant events into our everyday consciousness, and by expert systems of knowledge and practice, which are narrowly focused and thus tend to have unforeseen consequences outside their sphere of competence, which is often also bureaucratically defined so that experts do not bear the consequences of these indirect effects. In late modernity, most aspects of human activity and relations are subject to chronic revision in the light of new information or knowledge, delivered to us in disembedded and disembedding form, with the effect that we are forced to acknowledge that our lives will not follow a predictable course, that all aspects of our life are open to revision. The resulting reflexivity, our reflection on such necessary revisions, a process of ongoing reconstruction of our expectations of ourselves and others, extends into the core of the self, which becomes a reflexive project, continually liable to be undercut by changes at the level of abstract systems. However, because of de-traditionalization, we are also more than ever dependent on those abstract systems as our source of self-identity (Giddens 1991).

These shifts in the way that we know and understand ourselves as social and political actors are reflected or expressed, Giddens argues, in shifts in politics, because they are changes in the way that people understand themselves as possessing and exercising agency, the capacity to act upon society. The shift takes the form of what Giddens describes as a move from emancipatory politics to life politics, so that issues shift from the question of the distribution of resources for collective realization of given identities to questions of the opportunities for self-creation. Disembedded from traditional forms, all issues take on a fundamentally ethical aspect. As a society, today we question ethics everywhere. We are essentially ethically challenging individuals in an ethically disoriented society. Life politics should not be dismissed lightly as simply substituting the subject of self-interest for collective interests and issues of consumption for distribution; life politics puts fundamental ethical questions on the political agenda, such as questions of our responsibility for our actions in relation to nature, or of rights to life and death (Giddens 1991).

This concern with existential questions contains the possibility of a reflexive awareness of the construction of identity through such action. In this sense, Giddens's concept of life politics is compatible with Melucci's concept of the latent phases of social movements, when people continue to challenge the given order of society, but in everyday life rather than through organizations. The reflexive self, it can be argued, is inherently political, requiring continuous choices. However, where Melucci's analysis of this condition of the subject focuses on its creative potentiality, Giddens focuses on reflexivity as a response to ontological threat. These may each be the obverse of the other, but face in different directions and give rise to different politics; in the first, a politics of self-construction in the open possibilities of becoming, in the second, a politics of recuperation, always searching for the recovery of a lost sense of certainty. Reflexivity perhaps produces nothing more than the demand for increasingly individualistic recognition, for universal pluralism, for choice in place of direct provision of resources, and thus, ultimately, for the kind of options that are modelled on the consumer, rather than on the citizen guided by an understanding of the common good – or even Melucci's player of the self who is concerned to maintain a social field that is free of the enclosures of normalization.

As Zygmunt Bauman has observed, the endemic insecurity of reflexivity makes choice imperative, but this does not necessarily politicize issues of life. Indeed, the effect may be the Hobbesian reverse, to close them down, since 'at the heart of life politics lies a profound and unquenchable desire for security; while acting on that desire rebounds in more insecurity and ever deeper insecurity' (Bauman 1999: 23). This individual insecurity, Bauman points out, is easily appealed to as an electoralist ploy by post-ideological political elites laying claim to the function of protecting public safety. The perception of insecurity produces a demand for increasingly widespread issues to be treated as security issues – that is, outside the parameters of the political in which aims, objectives and means could be challenged.

However, Bauman's reflections remain fragmentary and, while they offer us plentiful insights into the contemporary social condition, he provides no comprehensive perspective for understanding politics and society today. He has no such aspiration, despite his most recent repackaging of postmodernity as liquid modernity (Bauman 2000), but Beck's theorization of risk society does promise to offer a systematic perspective for understanding such a world of chronic uncertainty.

Limits

Beck's risk society approach has been applied far more widely than to ecological issues. 'In a world risk society, we must distinguish between ecological and financial dangers, which can be conceptualized as side effects, and the threat from terrorist networks as intentional catastrophes; the principle of deliberately exploiting the vulnerability of modern civil society replaces the principle of chance and accident' (Beck 2006b: 329).

In the credit boom of the first decade of the millennium, all banks knew the risks to which they were exposing themselves and the world financial system when they over-invested in the sub-prime mortgage market in the USA, but their financial expertise told them the situation would be sustained at least long enough to enable them to divest themselves of these debts before the repayments dried up, with the ruination of the debtors. When this indefinitely postponed future arrived, the threat posed to the world financial system by the banks' insolvency was such that states ultimately intervened to prop them up (as has happened in the USA, the UK and to a lesser extent in France), but questions remain over the viability of even that last-ditch attempt to sustain the illusion of value. Naomi Klein (2008) has recently argued that the strategy of inducing, risking and then profitably unloading the consequences of such financial catastrophe has become normalized as a new form of 'disaster capitalism'.

Even if we revert to Beck's original example, it is difficult to continue to refer to ecological dangers as side-effects when there is overwhelming evidence of the clear and present danger of socially induced climate change, but the problem remains unaddressed in the only way that would make any difference – by planning and implementing massive changes in living, working and distributional arrangements on a global scale, across all advanced societies simultaneously. Despite Beck's argument for the politicization of technology and development, so that these would become subject to political debate in the public sphere rather than split between the imperatives for or against, as in modern instrumental and radical ecological approaches, the gap between acknowledged reality and policies to address the looming catastrophe seems to indicate that politics are already at work, at least in so far as denial is a form of the politics of truth.

In a reformulation, Beck (2006b) differentiates between risks from unintentional 'side-effects' and those from intentional threats, but this introduces a number of contradictions into his original theory of risk society. Firstly, differentiating between risks in this way seems to contradict the central tenet of his original thesis – which is that risk per se, or even 'risk consciousness', is what characterizes our age, rather than particular risks. As he says in the same lecture: 'Risk does *not* mean catastrophe. Risk means the *anticipation* of catastrophe' (ibid.: 332). In its original, generic formulation, risk society theory provided an explanation of the phenomenon of increasing fear in societies where causes of fear are actually decreasing; risk perception does not have to correspond to particular phenomena. But the latest formulation, as it attempts to move from an analytical to a normative stance on immediate issues, refocuses attention away from societal perceptions onto 'real risks', onto 'risks themselves', producing a less sociological, less general analysis which does little more than make a value distinction between sets of risks that are reported to be facing global society. Unlike his original theory, Beck's reformulation is no longer a general theory of society and is quite unable to encompass phenomena such as fear of crime or paedophilia, the crisis of debt or concerns about obesity, but simply posits a hierarchy of terrorist, financial and ecological risks for policy-makers.

It is also unclear whether the concerns Beck highlights really can be separated as he suggests. Risk of terrorism and environmental risk, for instance, are unintentionally connected because security measures taken in one sphere affect the others – for instance, responding to energy and environmental insecurity by resort to a nuclear energy programme, as in the UK recently, actually heightens the risk posed by terrorism. Furthermore, anti-terrorist policy is combined with policies on energy security, particularly with regard to the energy-reserve-rich Middle East and Central Asia. Similarly, on a relatively micro-scale, the police control of ecologically oriented domestic protest now routinely utilizes logic and legislation originating in attempts to control terrorism.

Securitization

Despite his attempts to argue that we must repoliticize issues of risk, Beck's analysis of risk perception as the manifestation of a new social era has the effect of depoliticizing the overall framing process simply by accepting its construction as a given social fact. Beck expends relatively little time in exploring the politics of the discursive framing process, but skips directly to its effects.

The tendency for policies and politics to address all issues in terms

of risk has been identified independently by the international relations theorists Buzan, Waever and de Wilde (1998) as securitization.
Their conceptualization focuses explicitly on the politics of framing
issues as security issues. Their context is the discourse of security
studies after the end of the Cold War, and thus they are concerned
particularly with the implications and effects of extending security as
a frame for the way that issues are conceptualized beyond the military
sector.

Security studies had narrowed its scope in the Cold War to military and nuclear strategic concerns (Buzan et al. 1998: 2–5), but this
theoretical focusing was challenged by a number of factors that can
be associated with postmodernization and globalization, such as the
development of international institutions and policies to regulate a
globalizing economy and transnational crime, and the displacement
of the issues of the politics of distribution by issues such as identity
and the environment, which were unaddressed in the welfare state
settlement of the earlier 'social question'. Security had become a
much more diverse field of concerns in practice by the time that the
break-up of the Cold War bipolar world order finally forced security
studies to address these wider issues, so that theoretical concerns
within the discipline over the loss of specificity of the core concept of
security with its extended application were already overtaken by the
designation of, for instance, the Reagan presidency's pan-American
'war on drugs', which clearly framed that issue as a security concern.

If the concept of security is to be extended analytically, however,
it must convey some more specific meaning than simply treating an
issue as a threat or problem, because it must be differentiated from
the normal scope of the political as referring to issues that need to be
addressed from the perspective of some higher-value criteria. Buzan,
Waever and de Wilde argue that securitization refers to a process in
which issues are presented as 'existential threats to a referent object
by a securitizing agent who thereby generates an endorsement of
emergency measures beyond rules that would otherwise bind' (Buzan
et al. 1998: 5), which are clearly the same grounds that Agamben
(2005) has identified as the foundation of modern sovereignty in the
state of exception. '"Security" is the move that takes politics beyond
the established rules of the game and frames the issue as either a
special kind of politics or as above politics' (Buzan et al. 1998: 23).

The presentation of an issue such as security implies a complex
bundle of associations: that the issue is an existential threat to the
very existence of the referent object, that it has priority over other
issues, and that its threat legitimates 'extraordinary means' (Buzan

et al. 1998: 24). However, Buzan and his colleagues recognize that issues cannot be securitized by diktat; any claim also needs to gain acceptance. The field in which such acceptance is to be gained is not specified, but we can assume the authors refer to public acceptance, in which the framing of the issue as security and the construction of the referent object that is under threat are 'negotiated between securitizer and audience – that is, internally within the unit' (ibid.: 26). However, although they identify these politics of security, they also imply a more discursively deterministic command-like model in which they describe the process of securitization as like a speech act (ibid.), as performative in the sense that the utterance itself articulates the definition of the situation. The concept of a speech act does not allow for negotiation.

Accomplished securitization depoliticizes by removing issues from challenge or contention, because it defers political discourse on issues to expertise and relieves securitizing actors of the need to gain consent for the deployment of special means, thus legitimating a quasi-sovereign authority in any sector in which it is asserted, as in the definition of a psychiatric episode as psychosis, which legitimizes the authority making the pronouncement and sanctions their compulsory detention and treatment of the subject of the episode. The conventional referent objects for security discourse have been the state, its sovereignty, the nation and identity, but, if the critique of securitization is extended beyond the military sector, the referent object may be something other than the state or nation. Securitization analysis suggests anything can be constructed as the referent object.

Though some construct claims are much more likely to succeed than others, the securitization approach is 'constructivist' (Buzan et al. 1998: 204) in the sense that its theorists do not seek to identify an underlying 'reality' against which to evaluate claims to security, but rather focus on the securitizing process or presentation, framing or staging – i.e. on security as discursive. The constructivist perspective of Buzan, Waever and de Wilde's securitization thesis is shared by other international relations theorists, such as Campbell: 'security . . . is first and foremost a performative discourse constitutive of political order' (Campbell 1992). That perspective, in which both security and its referent objects are seen as constructs, accounts for the apparent imperviousness of the discourse of security to empirical challenge.

Securitization as a critical theory

In Buzan, Waever and de Wilde's account, however, there is a further contradiction. On the one hand, they argue (contra the Hobbesian view that security is the necessary basis of all order) that securitization is not always a good thing, if only because it simply freezes relations of conflict, leaving immediate causes and contributory factors unaddressed. Securitization may also undermine what it is intended to protect, as liberals argue that too much market security undermines the function of the market for economy – an argument that Norbert Elias has implicitly extended to everyday life in civilizing societies, where the threat of violence has been effectively removed. Elias (2000) pointed out that the capacity to deal with conflict depends on potential for conflict in society, so securitization, the (at least discursive, conceptual) removal of violence from everyday life under a state, will produce insecurity as it constructs citizens as potential victims in need of the protection of the state, thereby legitimating its 'exception' to the rule of law and enabling unlimited violence against citizens who are deemed to threaten the state.

Although acknowledging that security is a construct, Buzan, Waever and de Wilde do not attempt to envisage a politics beyond or without this interventionary clause, but seek only to delimit its scope, through desecuritization: 'shifting issues out of the emergency mode and into the normal bargaining processes of the political sphere' (Buzan et al. 1998: 4). This shift is clearly predicated on prior securitization, suggesting that they ultimately accept the core of the Hobbesian approach, which argues that securitization is necessary to secure the grounds for the political process. They argue that 'excessive and irrational' securitization can be dysfunctional for individuals, civil society, the economy, the state and international relations, but they imply that proportionate and rational securitization could be functional and legitimate while providing no normative criteria for evaluation. Since the process is, as they say, self-referential, sovereign power would have to decide for itself on due proportion, a role they effectively affirm as the task of limiting claims to security to maintain a balance between the costs and benefits of securitization (ibid.: 209).

Buzan, Waever and de Wilde seem to aspire to the neo-liberal narrative in which security through Leviathan (realized in the form of the Westphalian state, with its progressive monopolization of the means of legitimate violence) stands as a necessary condition for the development of civil, desecuritized pacific society, which ultimately makes violence anachronistic, extending desecuritization to military–political relations that have through this historical process become marginal and even redundant. However, although in the period between the end of the Cold War and 9/11 there was some degree of desecuritization in the military sector, as military forces focused on a new role as peacekeepers, and even in disaster relief, securitization shifted to the economic in response to the global opening up of opportunities for illegitimate economic activity in the 'dark side of trade, i.e. criminal activity in drugs, weapons, and other banned products' (Buzan et al. 1998: 211). The door of sovereignty is always open to securitizing discourse.

In the post-9/11 world, securitization can be seen as a strategic attempt to recuperate authority in a national formal political context, the means for a strategic project of relegitimation after the decades of the crisis of authority following '68. Emergency legislation has been routinely used by 'protecting' agencies to control opportunities for life, just as psychiatric discourse readily becomes a means not merely of treating sufferers from mental illness but of normalizing conduct across society, pathologizing difference as deviance. Already in the 1980s in the UK, criminal justice and public order legislation was being used to exert control over communal attempts to live differently, whether on a permanent basis, as in the 'peace convoys', or in what were effectively 'temporary autonomous zones' of rave culture, where people experimented with new ways of being together and simply of being (McKay 1996; Jordan 2002; McDonald 2006). More recent anti-terror laws, passed in the wake of 9/11 and in the context of the resecuritizing war on terror, overspill the 'sectors' of Buzan, Waever and de Wilde's analysis, linking together control functions across areas that were hitherto separate and enabling a wide range of measures to be deployed against diverse threats.

The result is not simply a more integrated security system, but a new phenomenon. The old divisions of control functions, into military, economic, political, societal and cultural sectors, were not simply those of security studies analysts, but were actually embedded in different agencies subject to constitutional check by the limitations of, in Weberian bureaucratic terms, their jurisdictional competence. A unified security sector means the redundancy of many of those limits that theorists such as Buzan, Waever and de Wilde take for granted. However, rather than seeing this new phenomenon as a conspiracy, in the perspective that is frequently promoted by what used to be 'the left' (e.g. Bauman 1999: 52), their analysis enables us to see how securitization follows a logic of constituted power in the form of sovereignty, which perceives constitutive power wherever it arises as an ontological threat to its legitimating protector function, with the result that the response of control is not conspiratorial, but imperative for existing power.

9
Cosmopolitanisms and Postnational Formations

Globalization is frequently introduced using conventional categories of social science which were developed to analyse distinct aspects of social life within discrete, national societies, categories that had largely developed from the different fields of activity identified for state intervention: economic, social, political and cultural. These distinctions were always difficult to maintain in sociology, since these kinds of activity are differentiated in reality only in so far as the analytical distinction is embedded in institutional forms. Such institutionalization was most advanced in the state, as a relatively artificial assemblage of agencies developed specifically to address issues that had been identified using the conventional distinctions of social science. More recently, globalization has problematized the national frame of those analytical distinctions, while postmodernization makes them even more difficult to analyse separately, especially in so far as they are no longer susceptible to state intervention. The conventional approach used to analyse globalization by dividing it into these categories is thus undermined by the process itself.

Globalization is often seen as a process driven by economic developments, disrupting, disembedding and even destroying cultures, creating powerful social forces and producing political institutions at a new global level while also reorienting social movements and civil society to this new context. However, the extent to which globalization is economically driven is contentious both in theory (Scott 1997) and in practice. Different elements of civil society have both promoted and challenged this economic determination along ideological lines, as neo-liberal 'globalist' proponents and as 'anti-globalization' protestors (Held and McGrew 2007). The social effects of globalization are often understood as a response to economic processes, as the unintended effects of local exploitation of resources by transnational corporations which are largely impervious to the influence of the states where they locate their activities (Sklair 2000). The mobility of capital has resulted in the effective economic stagnation of some areas, while others enter into headlong development at a rate unseen since the early stages of the industrial revolution and on an unprecedented scale; the result is the redundancy of entire populations, producing large-scale labour migrations which seem to challenge the regulatory capacity of territorial states every bit as much as does the mobility of capital.

Dimensions of globalization

The economic dimension of globalization is considered predominantly in terms of the domination of states and markets by 'transnational corporations' (Sklair 2000), including multisectoral conglomerates in which the service sector may be the dynamic element driving mergers, takeovers and extensions into other fields of economic activity. Globalization refers also to the intensification of international trade (distance and frequency), both licit and illicit, and the large 'grey' area of transactions and activities in between. The implications of the transnationalization of capital, on the one hand, and the intensification of trade, on the other, include primarily the state's apparent loss of economic sovereignty, as government becomes a balancing game between the interests of capital and citizens. This takes place in the context of an asymmetry of power, in which capital has the capacity to hurt the state and its citizens, for instance by relocating its activities elsewhere – a capacity which is reciprocal only to a limited extent, such as the UK government's freezing of assets of bankrupt Icelandic banks in 2008 using anti-terror legislation. In more usual circumstances, states are constrained in their actions against capital by international law, in which the hegemony of neo-liberalism is embedded in the sense that each state's guarantee of market relations is the condition of its international legitimacy. That hegemony is embedded and maintained through the institutions of global economic regulation, such as GATT, the World Trade Organization, the World Bank and the IMF, which are able to operate globally in the sense that, within their jurisdictional competence, they have authority over their signatory states.

Cultural globalization can be considered in two ways. Firstly, it can be seen as homogenization, a simplistic approach that also follows the logic of modernization theory, such that globalization inevitably erodes cultural difference, producing a 'global culture', which some critics see as Westernization, or even Americanization. A tradition of nationalistic resistance to the displacement of national and local differences by 'Coca-Cola culture' dates from at least as early as the end of the Second World War, when the structural erosion of tradition in Western Europe coincided with the arrival of US servicemen with access to US-produced consumer goods and relatively high levels of disposable income, in relation to a Europe struggling to reconstruct itself economically. Against cultural homogenization, local or national particularities may be elevated as values under threat from homogenizing globalization processes, or diversity in general can be considered socially valuable. Against cultural homogenization, then, we can assert the value of local distinctiveness, but we can do so either as protection of a particular culture or in a global context, as defence of diversity in general. The resulting debates are then essentially the same as those confronting multicultural citizenship.

Cultural globalization can be understood in a more sophisticated sense as heterogenization, a process in which globalization highlights difference or produces increased awareness of diversity, as different cultures come into contact. Through globalization, the old sealed 'containers' of nation-states, in which a sense of cultural homogeneity had been constructed, usually through explicit state policy as well as through populist nationalism, become porous to other cultures. Heterogenizing globalization can produce cultural reaction through social closure around exclusive cultural identifications, as in the politicization of religion or in neo-fascism. It could also produce desires and drives for multiculturalism, with its fixing of identities into distinct but equivalent communities, and could disembed local cultures so that they become just another style in global context, something that can be commodified and marketed. All three of these effects of the heterogenizing force of globalization may overlap or contend with one another, but all ultimately result in a more subtle form of homogenization, in which places and peoples appear to retain their local/national distinctiveness but become merely category variants, whether as distinct nations, communities or lifestyles, in a global mosaic.

However, cultural globalization can also be understood as hybridization or 'creolization' (Friedman 1995; Hannerz 1996). Stuart Hall discussed the hybridization of ethnic identities in the UK (for instance, British Caribbean, British Asian), and further studies have revealed still more localized identifications, with precise localities, with some form of subcultures or even with a neighbourhood or a street gang (Back 1996), so that the result is a complex overlaying of identifications which refuse reduction to the kind of hierarchical equivalence required for racism to operate, though they may none-theless be exclusive and antagonistic. In this perspective, the diffusion of Western culture results in its 'indigenization' (Appadurai 1996) as it is adapted to the local culture, which also changes (Nederveen Pieterse 1995). This perspective highlights the social constructedness of culture – that it is what people do rather than being something given – suggesting that culture is always and already hybrid and that homogenization and heterogenization are simply an effect of the use of culture in hegemonic projects, such as the nation or community, in which there is an attempt to fix something that is organically fluid.

Political globalization refers to the development of a level of politi-cal action (whether formal or informal) beyond the state and inter-state relations. We can understand this in a number of ways, firstly, as a reflection of underlying processes, whether economic or cultural, on the model of a political sociology of global postmodernity, which uses the old approaches developed in the context of the nation-state and its attendant assumptions (given identities, contained social forces and a bounded society consisting of fixed interest-groups) to look at global political institutions as reflections or expressions of social forces and identities that exist independently of their repre-sentation. Alternatively, a global and postmodern political sociology sees global political action as constituting new actors and politics in representation and enactment, rather than reflecting supposedly underlying identities and realities.

Political globalization can be understood as a function of economic globalization, the generation of new political institutions to meet the needs of the emergent global economy, an approach often labelled as 'globalist' or 'globalizing' (Held and McGrew 2007). The develop-ment of institutions of global governance from international treaties (e.g. GATT, the WTO, the World Bank) could be explained in this way. In this process the state takes on new roles with the delegation of functions of global governance, so they become powerful in rela-tion to their subjects even as they lose autonomy in global context. However, a contrary view sees economic globalization as a politically driven process deriving from the activities of states, often using the term 'internationalization' rather than 'globalization' to indicate that the global is predicated on the interaction of national units. The debate is then over whether and to what extent the state's role is transformed by this process, in which states act as the agents of globalization (Scott 1997; Sassen 2006).

Political globalization can also be understood as a reactive expression or reflection of cultural globalization, or of culture lifted into a global dimension, to account for the political representation of transnational identities of ethnicity, religion, etc. – not only religious fundamentalisms, but the reappearance in politics of 'tribal' identities of all kinds and the way in which other 'cultural identities' become represented, as in the idea that the EU represents some common European cultural identity (Outhwaite 2008; Levy et al. 2005) and the claim to a common Asian identity in the 'Asian values' debate. These approaches are, however, hampered in so far as they direct us to seek to identify causes and effects, though critics of essentialist notions of cultural identity have pointed out how such regional identities are consequent upon and rationalizations of, rather than the grounds for, political organization (Lawson 2003), with the implication that such identities are necessarily hybrid, imaginary constructs, though they can be none the less powerful political forces for all that (Ong 1999).

An alternative intellectual response to the effect of globalization has been the revival of the discourse of political economy. However, political economy has been unable to return to its older frameworks, which had developed out of and in critical response to the regulatory practices of the state, because the state as an institutional form is no longer able effectively to influence economic processes which take place at the global level, while global institutions of economic regulation lack theoretical models and are thus constrained to operate as if regulating a national economy writ large, usually adopting ideologically oriented theories, principally those of neo-liberalism or neo-Keynesianism.

If the state fails in purely economic terms today, then attempts to deal with the social effects of globalization that produce migration flows through national immigration policies, even when packaged together, as in the EU, similarly seem to fail in the face of people driven to escape the ruination of their localities by globalization. In both cases, the constituted power of the state clearly fails because it is attempting to exert control over a phenomenon emerging from the constitutive power of social forces operating at both the global and the local level.

Political economy approaches try to imagine the politics of globalization as the politics of the nation-state writ large, so that, where the nation-state contained an unequal division of labour, globalization

equates to an international division of labour with attendant inequalities distributed between localities, or even, crudely considered,
between nations or regions. This approach is theoretically problematized by its assumption of a universal standard against which
inequality can be adduced. In the nation-state, universality was
posited first in citizenship, and especially in its military mobilization,
which rendered all (male, adult, racially and culturally majoritarian)
subjects as equitable in terms of obligation, furnishing the grounds
for the extension of claims on the state to secure equity of entitlement and producing the politics of distribution pursued through
the state. Citizenship thus provided a standard of interchangeable
subjecthood as a basis for just comparison that is absent in the condition of globalization. No such universal criteria exist on a global
scale, across divergent localities. The concept of human rights as an
attempt to substitute for citizenship is problematic because it inevitably constructs a passive recipient of rights, inherently (in order for
the concept to be all-inclusive) without obligations and therefore
without a political dimension.

Thus, both qualitative and quantitative understandings of just
entitlement confound these attempts to extend the analysis of
national economy to the global. The norms (i.e. the common expectations) and values (the criteria of justice) may each or either differ
between the social context in which labour is performed and that in
which the subject is embedded, as in the case of migrant workers
who may have diverse expectations of economic reward and different
understandings of entitlement to those of the workers with whom
they are competing in a globalized labour market. Internalizing the
'higher' standards of the 'host' society would effectively disadvantage
these workers in their local context. Understanding global political
economy as the national writ large is also severely compromised by
empirical factors, which show it to depend on gross oversimplifi-
cations. Post-industrial development through services rather than
manufacturing industry applies also to generally less advanced
economies such as India and China, where it proceeds alongside
industrialization rather than following from it as a further stage of
development, rendering the stages models of growth of modernization theory redundant. Similarly, conventional distinctions between
the First and the Third World are confounded by the fact that wealth
and opportunity, and also inequality and poverty, are not distributed
on international lines. By the 1980s it was clear that some groups or
classes even in the advanced countries were being left behind by the
economic development going on around them. In particular, such

'combined and uneven development' has produced not a world revolutionary class of dispossessed producers, as envisaged by Marxists, but the phenomenon of economically surplus populations, whose geographical location does not correspond to the shifting patterns of demand for labour.

The 'global division of labour' evaporates when we look at it in detail, both as a critical concept and as an empirical reality. Impoverishment as a consequence of globalization and post-industrial development is relative, and as such it can be seen as a common feature of the emergent global order, cutting across national divisions. The only response to local impoverishment – migrant labour – is similarly a phenomenon not only between globalized states but also within them, and is particularly significant in China, where there is migration for work from rural to urban regions. We could generalize by saying that the social effects of globalization are thus 'glocal', both global and local (Featherstone et al. 1995). Even within nation-states the social division of labour of industrial capitalism has given way to a new order.

Changes in class composition have been theorized variously, but are most frequently related as the changes to the organization of production known as 'post-Fordism', which also play a part in and are part of globalization (Harvey 1989). These new strategies of organizing capitalist production have been promoted via global corporate capital and are quite distinct from the older, Japanese, German, Anglo-American national or regional modes of organization (Lash and Urry 1994). Post-Fordism produces on a 'just-in-time' basis, enabling production to be tailored more neatly to niche markets and fashions than old-style mass production on the assembly-line model. However, where Fordist production demanded a steady supply of labour that was adjusted to the regular demands of mass production, post-Fordism requires flexibility in the supply and the quality of labour. Many workforces become divided into core employees who embody essential skills and thus enjoy security as well as welfare benefits and a periphery of unskilled casualized workers whose employment fluctuates with demand. However, in the recession consequent on the global credit crisis of 2008–9, core workforces have entered into a new compact with capital in response to the threat to the survival of the enterprise as a whole, accepting short and flexible hours in exchange for continuous employment. This has produced a *crisis corporatism* extending across many hitherto advanced economies, as this alliance of labour and capital has pressured governments to provide popular bail-outs for their declining industries, drawing national states and their resources into new, short-termist and speculative capitalism as the local underwriters and agents of global markets and their regulation.

Where modern capitalism previously produced long-term strategic rationality, geared towards expectations of an investment in stability, the new capitalism that has developed since the late 1970s, it is argued, has reversed that. It favours and generates instead short-term rationality as an effect of the intensifying commodification of capital itself, in the form of speculative short-term investments aiming only to maximize immediate profit, which is the capital-side corollary of the casualization of labour (Sennett 2006; Klein 2008).

Hitherto, the mobility of manufacturing production and services meant that it had little intrinsic reason to develop particular relations to any population or state, producing a tendency for production to become 'disembedded' from its social context, but the effects of the credit crisis make relocation, which was usually dependent on loan capital, an unfeasible response for enterprises, thus creating the magical conditions under which the zombie category of national economic policy appears to rise again. There is now a considerable sociological literature on the 'new capitalism', which notes in particular its tendency towards contingent and short-term strategies at every level of analysis, from the 'casino capitalism' of the Davos-level corporate executive globalizers (Strange 1997; Nederveen Pieterse 2005) down to the life strategies of casualized workers at every level of employment, where the experience of short-termism is called 'precarity'. Precarity is a concept that was initially developed in European sociology and has most notably proved a mobilizing focus for political organization across Europe, which some theorists have seen as manifesting a new political subject, the 'precariat' (Raunig 2007b; Negri and Scelsi 2008).

These observations imply an enormous historical shift as radical reorientation of the structure of subjectivity that Max Weber identified as the subjective precondition for the development of modern capitalism per se, in the form of the Protestant work ethic of early modern Europe, which was subsequently emulated globally as a strategic necessity in the context of competitive markets (Sayer 1990). The new structure of subjectivity produced by new conditions of work, Sennett argues, favours short-term relationships over long-term commitment as a functional adaptation, a preference that translates throughout social life, just as did the older subjectivity, to produce new norms of relationship which extend across the social forms of family, friendship and civic association, as each of these becomes remodelled and reconceived along the lines of a contingent and probably finite project rather than of a lifetime commitment. This is a reconfiguration that Bauman has conceptualized as the 'liquidification' of society, though in his analysis the determinant process is the organization of consumption rather than of work (Bauman 2000, 2007; Bauman and Tester 2001).

However, where Bauman and Sennett see loss of social solidarity, proponents of 'post-Marxism' as a guide for resistance have followed the same lines as Melucci, to argue that precarity provides the potential for a new social condition for the radical organization of life. Rather than retrenchment in the classical condition of contending the rate of exploitation of labour, the contention of precarity in favour of the radical reorganization of society and the abolition of distinction between work and life can take the form of a reappropriation of the actual conditions of *social* production. It is thus the evolution of the Marxist project of self-emancipation in a postmodern context, where the proletariat has been displaced in new relations of production for a more general social subject whose 'labour' consists in the production of everyday life, not merely in the form of objects, but as services both commodified and uncommodified, in everyday life as it is lived (Virno and Hardt 1996).

Many of the conditions of globalization and the new capitalism are technological, and thus draw attention to the extent to which all social and political formations are assemblages: information communications technology, containerization in shipping, increased levels of air transport, electronic digitization of information, and so on. Furthermore, the driving factors of demand for consumer goods and consequent labour demand, the erosion of national sovereignty, political instability, the international 'grey economy', satellite TV, the commodification of culture via tourism and the culture industry, and other examples, all traverse the categories we would conventionally use analytically to isolate the technological from the political, economic and cultural dimensions of change.

The global and the social as units of analysis

Most of the massive profusion of literature on globalization and its implications continues to operate through those conventional categories that were used to analyse processes of social development at the level of the nation-state, but John Urry's (2003) analysis of the literature identifies within this five major debates which each relate in different ways to his question of whether we can still use the concept of the social, grounded as it is in the assumption that a society is a bounded entity (on the model of the nation-state), as the integrating concept, the context in which these analytical categories interact.

In *Global Complexity* (2003), the concept of society is shown to be inadequate for thinking through the global, which is not another qualitatively equivalent level to the social-national but a categorically distinct phenomenon, something entirely novel and new with which the social sciences must engage by developing entirely new metaphors for understanding, since globalization transforms long-standing debates and conventional concepts in the social sciences. Globalization, Urry argues, is complexity, and functions at a different categorical level. Where some approaches take globalization to mean a new variable for pre-existing concepts that developed in relation to the national formation of modern society, as in 'global modernities', 'global civil society' or 'global movements', and others see it simply as a new context for existing concepts, as citizenship, power or the state 'in a global age', Urry's title indicates that globalization in his analysis is more than a variable or a context, and fundamentally changes the objects for what we have hitherto called social science.

This is particularly evident in relation to power. Globalization as complexity cuts across the structure–agency divide in sociology, escaping the dichotomy of cause and effect that is embedded in the contrasting views of globalization as, on the one hand, a structural process that determines options for actors and, on the other, an effect of the exercise of agency by social actors. Thus, Urry argues, globalization disconcerts the dichotomy of mainstream sociological understandings of power as either structural power (as in Lukes's third dimension) or power as a possession, in which it is attached to the concept of agency. In those formulations, power had always been related to co-presence but has now become exercised virtually, effective and secured through avoidance of engagement. Power is now indexed to what Giddens called disembedding, while it was hitherto magnified and secured through embedding itself in enduring structures, relations and identifications. In particular, Urry points out the mediatization of power characteristic of our age, whereby the power of representation and discursive construction no longer depends on the social chains of distribution that have characterized modern society since its development from the early Middle Ages – chains which Elias saw as the underlying condition of the civilizing process whereby people came to act with a view to the social consequences of their actions (Elias 2000).

However, Urry's focus is on the conventional public sphere, the media conceived as structural, but elevated to a global scale. His analysis thus neglects the agential elements of mediatization, the ways in which new technology has been used effectively to outflank the blocs of corporate and state media since as early as the 1989 Tiananmen Square protests in Beijing, where protestors communicated with the world using fax technology developed for office communications, while the corporate media were mostly successfully blocked out by the Chinese state. Similarly, in 2009–10, the opposition to Ahmadinejad's questionable re-election as president of Iran used internet blogs to circumvent surveillance and censorship. Under such conditions, open access to the means of representation becomes a prerequisite for effective resistance to power constituted in institutions such as the state or corporations, and Melucci's argument about the resources of an information society escaping their intended uses seems played out in such events.

Less spectacularly, new technology is also used to extend 'community gossip' across geographical space and political divisions through networks linking distant localities. These lines of diasporic communication are not equivalent to a modern public sphere, in the Habermasian sense, and nor are they social movements per se. However, in the sense that migrant labour is always hybridizing identities and experimenting with novel deployments of resources, and as such has historically been a rich source of cultural and political innovation in modern times, we could liken these instances to the 'latent' phase of Melucci's analysis of new social movements.

Cosmopolitanism and its imaginaries

Urry outlines for us a politics of globalization itself, or at least a politics of the discourse of globalization, in which its meaning is contested in much more complex ways than the superficial opposition of neo-liberal globalizers and the 'anti-globalization' movement. Between those reductive positions, cosmopolitanism appeared as the equivalent of a 'third way' between right and left, in which globalization appears to open new democratic possibilities. However, it finds itself contending the mantle of universalism on the global stage with religious fundamentalisms.

Delanty (2000) addresses the issue of the subject of globalization through the concept of citizenship, distinguishing between four frames of cosmopolitanism: international legalism, global civil

society, transnational communities and postnational constitutional-
ism. The first, international legalism, sees cosmopolitanism as an
aspiration and the possibility of cosmopolitan citizenship as emerging from the process of internationalization of society, on the model
foreseen by the Enlightenment philosopher Immanuel Kant. Kant
([1795] 1970) considered that rationality in power and the reduction of all states to an equivalence in the Westphalian order would
produce an eventual outcome of perpetual peace and concord among
states such that their differentiation would cease to be significant.

The second approach envisages cosmopolitanism and its possibilities as emerging from processes of civil society. However, referring to
the concept of civil society means that it must be conceived as distinct
from communities, and thus global civil society is often traced to the
institutionalization of networks in international non-governmental
organizations (Keane 2003). This perspective seems to privilege the
point of view of a global elite, able to travel and re-embed themselves in the formation of global networks, while the most influential
networks actually appear to be those informal transnational links of
diasporic communities developed by those who are compelled to
move by violent disembedding processes (Calhoun 2003; Bauman
1998).

Thirdly, Delanty presents the postnationalist perspective that has
emerged in particular from the work of Jürgen Habermas (2006) and
is shaped by its context in the EU as a constitutional sharing of sovereignty between member states. Delanty assimilates the EU to the
concept of the state, but this is not necessary and may even introduce
implications which undo the Habermasian hypothesis that the new
commitment to a purely constitutional construct finally realizes the
promise of political modernity in a subject free from the trappings
of irrational nationalism and cultural identification. It consists in a
purely constitutional patriotism, in which procedure and its performance on the basis of a shared political culture embed solidarity in 'a
politically constituted global society . . . without having to assume
the state-like character of a world republic' (Habermas 2006: 136–7).
This perspective, however, is peculiarly European and difficult to
generalize since, while the history of the emergence of a global states-
system may be traced to Europe, there is no reason why future tem-
plates should follow a European model in a postcolonial, globalized
world where informal transnational networks seem to be a more
influential source of identification for disembedded populations.

Delanty (2000, 2001) projects each of these global visions onto the
notion of cosmopolitan citizenship, which sets his notion of globaliza-

tion firmly in a progressive narrative, with citizenship as the missing subject of the emergent cosmopolitan global order. However, this requires him to assimilate the global to the national, the postnational constitution to the state. Delanty assumes that we can only conceive of the subject of globalization normatively in terms of citizenship, as a relation to the state or to the national civil society writ large. As Urry has pointed out, the global is not the national raised to a higher scale. The constitutional EU is not a state, and global civil society cannot be modelled on national society writ large. These perspectives also all emphasize structure over agency and look for the appearance of constituted power, even in the concept of global civil society as an entity rather than as a process.

Another approach is taken by Ulrich Beck, who has undertaken a systematic attempt to theorize globalization free of the anachronistic constraints of the national model (Beck 1999, 2005, 2006a). Earlier, we looked at his idea of risk society and sub-politics – where he argues that the apparent depoliticization of politics in modernity actually produces an awareness of 'risk' and leads to the revival of political activity at grass-roots level, around new issues. In his more recent work, he has argued that risk politics escapes the frame of nation-states, resulting in a 'world risk society', where all political issues have a global dimension, which leads to an ethical awareness of inequalities and injustices on a global scale. Still more recently, he has applied the same logic to cosmopolitanism.

In this analysis, the logic of control characteristic of modernity took the form of imperialism – the idea that 'civilization' in the sense of the dominant culture of economically advanced countries could be extended to 'primitive' peoples by controlling them. This was later extended through the concept of 'modernization theory', which argued that developing countries would have to follow the path that had been taken by the developed First World, or 'the West'. This project imploded because it produced its own 'risks' in the form of Third World national liberation movements but also environmental degradation and other costs of industrialization. Beck, however, argues that the effect of global risk society can produce a revival of ideals of progress, social justice, pacification, and so on, albeit in a new form – such as the ideal of sustainable development. He envisages global cosmopolitanism as a kind of new Enlightenment, with new universal criteria of emancipation (Beck 2005). So far, however, such situations seem preoccupied with the old issues of reconciling contradictory ideologies of distribution and its discontents, as in the attempts to engineer reconciliation in South Africa and Nepal.

Beck, then, like the theorists Delanty classifies, sees new cosmopolitan ideals as arising from wider global social processes. In contrast, we can group together approaches which see this process as arising 'from below', as a new global cosmopolitan consciousness. This approach of cosmopolitanism from below is closer to being a postmodern political sociology of global civil society, with more emphasis on agency and less on structure. Those who argue this perspective are divided on many counts, but principally along the lines of whether the constitutive effect (i.e. the development from below) will arise (a) from a new global consensus (e.g. on values, such as human rights or democracy), (b) from a global reinvigoration of agonistic politics of contention, or (c) out of new social conflict.

Constitutive globalization

In the first view, transnational networks of international non-governmental organizations and environmental campaigners, enabled by new communications technologies, emerge from diverse 'resistance' to unaccountable transnational corporations and global governance processes. Out of these networks new values arise. The scope of this approach can be wide, encompassing the activities of a very broad range of global actors, from anti-capitalist anarchists, through grassroots globally connected networks of local activists, to 'superstar' moralists such as Bob Geldof and Bono. However, practical political attempts to set up institutions to articulate this 'global civil society', such as the World Social Forum, have problems in dealing with the politics of scale involved (who or what kind of bodies should have the right to organize sessions, to speak). Such approaches do, however, provide a basis for analyses that can be seen through the approach of a 'postmodern political sociology', in which these emergent global politics, in grappling with such issues, developing new relations, protocols, procedures and political culture, actually constitute new actors, identities and politics, rather than simply reflecting preexisting realities.

So far, we have considered global civil society only as an organic, structurally emergent formation, but it can be understood also in the sense intended by Vaclav Havel, as a network of activism that produces rather than merely expresses identities. In this sense, global civil society poses 'a bold new ethical project for global democratization' (Munck 2006), and is associated with democracy as an active conception of engagement and activity with the political in the sense of the contention and creation of possibilities, rather than as a passive plebiscitary performance. Human rights provides an ideology for cosmopolitan aspirations – the idea of a universal 'human rights regime' promises the defence of individuals against corporate bodies such as the state and transnational corporate capital without (in theory) requiring a global state. Cosmopolitanism is idealist in so far as it argues that universal values must emerge, but neglects the institutions necessary for them to achieve political articulation. Attempts to engage more sociologically with cosmopolitan ideals (to explore whether they are actually emerging from globalization processes) tend to become reflexively critical of cosmopolitanism and even of human rights as a grounding for that project.

Social movements can be seen as expressions of civil society that become institutionalized as non-governmental organizations, so that international non-governmental organizations are often seen as an indicator and an expression of global civil society, especially when concerned with global 'citizen-making' (of donors and recipients). However, INGOs operate according to particular strategies, and elevate a particular conception of citizenship (the passive, needful recipient subject of charitable aid) as their global project. Ostensibly producing global civil society, in effect INGO activities thus structure it as Western or even US hegemony (Vogel 2006). By undermining local authority, confronting national political institutions and substituting functions of the state with their provision of goods or services in underdeveloped or de-developed areas, INGOs at once promote human rights and effectively erode resistance to capitalist globalization and US hegemony, and their operations can even be seen as a part of a process which reproduces the conditions for civil war (Duffield 2001, 2007; Chandler 2006).

However, global civil society is not the only model of the emergent global subject. Social movements do not necessarily become institutionalized but may seek to resist such 'professionalization', with its elite connotations. Some elements of new social movements have developed strategies and modes of political practice specifically geared to avoid ossifying into institutional structures which would continually defer their ultimate objectives (Agamben 2000). Instead, radical movements began to generate a perspective in which action in itself became the end, self-emancipatory and realizatory. If these movements are constitutive of new identities and new possibilities, then the globalities they produce will be very different from the civil society of the INGOs or the World Social Forum.

Direct action is the idea that political action should express and exemplify those values of the objective of the movement, in contrast to instrumentalism, and has thus evolved anti-hierarchical forms, most notably the form of the affinity group, which is also a tactic of protesters precluding the identification of 'ringleaders'. McDonald (2006: 32–3) points out how strategies such as these have in turn re-oriented social movements away from effectiveness in the traditional sense of impacting on policy, or even on wider society, towards personal transformation through participation, so that they become both movements of experience and experiments in the politics of the self – experiments in subjectification, of new ways of relating to others, to the environment and to oneself in the moments of opportunity opened by protest as temporary zones of autonomy from all given forms and authority.

One of the results has been the 'deterritorialization' of social movements, as these become practices of fluidity, 'nomadic' in the sense that they derecognize boundaries in the form of norms as well as the territorial spatializations that conventionally contain politics within the nation-state, ideology within the party-form, and subjectivity within the monadic individual. As Melucci pointed out, these practices reflect the social conditions of the 'new capitalism', as identified by Sennett (2006) and Boltanski and Chiapello (2006). Proponents of 'post-Marxism', such as Negri and Scelsi (2008) and Virno and Hardt (1996), see in these features the conditions of possibility of new forms of social life which would liberate the social subject from the shackles of identification and representation. The 'global anti-capitalist' movement in particular understands itself as a constitutive force that is something entirely different from the civil society of nation-social formations, INGOs or global elites, pioneering an alternative process of globalization from below that is unfinished, uncontained by any institution or form, in a state of continuous contention and thus inherently political in an entirely new sense.

However, this 'movement of movements' (Agamben 2000) invokes an automatic reaction of the control function of constituted power, irrespective of whether it poses any realistic risk to global capital formations and flows. Local policing of globally oriented protests in this sense becomes an agency of globalization from above, providing the security function for capitalist globalization in the forms of summit leadership, transnational corporate development, and the logistical demands of global trade, against their counterparts from below. As Agamben points out, such public order policing operates at the precise node where violence and right are exchanged, where the legitimation of force and the delegitimation of violence 'take place', and is therefore precisely where sovereignty, grounded in the monopoly of legitimate violence, is produced and reproduced (ibid.: 104). As local or state policing becomes increasingly global policing, so, just as the state comes to act as an agent of globalization, that policing becomes the point of emergence of a globalized sovereignty, which has been termed 'empire' by its critics, such as Hardt and Negri (2000).

That policing takes place through continuous 'intelligence' operations, like a state of continuous war preparedness, rather than episodically, and as such transforms the conditions of civil political life in global empire, since activism per se becomes suspect, and therefore effectively (for police purposes) illegitimate. As the technologization of political administration in governance demands that the technicians of police be able to operate without hindrance from relatively arbitrary political concerns, so sovereignty is strengthened at the expense of the constitutive elements of the political establishment, such as the legislative and the judiciary. The growth of police power is a corollary of the extension of executive power that has been remarked as one of the key features of twenty-first-century democratic political regimes, most notably in particular in the USA, the UK and Italy. It is closely linked to the emergent gulf between political institutions and their constituencies, a gulf that is perilously bridged by a reappearance of the phenomenon of 'Caesarism' that Max Weber identified as a tendency of democracies dominated by political elites, where political participation withers into plebiscitary electoralism in which the voters may have rapidly declining illusions, while the forces of public order function to contain politics to those given institutions of largely discredited, increasingly tenuous legitimacy.

10

War, Terror and Security

The armed forces and police, whether acting within the ambit of their specific areas of competence or in joint operations, always observing the most rigorous mutual respect and avoiding any arguments over precedence that would be prejudicial to their aims, are charged with the patriotic duty of leading the lost sheep back to the fold . . . (Saramago 2007: 56–7)

. . . the police are at the end of the assembly line (Saramago 2007: 177)

Saramago puts these comments into the mouth of his character of the prime minister in a rousing speech to a despairing and fractious cabinet confronted with a non-conspiratorial refusal of the authority of political representation, an executive denuded of conventional legitimacy whose only hope lies in the gamble of the assertion of sovereignty. The speech therefore appeals to the inner values of the 'protector' services of modern society, invoked in coups d'état and military dictatorships to justify emergency powers such as the military order to close down civil society and the curfew, in which public life is closed off as all subjects are confined to their private lives, while the military and police forces, usually themselves 'confined to barracks' (in Norbert Elias's (1988) memorable phrase), instead patrol the streets. That closure of public space, along the lines traced by Foucault in his analysis of the plague order of the city as the template for disciplinary society (Foucault 1977), together with the opening of the barracks that contained the forces of legitimate violence, classically marked the distinction between peace and war, but the same procedures are enacted against disease and sedition, just as against an external enemy. This caesura between civil and military order is one of the fundamental divisions of the political structure of modern society.

Increasingly, today, this division becomes blurred, especially since the acceleration of securitization after 9/11, as emergency powers have become normalized as a condition of society. Security forces stand guard outside public institutions and inside the nodes of circulation of everyday life, where passes are required for entries and exits, to access and to disengage, to make use of opportunities or to forego them, with each choice electronically monitored, as well as the flow itself and its disturbances. In the past decade we seem to have left Foucault's disciplinary society and entered into Deleuze's society of control. Though some critical approaches associate these developments with neo-liberalism (Neocleous 2008), the shift appears to function regardless of ideology. Sociologically, in this new constellation, the military and police functions, carefully demarcated into distinct bureaucratic jurisdictions of competence in democratic societies, blur into each other, becoming the more amorphous charge of 'security'.

Civilizing security?

The criminologists Ian Loader and Neil Walker (2007) have attempted critically to dissect this phenomenon from a different angle, refusing, they claim, the dichotomy of security and liberty, the options usually presented between security at all costs and the rejection of constraint on liberty at any cost – in effect reconstructing the argument of Thomas Hobbes for the twenty-first century. Just as Hobbes argued that it was rational and therefore necessary for subjects to acquiesce to a power over all as the guarantee of security in all other social relations, so Loader and Walker argue that security is the precondition of all social life today. The social is ambiguous and never clearly specified in their argument, sometimes being represented in terms of community, a relatively static and conservative concept, assuming homogeneity and consensus, in contrast to the concept of society, which can accommodate conflict and contention, but elsewhere being defined as civility, a more inclusive term which acknowledges the need in a complex society to recognize and respect difference. Throughout their book, the concept of security itself is an abstraction, but also unstable and inconsistent. In one instance they use the term in three different ways consecutively, indicated in print as security, Security and 'security' (Loader and Walker 2007: 12). This conceptual instability is particularly critical since the definition of security was one of the main contentions in the politics of distribution, the question of whether it referred only to the security of body and property, as in liberal formulations, or should be interpreted more widely to include social security, the absence of which would produce the anxieties and fears that Loader and Walker, like Hobbes, see as undermining the conditions of civility or community. In so far as they do specify security, the references are mostly to policing, which is assumed to be apolitical, consisting of systems of normative ordering and their co-ordination as purely technical practice and process with aims that are self-evident (ibid.: 189–90).

Ignoring the status of security as an 'essentially contested concept' in Gallie's sense (1964), and assuming its content as given in technical expertise rather than as political, Loader and Walker thus posit a prior value of security as a public good that is a condition of social life, then identify the state as the 'prior' agent of delivery and proceed to announce imperatives which displace politics and the political from everyday life, with the explicit aim of containing contention within the given institutional parameters of formal political practice, though these are precisely the channels that have been disrupted by the politics of identity, new social movements, representation, culture and globalization. The parameters of the political thus become the parameters of control, a new front line on which the task of security is to constrain and contain the possibilities of social life within given limits, thus establishing set conditions for living. Loader and Walker thus subordinate classical questions of the political – questions of how we should live – to the technical prerequisites of security, its maintenance and guarantee.

The state provision of functions of security, we are told, is essential because 'they entail the crafting of stable identities' (Loader and Walker 2007: 172), thus precluding hybridity, fluidity and creativity of identification. For Loader and Walker, identity, both personal and social, must be indexed to the apparatus of the state lest it undermine the latter's capacity to fulfil its functions in providing security. The argument becomes doubly tautological when they discuss why the state is the best means for the provision of security, since it appears that the state alone produces identities which constitute an environment that enables security (ibid.: 172–6). The politics of self and social identity, in the sense of the contention and challenge of conventional forms, are thus off-limits, illegitimate and even dangerous, since politics are to be restricted to the politics of distribution (in their terms, the 'delivery of public goods'). Restricting the political to such questions means rolling back its parameters to exclude the contention of authority. As we have seen, that contention is implicitly marked not only by 1968, but also by the revolts of 1989 and the

reassertion of civil society as a space of freedom against the determinations of the state, since the necessary attributes of the state's
provision of security 'require the priority of the state as a site of political identity over others to be internalized' (ibid.: 181). The task of
democratic governance then becomes the improvement of security,
state and police, a structural order of precedence in which the political – the question of how we should live – becomes conditional on
given technical prerequisites of how we *must* live, without any scope
for challenging those norms which are assumed, *a priori*, as given.

Once they have established this imperative of police security and
the essential priority of the state in its legitimate provision, Walker
and Loader note four cautions against the untrammelled operations
of security forces, which necessitate the civilizing of security, but,
whereas as security provides the condition for civility, democratic
governance is clearly predicated on security, and these 'pathologies'
are as much those of governance as of security (Loader and Walker
2007: 196–212). The risks are the tendencies of policy drift to 'professional paternalism' (which indicates security-sector technocracy,
the only one that is truly a risk or pathology of security itself), to
consumerism (particularly electoral pandering to populism), to
authoritarianism (which can arise from either of the former paths)
and to fragmentation (in which either consumerist individuals or
interest groups particularize security, contravening its function as a
common good). However, each of these is ultimately dismissed as a
second-order concern, after security, which is to say they are risks
that must be taken, a conclusion in stark contrast to the imperative
basis of security as an essential and preconditional public good. The
practice of civilizing security subsequently turns out to mean the use
of the state and its ordering capacities to constrain popular demands
for security, which is in effect a further security function.

For Loader and Walker, police ordering operations and the security
of the state apparatus that provides this function are the precondition
of democracy and politics, rather than vice versa, so that democratic
governance of security is conditional on the technical prerequisites of
police security and the state, precluding social experiments in identification, representation and living arrangements. In attempting to
develop normative guidelines for securitization, Loader and Walker
thus seem to have reconstructed in abstract the logic of the security
reflex which converts protest or resistance into terror, so they appear
as an ontological threat to the given order and its parameters of the
political. Such forces of the creation of identity and the opening of
new possibilities for life can be understood as exercises of constitutive

power, in contrast to the constituted power of established institutions and given relations, but these are two moments of power, not two opposed forces; they are incommensurable and therefore cannot be brought into 'balance' as security and liberty, a formulation which misunderstands the contemporary political situation, reducing it to the dichotomy of norm and deviance.

When their order of precedence is extended to the global dimension, Loader and Walker are clear that security is not only prior to society, but if necessary it must be imposed. In their reasoning, global security order could be established as a public good on the basis of the shared understandings of national state security apparatuses quite regardless of the conventional requirements of democratic consent or legitimation (2007: 262). However, if security is also enabling and even productive of identities, opportunities for global identity formation and new forms of association would remain containerized within nation-states. The common functions of states as security providers, and the technical expertise invested in that provision, would establish an integrated grid of security for a subject which will internalize the identity given by that grid, just as the national citizen is normatively expected to internalize a love for their nation-state. The subject of global order is thus the subject of security, which is constructed by channelling political action into given institutions and by controlling the parameters of the political to maintain given constraints, producing a naturalized antagonism to anything outside those parameters.

For all their assertion of the priority of the state, Loader and Walker neglect that the state's sovereignty consists not in its institutions, but in the distinction between force and violence, peace and war. It is precisely that sovereign distinction that has been under challenge since 1968 and again since 1989. On the one hand, the legitimation of the state and its force has been challenged, exposed as violence, in countless struggles against given authority over the intervening decades, ebbing and flowing but never dying away entirely. On the other, the distinction between peace and war has been eroded by failures of the security state in its own terms, resulting in serial mis-interventions and the proliferation of civil war, with the unintended consequence of permanent global insecurity.

New and old wars

The end of the Cold War in 1989 produced hopes for a world in which democracy would become a global norm and war would become obsolete as a means of achieving strategic objectives. The impasse of the Cold War nuclear stalemate had already led many to conclude that war was no longer an effective means of strategic action. Since many of the actors involved in sub-nuclear conflicts around the world were ideologically and politically aligned with the Cold War bipolarity and were dependent on external support from one of the superpowers, it was assumed that many of these conflicts would also come to an end. With the ebbing of the risk of interstate war, a new role was envisaged for armed forces, co-ordinated by the United Nations, in peacekeeping, emergency relief, and the provision of security for NGOs operating where national state provision was uncertain – roles to which 'post-heroic' military professional forces were not averse (Shaw 1991).

However, 1989 seems instead to mark a transition from one typical form of conflict to another. Some existing conflicts, even if originally superpower wars by proxy, seemed to have developed an independent internal dynamic, while new conflicts broke out from 1990 onwards. Three types of conflict seemed to proliferate in place of the old ideologically aligned wars of the Cold War era: firstly, contentions and fragmentations of sovereignty, most often on the fringes of the old Soviet hegemony, as in the Balkan wars of 1991–5; secondly, sometimes crossing over with the fragmentation of sovereignty, ethnic conflict, as in the Rwandan genocide perpetrated by Hutu militias in 1994; and thirdly, the reconfiguration of proxy struggles, epitomized by the case of Afghanistan, where mujahedin resistance to Soviet domination translated after 1989 into internecine strife between tribal warlords and subsequently the takeover by the non-state forces of the Taliban, followed after 9/11 by US-led occupation, producing further, ongoing, armed resistance. These three forms – fragmented sovereignty, ethnicization and state collapse – all inaugurate a common condition in which the fundamental distinction between force and violence, peace and war, becomes lost.

For all its horrors, war between states had produced stable institutions and identities in the nation-state and the modern states-system, but new forms of armed conflict after 1989 produced the disintegration of the state as a functional territorial unit of administration, including loss of its monopoly of legitimate violence. In the early nineteenth century, Carl von Clausewitz ([1832] 1984) had analysed a new modern form of warfare that swept Europe with the forces of Napoleon Bonaparte after the French Revolution. The unprecedented success of the new tactics and strategies of the Napoleonic forces were, he argued, evidence of a number of consequences flowing

from the overthrow of the ancient regime of monarchy and aristocracy and the modern institution of the nation-state. Modern warfare
would tend to be decided by battle, because mass national conscrip-
tion for military service raised unprecedented forces, but with economic costs that precluded the long, protracted campaigns possible
with mercenary professionals. Warfare had hitherto been a monarchical prerogative but now became subject to a 'trinity' of government,
the national people and the military command, so that war became
'politics by other means'. This new political constellation destabi-
lized the old strategic equilibrium of European states, producing a
militarily competitive environment in which all states had to adopt
similar forms or perish, reproducing the symmetrical form of states
and military forces in all conflicts. The expectation of encountering
a similar enemy in the field informed the development of modern
military weaponry, organization and strategy. However, guerrilla
warfare developed as a parallel counter-strategy from the start, in the
resistance to Napoleon's campaigns in Spain, a development that was
advanced further in the twentieth century as a means for national liberation from colonialism. For resistance fighters, the conduct of guerrilla war was an integral and necessary stage of the process of forming
a new autonomous, territorially integral state, rather than restoring a
subjugated regime or taking over an existing state apparatus.

Even those struggles, however, were binary, consisting of a confrontation, however unequally structured, between mutual enemies,
but in post-Cold War conflicts that binary order became subdivided
as conflict fragmented into antagonism between multiple protago-
nists in sometimes unclearly defined confrontations, where the
forces involved also lacked the disciplined form of military bodies.
The objectives, too, shifted from national territorial integrity to local
ethnic homogeneity. Forces involved in these 'new wars' (Kaldor
2006; Münkler 2005) are thus engaged in entirely different modes of
warfare from the forces of global interventionary alliances, which are
invested in risk-avoidance strategies of the 'new Western way of war'
(Shaw 2005) aiming to create conditions for the security of distant
locations, usually by fostering the development of local state security
agencies.

New forms of violence

The distribution of the new violence was seen as indicative of a new
world (dis)order dividing global space into 'tame' and 'wild' zones,

as advanced, post-industrial societies sought to enclose themselves against the effects of their own exploitation of the world via the hegemony of neo-liberal economic globalization (Luke 1995). This self-enclosure could be seen on a grand scale in terms of immigration control policies and discursive constructions of 'the West' and also 'locally' in the withdrawal of economically privileged elites into exclusive 'gated communities'. Global, national and local exclusions thus all appear as part of the same phenomenon of construction of a spatial division between 'tame' and 'wild' zones and populations (Bauman 1998: 20–2, 126). However, the shift from isolationism to global interventionism by established powers since 9/11, led by the US and closely followed by the UK and drawing in other NATO allies, has shown the limitations of this perspective both as a way of conceptualizing reality and as the basis for practical action.

In post-1989 outbreaks of violence, the erosion of demarcations between military force and other forms of organized violence, and the growing informality and indiscipline of military forces involved, prompted Wolfgang Sofsky's development of an alternative ideal-type approach to the social forms perpetrating what he described as 'wildcat wars' (Sofsky 2003) – or, in Hans Magnus Enzensberger's terms, postmodern and even 'autistic' violence (Enzensberger 1994) – a symptom of the general loss of hegemony of Enlightenment reason as the basis for action. The new violence of distant, fragmentary wars and of the metropolitan city centres thus appeared as a singular phenomenon, very different from modern forms of violence practised for instrumental reasons to achieve ends extrinsic to the practice itself. However, closer studies of 'new wars' reveal that their violence remains irrational only when viewed from a 'safe' distance. Paul Richards, for instance, has shown how the apparently random brutality of the rebels in Sierra Leone who amputated the limbs of their civilian victims during the civil wars of 1991–2002 had its rationale in the particular social, cultural and political context (Richards 1996). Appadurai observes that the new forms of violence are usually inflicted on minorities within a nation-state, which both makes a national 'people' and reveals the limits of the nationalist project in its surveys, censuses and citizenship (Appadurai 2001). Appadurai (1998) raises the question of the *identification process* which transforms 'neighbours and friends into monsters', pointing out how acts of genocide often have a ritual quality as an attempt to 'fix' identities. He thus enables us to trace the politics of representation even in genocide, where all representations can appear as merely a cover for manifold psychological and individual motives.

Reducing the phenomenon to underlying self-interested individual motives may explain why, in the Bosnian War of 1992–5 and in the Rwandan genocide in 1994, neighbour attacked neighbour, friendships split asunder and even families divided into warring parties, but we require stronger sociological explanations of how the violence spreads, of how hatred apparently becomes contagious. Bauman has also pointed out how the new forms of organized violence use ritualization to create a 'majority' identity. When ritual humiliation, debasement and violence become public, they are implicitly legitimated and thereby authorized by those who do not speak up, a 'public' which become party to the acts by virtue of their silence and inaction. Genocidal processes similarly create a 'majority community' by coercing participation, creating a commonality of interest which includes the coerced participants, since external condemnation is applied to them, too, in addition to their own inner sense of guilt (Bauman 2000). However, these explanations of the intersubjective dimension do not explain the new macro-structures of violence that have emerged in the post Cold-War world.

New wars

Kaldor's (2006) analysis of 'new wars' depends on a contrast with old wars, but the contrast is between a highly detailed account of new violence that identifies many significant factors and an idealized and normative account of the old. Kaldor accepts Clausewitz's early nineteenth-century description of the old form of war as 'politics by other means', arguing that, on this basis, war appeared as a progressively less effective and therefore less legitimate way of pursuing collective interests. After 1945, 'the integration of military forces on a transnational basis' in military alliances such as NATO and the Warsaw Pact also made war less practical. Kaldor sees such international military integration as part of a wider process of political globalization, providing institutional forms to match ideological cosmopolitanism. This perspective assumes that developing states will follow the same trajectory of development as that taken by the advanced economies. However, hegemonic actors can manipulate alliances to make weaker parties reluctant participants in foreign policy adventures over which they have little control.

While Kaldor identifies a tendency towards the increasing obsolescence of war as an effective means for advanced, post-industrial states to pursue their political ends, she notes that the predominant

Clausewitzian concept of war ignored the widespread 'irregular, informal' warfare of the second half of the twentieth century. Over the course of the twentieth century, guerrilla struggles against colonial domination developed alternative strategies that have been taken up today by actors who do not share their aspirations to statehood; they are motivated by particularistic identity politics rather than by political ideologies which always aspire to universalism. Within this normative framework, Kaldor analytically differentiates old wars from new in terms of goals, finance and methods.

In direct contrast to the Clausewitzian model of war, guerrilla and resistance movements strategically avoid direct armed confrontation, aiming instead to prevent the enemy from achieving territorial domination by exercising control over populations, an approach also adopted by the opposing counter-insurgency forces of colonial powers. For both sides, terror was often a more expedient means of control than ideological indoctrination. Terrorizing a population has therefore become the usual military operation in the new wars, with the effect that the civilian population becomes the primary target of military operations, reversing the ratio of military to civilian deaths that characterized the old forms of war. However, Kaldor's comparison seems selectively to omit the casualties of mass aerial bombing in the 'post-heroic' phase of old wars, and even her use of the term 'war' follows a selective logic that does not include the 'police actions' of imperialism, thus excluding the campaigns of genocide undertaken by military forces of the colonial powers against native peoples.

Kaldor's analysis depends on contrasting the military forces of the old wars (homogeneous, centralized, well-disciplined, heavily armed and ethically commanded) with the forces of the new (disparate, decentralized, informalized, unethical and lightly armed). The 'privatization' of the forces of the new wars is similarly contrasted to the contemporary interventionist attempts to re-establish public authority with a monopoly of violence, as in Afghanistan today. Economically, old war stimulated production and development, but, where forces aim at control of population rather than of territory, the destruction of economic resources serves to make populations dependent and removes means of resistance. Plunder and the black market substitute for taxation and commerce as sources of funding, especially in the context of economic globalization, which reduces legitimate local economic opportunities and also produces diasporic communities of migrant labour, who are more prone to the lure of imaginary community and the solidarity of hatred, providing a source of expatriate finance and a reservoir of socially disembedded recruits for the new wars. In Kaldor's analysis, ethnic or particularistic, exclusive nationalism has filled the vacuum left by the retreat of ideology and the ebb of class politics, utilized cynically by elites as a strategy for legitimate domination when old political systems collapse. Exclusive nationalist rhetoric appeals especially to disembedded elements such as migrant labourers, whose 'imagined community' is detached from the reality of their everyday lives. In Kaldor's analysis, these diasporic networks link the new wars to a grey area of quasi-legitimate economic activities, merging into the black economy of transnational organized crime, such as drug smuggling and people trafficking (Kaldor 2006).

Kaldor identifies a global 'political cleavage' of late modernity between cosmopolitanism against particularism, but her arguments for humanitarian intervention illustrate how cosmopolitanism can actually function as simply another particularist ideology, the worldview of a globalized, liberal Western middle class, to legitimate humanitarian military intervention. Critically, however, the sovereign act of differentiating legitimate force from illegitimate violence is thereby reproduced along a new normative axis, justifying a new 'cosmopolitan' imperialism.

Münkler's (2005) more objectively comparative approach integrates the same factors, but in the frame of state-formation/ disintegration processes. Historical sociology (e.g. Tilly 1992; Giddens 1985) explains how the wars characteristic of early European modernity produced processes of state formation, while the typical forms of war today produce processes of state disintegration. The early modern European state-formation process was shaped by two military conditions which are absent in new wars – discipline and systemic technological development. In early modern European warfare, gunpowder weapons systems, including complex logistical supply trains, and forms of discipline recovered by the Renaissance from classical sources combined together in new forces which were vastly superior militarily to those of feudal society. These developments required regular and long-term investment of resources that could be extracted from society only by turning extortion into legitimate taxation through the state; non-state political entities such as city-republics were eliminated and states became consolidated into centralized national blocs. War thus became a symmetrical confrontation between states, ensuring the rationality of actors, since each could calculate the others' likely responses. This process eventually produced the binary stand-off of the twentieth-century Cold War, when war became rationally unthinkable because it would produce 'mutually assured destruction' (Münkler 2005: 51–73).

However, the conditions of discipline and technological development have gradually become dysfunctional as resistance to domination by constituted, imperializing states developed new strategies such as guerrilla warfare, utilizing asymmetries of force, firepower, strategy and rationality. As these struggles have drifted into stasis, where neither side can achieve decisive victory, the effect has been to reverse the state-building function of war, producing a state-disintegrating process in which war comes to displace politics as a means of getting things done, or at least of preventing others from achieving their objectives.

In new wars, any residual ideological goals are displaced by the priority for the survival and continuation of the forces of war themselves. Discipline and training then become rudimentary requirements for forces armed with light, user-friendly weapons engaged in the intimidation of civilians, and even children make suitable disposable soldiers under the loose command of a permanent cadre. Because such forces can maintain themselves by immediate extortion and involvement in grey and black global economies, they need no revenue support system, popular legitimation or permanent administration, and can even undermine the local markets that were both stimulated into growth and positively regulated by the logistical demands of the early modern European war-state. Münkler argues that new wars come to be self-sustaining 'open war economies', in which war thus becomes both rational and economic, no longer a means to an extrinsic end but a way of life for its participants, generating a socially endemic culture of violence and a downward spiral that can be reinforced rather than alleviated by asymmetrical intervention and aid relief (Münkler 2005).

Münkler argues that the favoured European approach to intervention with the aim of strengthening the state, rather than the Anglo-US approach of aiming to defeat an enemy, can address the underlying conditions of new wars, but the difference between these strategies is reduced if we see them in terms of securitization, as simply operating respectively more restricted and wider definitions of security in framing the conflict for policy development. The prospects of constructing either kind of security regime are not good. Globalization makes it increasingly difficult to define and establish the state in its classic form. If even highly developed polities such as the UK require integration in transnational units to sustain the effective sovereign functions of statehood, what hope have fledgling regimes of accomplishing the goal of stable territorial sovereignty? The Westphalian order's requirement of mutual recognition of statehood has itself become a source of conflict, since it configures alternative forms of political organization as illegitimate or dysfunctional rivals to be eliminated, such as the rule of the Islamic courts that briefly brought relative peace and stability to Somalia in 2006.

Kaldor recognizes that intervention in the wrong form, of unrevised old war, as in the invasions of Iraq and Afghanistan, will be ineffective in terms of cosmopolitan aims. Münkler reverses the logic of this argument, asserting that it is the situation of new wars themselves that makes external intervention complicit in the endemic violence. However, both analyse the phenomenon of new wars as an intrinsic process, in isolation from developments in the formal military forces of constituted state powers – the forces of intervention that have themselves undergone enormous transformation since the end of the Cold War in 1989.

New ways of war

The military forces of the economically advanced world today are very different from the military forces of nation-states in the nineteenth and the earlier twentieth century, not least because they now operate usually only in some form of alliance or coalition rather than unilaterally as forces of a sovereign nation-state. Those transformations have been linked to wider social and cultural changes by being analysed through theories of postmodernity, in which representation becomes an increasingly important part of and may even substitute for social reality (Baudrillard 1983). Postmodern approaches argue that war has become for Western societies primarily a media spectacle, rather than a lived experience (Virilio 1998; Baudrillard 1995), conducted only nominally by nation-states, remotely performed by professional specialists, and legitimized though the expertise of executive power, spectatorship and technology rather than through the emotive appeal of patriotism, citizenship participation and mass heroism, as in the age of nationalism. Baudrillard (1995) analysed the first Gulf War of 1991 as the flawless enaction of a simulation, and Kellner (1992) referred to it as ideological spectacle, while Ignatieff (2000) wrote of the 1999 Kosovo intervention by NATO as 'virtual war'. Mann (2003) described the invasion of Iraq as akin to spectator sport, and Der Derian (2009) characterized it as 'virtuous war', in which the impact on civil populations is excluded from media representation, thus making highly technological and politically undercontrolled warfare appear ethical.

Hirst (2001) addressed transformations of war and military power from the point of view of the state's military developments in the context of the international system. For Hirst, the effects of the military revolutions of early modernity that produced the Westphalian system (in which states recognize one another's sovereignty) provide a template for the analysis of the effects of subsequent military developments, through Clausewitzian total war to the revolution in military affairs (RMA) of the late twentieth century. The RMA is controversial even among military strategists, but Hirst provides a summary analysis of its developments and implications, envisaging a scenario in which largely automated military powers confront low-tech opposition that remains indistinguishable from its civilian context while engaged in spectacular acts of terrorism and information warfare designed to delegitimize the military superpower (Hirst 2001, 2006). While this vision seems increasingly borne out by developments in the 'war on terror' and associated conflicts such as in Palestine, Hirst's focus on the state directs analysis away from new forms of social (dis)organization that might arise where warfare becomes indefinitely protracted and legitimation fails.

The emergence of such situations may be seen as an aspect of risk society. Shaw (1988, 1991) identified the late twentieth-century 'demilitarization' of Western societies, where military service became fully professionalized and separate from citizenship. By 1988, the increasing stability of the bipolar international system of the Cold War had produced a situation in which it appeared that military forces could be transformed into peacekeepers and disaster relief specialists. However, in response to new post-Cold War forms of violence, peacekeeping reverted to active military operations, initially indicated in NATO's intervention in Kosovo, and developed into pre-emptive warfare in Iraq and Afghanistan in response to the terror attacks of 9/11. But where old wars had been fought in the twentieth century as 'wars to end war', Iraq and Afghanistan are presented as 'wars to prevent terror'.

In *The New Western Way of War* (2005), Shaw uses Beck's framework of risk society to analyse these recent changes. He argues that the social composition of military forces and the way that warfare is conducted is a reflection of wider society. Where earlier forms of war in the twentieth century reflected and were structured by industrial capitalist society, today's global surveillance mode of war is characteristic of global risk society, with 'new wars' and a Western 'risk-transfer' way of war as two sides of the same phenomenon.

Since the end of the Second World War, many Western states have undergone a demilitarization processes that produces 'post-heroic' public attitudes to war, indicated by the end of compulsory military service and the near disappearance of military institutions from public life. In this process, soldiering has become increasingly specialized and professionalized, so service personnel become valuable assets who can no longer be deployed as 'cannon fodder', which in turn requires changes to military strategy and tactics, with military development aiming to minimize military losses while maximizing firepower. The professionalization of war and the elimination of its link to citizenship in the state means that war becomes legitimate only when it is fought by professional volunteer soldiers in distant lands, which also enables it to be presented as a media spectacle for Western societies to consume. The risks of war are transferred onto distant others, via intermediaries 'doing a job', who are themselves considered to be of greater value than the populations of war zones. This risk-transfer war takes place in the context of a global surveillance network, where access to information can no longer be controlled by states but is globally disseminated through horizontal networks such as the internet, functioning as a public sphere to constrain the conduct of war.

Western governments, now usually committed to war only as members of coalitions and alliances, balance international and domestic political risks with risks to life, enabling them to reduce the political control of warfare to the management of an imaginary 'risk economy' (Shaw 2005: 98). However, as the wars of intervention have become protracted, those policies have suffered from 'risk rebound' or 'blow back' of domestic disapprobation of soldier casualties and (to a lesser extent) of civilian deaths in the war zone, exposed by global media surveillance. However, Shaw's analysis of the new Western way of war neglects its interactive dimension, focusing on the interventionists' operational and strategic intentions at the expense of the effective reality.

Tarak Barkawi's study (2006) focuses on war as a medium of exchange, particularly cultural exchange and interaction. Barkawi extends the global perspective over the entire twentieth century, since the two European world wars entailed the mobilization of widespread empires. For Barkawi, imperialism plays at least as important a part as state formation in the development of war (Barkawi 2006: 59–90). The result is that 'new wars' figure in his account as the latest form of a long-term process in which war as a medium of cultural interaction and exchange has played an integral part in the development of global social reality at all levels, from geopolitics to the culture of everyday life.

Barkawi's cultural approach towards war as a facet of human experience and global narratives leads him to engage critically with dominant representations of both the 'war on terror' and the self-understanding of 'terrorism' as 'resistance'. His analysis highlights the effects of representation and discourse in war in shaping identity, enabling us to see war as a medium in which politics ceases to be about interests and becomes instead an interplay of imaginaries, where it functions 'as a globalizing force' (Barkawi 2006: 169).

Conclusion

We cannot consider latent functions of the 'war on terror' without the observation that practices and ideologies which deliberately foster insecurity in order to reconstruct legitimacy in a postnational context also serve to embed new relations of elite power and control in the social fabric, as the reconstruction of sovereignty in a global context around the responsibility for governance as a prerequisite of politics and society. Conventionally, we think of war as exceptional, as an unsustainable and hence asocial condition. However, this supposes a dichotomy between orders of civility (which we call social) and orders of violence (which we call asocial, so the notion of the social is moralized) that is called into question by almost every 'civilized' intervention into zones ordered by violence, because the intervention almost immediately appears as analogous to the forces against which it is (supposedly) deployed, feeding into the existing order of violence. Similarly, as Agamben (2005) has most recently reminded us, the 'state of emergency', the executive order of violence, is the necessary and continuously immanent condition of peace under sovereignty. If we abandon a state-centred approach, we can recognize the nominalism of the distinction between violence and force and focus on the multiple securitizational convergence between police and military forms and procedures. This is visible in a range of features: the function creep of anti-terror measures which become extended to ever widening areas of life and issues; a common police and military understanding of 'intelligence' as a representation of reality that does not require interpretation for action; technological interchanges (such as the unmanned drones developed to direct air strikes in situations where helicopters would be vulnerable to ground fire and the extension of their use in routine police surveillance of roads); and operational exchanges (such as the use of military helicopters to airlift civil riot police in paramilitary gear to the breach of the fence surrounding the G8 summit at Gleneagles in 2005).

Such convergences serve to illustrate how the bureaucratic and functional distinctions between police and military, and thus between war and peace, are giving way under the pressure of new demands of securitization in a global context. Diken and Laustsen take up Agamben's argument that sovereignty consists in the 'zone of distinction' that is found in the camp (in contrast to the city) and generalized in the state of emergency (the condition of curfew or quarantine, when the city becomes a camp). As they put it, 'the politics of security reduces security to a technological issue of risk-management' (Diken and Laustsen 2005: 137), blurring the distinction between war and peace, constructing an outside and an inside in relation to the institutions of the state alone, overruling political participation, suffocating political deliberation and redefining the political agenda in terms of institutionally given imperatives. In short, the politics of security are the institutionalization of control. However, we do not have to adopt terror as the given form for resistance any more than we have to adopt security at the cost of politics.

Loader and Walker (2007) make the important observation that security has a constitutive function, shaping identities, desires and possibilities, but they collapse the possibilities of critical analysis in their normative argument that security is essentially pre-political, a necessity determined by functional, technical requirements (such as the police or military techniques) that are subject to second-order constraint by given institutions only in order to maximize their function in producing subjects predisposed to security. Instead of their depoliticization of security-as-governance, a political sociology of security needs to show how the constitutive function of security makes it explicitly political in the sense of being continually subject to challenge, to contention, in terms of its constitutive operations, not simply in its application. If security shapes what kind of citizens we are, then it is political rather than technical. In doing this, however, we have to risk a continual questioning of the distinction between force and violence. It is precisely that question which articulates the issues of our times. The relation of security forces to the public is an aspect of the same issues as the relation of the global to the local, of the state to civil society, of protest to order, of the individual subject to the collective, of identity to representation, and of constituted to constitutive power.

Conclusion

The disjuncture between our political institutions and popular expectations and practice has begun to be explored seriously by social and political scientists in the past decade. However, much of that discussion still revolves around old concepts and retains an accusatory or tragic demeanour, often taking the form of retro-ideological denunciations of putative culprits, of the supposed death of politics or democracy, from one vantage point or another, whether as liberal condemnation of neo-conservativism or social democratic critique of neo-liberalism. Recycling old forms as solutions, it also neglects to acknowledge that such vantage points are today vacated by the class actors whose perceptions would in the past have resulted in action in the world to redress the wrongs identified in these diatribes (Keane 2009; Rancière 2006; Crouch 2004). Thus, as Beck observed, we still attempt, as social and political scientists, to animate zombie concepts whose real, effective purchase as means of understanding the world has eroded away along with the material realities that such concepts originally reflected.

Ideology and party, social class and the nation-state, are no longer the key concepts which would enable us to map the parameters of the political as it unfolds daily in events on both the grandest and the most microscopic social scale. If the concept of elites still serves us well, it is largely in so far as that concept is unattached to any grand explanatory framework, allowing us to identify relatively free-floating collective actors. Even in the case of those, we would perhaps have to recognize their radical, pragmatic contingency, and thus their brevity, in contrast to the elites of old that could lay claim to embeddedness in tradition. The Bush clique, predominant on a global scale for almost a decade, has bequeathed no lasting legacy, and Sarah Palin sets about reconstructing Republicanism more on the lines of the grass-roots, anti-elitist elitism of her rival, Barack Obama. Obama's electoral campaign was inflated by the rhetoric of hope that has animated all Western politics of modernity and has such clear religious resonance in the USA, but seems to be declining just as ingloriously in the failure of the constitutive power of his opposition campaign to translate into the constituted power of executive office.

Even as the executive of the world's (currently) single predominant superpower, Obama is struggling against the extent to which the nation-state, once the sole seat of the sovereign representation of the people, has become an agent of global processes, not only in an economic sense, in which states can no longer command their own fiscal policies, but also in the sense that states no longer represent any coherent cultural unity or even a sealed, contained population, but haemorrhage flows of all kinds, both out and in – more like leaky sieves than the steel containers of the early twentieth century that could still lay realistic claim to some status as personifications. Nevertheless, as agents of global processes, they continue to police the borders of the possibility of political organization, hence the wars of the 'global frontier-land' (Bauman 2002) in Afghanistan, Somalia and wherever else a real (but not necessarily better) alternative might arise that needs to be stomped on.

Within those states, citizenship, which once provided the subject for the politics of distribution, fails to keep up with a politics of representation in which its function is taken up by culture, even by the practice of everyday life, in representing radically pluralized, reflexively deconstructible social identities, constructed in order to be revalued and renegotiated, as mutant, chameleon, disposable effects of practices. Just as political action produces community, so cultural representation does not merely reflect but also changes and even constitutes its subject, the social identity it is conventionally thought to represent. Of these, nationalism is but another, a self-consciously false representation of collective identification to itself as a thing-like identity, the zombie form of the working class which was always, in a cultural sense, racialized and localized. Beck's analogy, intended to describe social scientific concepts, has a rather different purchase on social reality if we remember that zombies are not inert, but ambulant, animated and angered, in this case by the fantasies of identification that fill the vacuum left by ideologies which no longer describe the conditions of their existence.

Citizenship was refused and refuted, in a kind of ironic prefiguration of the eventual denouement of their own aspirations, by the theorists and practitioners of the movement of civil society against the Soviet-style state regimes of late twentieth-century Eastern Europe. For Habermas, the public sphere underpinned democracy, and its decline already presaged the stagnation of democratic institutions, but its technological equivalents today – the social networking sites and online databases such as YouTube and Facebook, and the internet in general as medium of two-way communication – seem more illustrative of Melucci's observations on the information society and its tendency to produce subjects who will utilize the skills demanded of them, by a system in non-systemic and even anti-systemic forms, to produce social identity performatively in the practice of everyday life, in ways that correspond to the latent phase of new social movements, rather than simply accepting co-option to corporate modes of existence. It is notable that the media used by such practices, and increasingly by the new social movements in general that today to some extent provide a basis for what, if anything, we could see as an immanent global civil society, are peculiarly subject to and even participate actively in new modes of control which characterize society and which may be, as Deleuze speculated, replacing the characteristic modalities of disciplinary society critically described by Foucault.

If disciplinary society in Foucault's analysis was characterized by the normalization of normalization processes, then the currently dominant political discourse of securitization could be said to normalize abnormalization, making fear and suspicion into existential civic virtues that once revolved around active service and participation in war for the passive enjoyment of peace, demarcating its subject by that distinction between the duality of political order which marked the sovereignty of power in its constituted sense, a duality undone today by securitization and the blurring of military and police functions. Loader and Walker inadvertently illustrate how attempts to reconcile securitization with a recuperated institutional politics of distribution, citizenship and sovereignty result in the resurrection of the Hobbesian spectre of the war of all against all, and also of Leviathan, the anti-politic. What Loader and Walker envisage in theory, however, is already occurring in practice, in interventions into situations that lead not out, but in, as the very conditions of instability and fragmentation become institutionalized in sham sovereignties that can never deliver what they promise and so condemn all to the insecurity of broken promises, the failures of redemption.

The keys and exits from the iron cage of modernity envisaged by Weber had already in his day become devices of constraint and delusion, and today are ever more clearly part of the cage itself. To exit, in order to pursue the political, to experiment and even to think about how we might live differently, it seems that we must accept that pre-carity, chronic uncertainty, is our fate, while making it our route of escape from the cage of our zombie institutions.

References

Abercrombie, N., Hill, S., and Turner, B. S. (1980) *The Dominant Ideology Thesis*. London: HarperCollins.

Adams, J., Clemens, E. S., and Orloff, A. S. (2005) 'Introduction: Social Theory, Modernity and the Three Waves of Historical Sociology', in Adams, J., Clemens., E. S., and Orloff, A. S. (eds), *Remaking Modernity: Politics, History, and Sociology*. Durham, NC: Duke University Press.

Adorno, T. (2001) *The Culture Industry*. London: Routledge.

Adorno, T., and Horkheimer, M. ([1947] 1997) *Dialectic of Enlightenment*. London: Verso.

Agamben, G. (1998) *Homo Sacer: Sovereign Power and Bare Life*. Stanford, CA: Stanford University Press.

Agamben, G. (2000) *Means without End: Notes on Politics*. Minneapolis: University of Minnesota Press.

Agamben, G. (2005) *State of Exception*. Chicago: University of Chicago Press.

Althusser, L. (1971) 'Ideology and Ideological State Apparatuses', in *Lenin and Philosophy and Other Essays*. London: New Left Books.

Anderson, B. (1983) *Imagined Communities: Reflections on the Origins and Spread of Nationalism*. London: Verso.

Appadurai, A. (1996) *Modernity at Large: Cultural Dimensions of Globalization*. Minneapolis: University of Minnesota Press.

Appadurai, A. (1998) 'Dead Certainty: Ethnic Violence in the Era of Globalization', *Public Culture* 10(2): 225–47.

Appadurai, A. (2001) 'New Logics of Violence', *Globalization: A Symposium on the Challenges of Closer Global Integration*, at: www.india-seminar. com/2001/503/503%20arjun%20apadurai.htm (accessed 8 May 2007).

Archibugi, D. (ed.) (2003) *Debating Cosmopolitics*. London: Verso.

Arendt, H. (1958) *The Human Condition*. Chicago: University of Chicago Press.

Arendt, H. (1965) *On Revolution*. Harmondsworth: Penguin.

Arendt, H. (1973) *The Origins of Totalitarianism*. New York: Harcourt, Brace, Jovanovich.

Back, L. (1996) *New Ethnicities and Urban Culture: Racisms and Multiculture in Young Lives*. London: UCL Press.

Bales, K. (2004) *Disposable People: New Slavery in the Global Economy*. Berkeley: University of California Press.

Barkawi, T. (2006) *Globalization and War*. Lanham, MD: Rowman & Littlefield.

Barry, A., Osborne, T., and Rose, N. (eds) (1996) *Foucault and Political Reason: Liberalism, Neo-Liberalism and Rationalities of Government*. London: UCL Press.

Bartelsen, J. (1995) *A Genealogy of Sovereignty*. Cambridge: Cambridge University Press.

Baudrillard, J. (1983) *Simulacra and Simulation*. New York: Semiotext(e).

Baudrillard, J. (1995) *The Gulf War Did Not Take Place*. Sydney: Power Publications; Aldershot: Arena.

Bauman, Z. (1991) *Modernity and the Holocaust*. Cambridge: Polity.

Bauman, Z. (1998) *Globalization: The Human Consequences*. Cambridge: Polity.

Bauman, Z. (1999) *In Search of Politics*. Cambridge: Polity.

Bauman, Z. (2000) *Liquid Modernity*. Cambridge: Polity.

Bauman, Z. (2002) *Society under Siege*. Cambridge: Polity.

Bauman, Z. (2003) *Wasted Lives: Modernity and its Outcasts*. Cambridge: Polity.

Bauman, Z. (2004) *Identity: Conversations with Benedetto Vecchi*. Cambridge: Polity.

Bauman, Z. (2007) *Liquid Times: Living in an Age of Uncertainty*. Cambridge: Polity.

Bauman, Z., and Tester, K. (2001) *Conversations with Zygmunt Bauman*. Cambridge: Polity.

Beck, U. (1992) *Risk Society: Towards a New Modernity*. London: Sage.

Beck, U. (1997) *The Reinvention of Politics: Rethinking Modernity in the Global Social Order*. Cambridge: Polity.

Beck, U. (1998a) *World Risk Society*. Cambridge: Polity.

Beck, U. (1998b) 'The Politics of Risk Society', in Franklin, J. (ed.), *The Politics of Risk Society*. Cambridge: Polity.

Beck, U. (1999) *What is Globalization?* Cambridge: Polity.

Beck, U. (2002) 'Zombie Categories: An Interview with Ulrich Beck', in Beck, U., and Beck-Gersheim, E., *Individualization: Institutionalized Individualism and its Social and Political Consequences*. London: Sage.

Beck, U. (2005) *Power in the Global Age: A New Global Political Economy*. Cambridge: Polity.

Beck, U. (2006a) *Cosmopolitan Vision*. Cambridge: Polity.

Beck, U. (2006b) 'Living in the World Risk Society', *Economy and Society* 35(3): 329–45.

Beck, U. (2007) *World at Risk*. Cambridge: Polity.

Becker, H. ([1963] 1997) *Outsiders*. New York: Free Press.

Bell, D. (1973) *The Coming of Post-Industrial Society*. New York: Basic Books.

Bellah, R. (1967) 'Civil Religion in America', *Journal of the American Academy of Arts and Sciences* 96 (1): 1–21.

Benjamin, W. (1973) 'Theses on the Philosophy of History', in Arendt, H. (ed.), *Illuminations*. London: Fontana.

Bennett, A. (1999) 'Subcultures or Neo-Tribes? Rethinking the Relationship between Youth, Style and Musical Taste', *Sociology* 30(3): 599–617.

Best, S., and Kellner, D. (1997) *The Postmodern Turn*. New York: Guilford Press; London: Routledge.

Bey, H. (2007) *T.A.Z.: The Temporary Autonomous Zone, Ontological Anarchy, Poetic Terrorism*. 2nd edn, Brooklyn, NY: Autonomedia.

Boltanski, L., and Chiapello, E. (2006) *The New Spirit of Capitalism*. London: Verso.

Bottomore, T. (1993) *Elites and Society*. 2nd edn, London: Routledge.

Bourdieu, P. (1986) *Distinction: A Social Critique of the Judgement of Taste*. London: Routledge.

Burchell, G., Gordon, C., and Miller, P. (eds) (1991) *The Foucault Effect: Studies in Governmentality*. London: Harvester.

Buruma, I. (2006) *Murder in Amsterdam: The Death of Theo van Gogh and the Limits of Tolerance*. London: Penguin.

Butler, J. (1999) *Gender Trouble: Feminism and the Subversion of Identity*. New York: Routledge.

Buzan, B., Waever, O., and de Wilde, J. (1998) *Security: A New Framework for Analysis*. London: Lynne Rienner.

Calhoun, C. (ed.) (1992) *Habermas and the Public Sphere*. Cambridge, MA: MIT Press.

Calhoun, C. (1993) '"New Social Movements" of the Early Nineteenth Century', *Social Science History* 17(3): 385–427.

Calhoun, C. (1994) *Social Theory and the Politics of Identity*. Oxford: Blackwell.

Calhoun, C. (2003) 'The Class Consciousness of Frequent Travellers: Towards a Critique of Actually Existing Cosmopolitanism', in Archibugi, D. (ed.), *Debating Cosmopolitics*. London: Verso.

Callinicos, A. (1990) *Against Postmodernism: A Marxist Critique*. Cambridge: Polity.

Callinicos, A. (2003) *The New Mandarins of American Power: The Bush Administration's Plans for the World*. Cambridge: Polity.

Campbell, D. (1992) *Writing Security: United States Foreign Policy and the Politics of Identity*. Minneapolis: University of Minnesota Press.

Canovan, M. (2005) *The People*. Cambridge: Polity.

Casper, G. (2007) 'Caesarism in Democratic Politics: Reflections on Max Weber', at: http://papers.ssrn.com/sol3/papers.cfm?abstract_id=1032647.

Chandler, D. (2006) *From Kosovo to Kabul (and Beyond): Human Rights and International Intervention*. London: Pluto Press.

Chatterjee, P. (2004) *Iraq, Inc.: A Profitable Occupation*. New York: Seven Stories Press.

Chernilo, D. (2007) *A Social Theory of the Nation State: The Political Forms of Modernity beyond Methodological Nationalism*. London: Routledge.

Clark, I. (2001) 'Another "Double Movement": The Great Transformation after the Cold War?', in Cox, M., Dunne, T., and Booth, K. (eds), *Empires, Systems and States: Great Transformations in International Politics*. Cambridge: Cambridge University Press.

Clausewitz, C. von ([1832] 1984) *On War*. Princeton, NJ: Princeton University Press.

Crook, S., Pakulski, J., and Waters, M. (1992) *Postmodernization: Change in Advanced Society*. London: Sage.

Crouch, C. (2004) *Post-Democracy*. Cambridge: Polity.

Dean, M. (1999) *Governmentality: Power and Rule in Modern Society*. London: Sage.

Debord, G. ([1967] 1992) *Society of the Spectacle*. London: Rebel Press.

Delanty, G. (2000) *Citizenship in a Global Age: Society, Culture, Politics*. Buckingham: Open University Press.

Delanty, G. (2001) 'Cosmopolitanism and Violence: The Limits of Global Civil Society', *European Journal of Social Theory* 4: 41–52.

Deleuze, G. (1995) 'Control and Becoming' and 'Postscript on Control Societies', in *Negotiations: 1972–1990*. New York: Columbia University Press.

Der Derian, J. (2009) *Virtuous War: Mapping the Military–Industrial–Media–Entertainment Network*. 2nd edn, London: Routledge.

Devine, F., Savage, M., Scott, J., and Crompton, C. (2004) *Rethinking Class: Culture, Identities and Lifestyles*. Basingstoke: Palgrave Macmillan.

Diani, M. (1992) 'The Concept of Social Movement', *Sociological Review* 40: 1–25.

Diken, B., and Laustsen, C. B. (2005) *The Culture of Exception: Sociology Facing the Camp*. London: Routledge.

du Gay, P. (2000) *In Praise of Bureaucracy: Weber, Organization, Ethics*. London: Sage.

Duffield, M. (2001) *Global Governance and the New Wars: The Merging of Development and Security*. London: Zed Books.

Duffield, M. (2007) *Development, Security and Unending War*. Cambridge: Polity.

Durkheim, E. (intro. and trans. S. Lukes) ([1898] 1969) 'Individualism and the Intellectuals', *Political Studies* 17(1): 14–30.

Durkheim, E. (1992) *Professional Ethics and Civic Morals*. London: Routledge.

Durkheim, E. ([1912] 1996) *The Elementary Forms of Religious Life*. New York: Simon & Schuster.

Eagleton, T. (1991) *Ideology: An Introduction*. London: Verso.

Eickelman, D. F., and Salvatore, A. (2002) 'The Public Sphere and Muslim Identities', *European Journal of Sociology* 43(1): 92–115.

Eliaeson, S. (2000) 'Constitutional Caesarism: Weber's Politics in their German Context', in Turner, S. (ed.), *The Cambridge Companion to Weber*. Cambridge: Cambridge University Press.

Elias, N. (1988) 'Violence and Civilization: On the State Monopoly of Violence and its Infringement', in Keane, J. (ed.), *Civil Society and the State: New European Perspectives*. London: Verso.

Elias, N. (1997) *The Germans*. New York: Columbia University Press.

Elias, N. (2000) *The Civilizing Process*. 2nd edn, Oxford: Blackwell.

Elias, N., and Dunning, E. (2008) *Quest for Excitement: Sport and Leisure in the Civilising Process*. 2nd edn, Dublin: University College Dublin Press.

Enzensberger, H. M. (1994) *Civil War*. London: Penguin Granta.

Evens Foundation (ed.) (2002) *Europe's New Racism: Causes, Manifestations, and Solutions*. Oxford: Berghahn.

Featherstone, M. (ed.) (1990) *Global Culture: Nationalism, Globalization and Modernity*. London: Sage.

Featherstone, M., Lash, S., and Robertson, R. (eds) (1995) *Global Modernities*. London: Sage.

Finer, S. E. (ed.) (1966) *Vilfredo Pareto: Sociological Writings*. London: Pall Mall Press.

Fletcher, J. (1997) *Violence and Civilization: An Introduction to the Work of Norbert Elias*. Cambridge: Polity.

Foucault, M. (1965) *Madness and Civilization*. New York: Pantheon.

Foucault, M. (1972) *The Archaeology of Knowledge*. New York: Pantheon.

Foucault, M. (1974) *The Order of Things: An Archaeology of the Human Sciences*. London: Tavistock.

Foucault, M. (1977) *Discipline and Punish: The Birth of the Prison*. London: Allen Lane.

Foucault, M. (1979) *The History of Sexuality*, Vol. I: *An Introduction*. London: Penguin.

Foucault, M. (1980) *Power/Knowledge: Selected Interviews and Other Writings*, ed. C. Gordon. Brighton: Harvester.

Foucault, M. (1982) 'The Subject and Power', in Dreyfus, H., and Rabinow, P., *Michel Foucault: Beyond Structuralism and Hermeneutics*. Brighton: Harvester.

Foucault, M. (1984) *The Foucault Reader*, ed. P. Rabinow. New York: Pantheon.

Foucault, M. (1988) *Politics, Philosophy, Culture: Interviews and Other Writings, 1977–1984*, ed. L. D. Kritzman. London: Routledge.

Foucault, M. (1991) 'On Governmentality', in Burchell, G., Gordon, C., and Miller P. (eds), *The Foucault Effect: Studies in Governmentality*. Chicago: University of Chicago Press.

Foucault, M. (2002) *Power: The Essential Works of Michel Foucault, 1954–84*. London: Penguin.

Foucault, M. (2007) *Security, Territory, Population: Lectures at the Collège de France, 1977–78*. Basingstoke: Palgrave Macmillan.

Fraser, N. (1992) 'Rethinking the Public Sphere: A Contribution to the Critique of Actually Existing Democracy', in Calhoun, C. (ed.), *Habermas and the Public Sphere*. Cambridge, MA: MIT Press.

Friedman, J. (1995) 'Global System, Globalization and the Parameters of Modernity', in Featherstone, M., Lash, S., and Robertson, R. (eds), *Global Modernities*. London: Sage.

Fukuyama, F. (1993) *The End of History and the Last Man*. London: Penguin.

Fuss, D. (1989) *Essentially Speaking: Feminism, Nature and Difference*. London: Routledge.

Gallie, W. B. (1964) 'Essentially Contested Concepts', in *Philosophy and the Historical Understanding*. London: Chatto & Windus.

Gamson, J. (1996) 'Must Identity Movements Self-Destruct? A Queer Dilemma', in Seidman, S. (ed.), *Queer Theory/Sociology*. Oxford: Blackwell.

Gellner, E. (1983) *Nations and Nationalism*. Oxford: Blackwell.

Gellner, E. (1997) *Nationalism*. London: Weidenfeld & Nicolson.

Giddens, A. (1985) *A Contemporary Critique of Historical Materialism*, Vol. 2: *The Nation-State and Violence*. Cambridge: Polity.

Giddens, A. (1990) *The Consequences of Modernity*. Stanford, CA: Stanford University Press.

Giddens, A. (1991) *Modernity and Self-Identity: Self and Society in the Late Modern Age*. Cambridge: Polity.

Gill, G. (2003) *The Nature and Development of the Modern State*. Basingstoke: Palgrave Macmillan.

Gilroy, P. (1992) 'The End of Antiracism', in Donald, J., and Rattansi, A. (eds), *'Race', Culture and Difference*. London: Sage.

Goffman, E. (1963) *Stigma: Notes on the Management of Spoiled Identity*. Harmondsworth: Penguin.

Goffman, E. (1969) *The Presentation of Self in Everyday Life*. Harmondsworth: Penguin.

Goffman, E. (1970) *Asylums: Essays on the Social Situation of Mental Patients and Other Inmates*. Harmondsworth: Penguin.

Goody, J. (2007) *The Theft of History*. Cambridge: Cambridge University Press.

Gramsci, A. (1971) *Selections from the Prison Notebooks*. London: Lawrence & Wishart.

Habermas, J. (1988) *Legitimation Crisis*. 2nd edn, Cambridge: Polity.

Habermas, J. ([1962] 1989) *The Structural Transformation of the Public Sphere: An Inquiry into a Category of Bourgeois Society*. Cambridge: Polity.

Habermas, J. (2001) *The Postnational Constellation: Political Essays*. Cambridge, MA: MIT Press.

Habermas, J. (2006) *The Divided West*. Cambridge: Polity.

Hall, S. (1991) 'The Local and the Global: Globalization and Ethnicity' and 'Old and New Identities: Old and New Ethnicities', in King, A. D. (ed.),

Culture, Globalization and the World-System: Contemporary Conditions for the Representation of Identity. Basingstoke: Macmillan.

Hall, S. (1992) 'New Ethnicities', in Donald, J., and Rattansi, A. (eds), *'Race', Culture and Difference*. London: Sage.

Hall, S. (1997) 'The Work of Representation' and The Spectacle of the "Other"', in Hall, S. (ed.), *Representation: Cultural Representations and Signifying Practices*. London: Sage.

Hamel, P., and Maheu, L. (2001) 'Beyond New Social Movements: Social Conflicts and Institutions', in Nash, K., and Scott, A. (eds), *The Blackwell Companion to Political Sociology*. Oxford: Blackwell.

Hannerz, U. (1996) *Transnational Connections: Culture, People, Places*. London: Routledge.

Hardt, M., and Negri, A. (2000) *Empire*. Cambridge, MA: Harvard University Press.

Harvey, D. (1989) *The Condition of Postmodernity*. Oxford: Blackwell.

Harvie, D., Milburn, K., Trott, B., and Watts, D. (eds) (2005) *Shut Them Down! The G8, Gleneagles 2005 and the Movement of Movements*. Leeds: Dissent.

Havel, V. ([1978] 1985) 'The Power of the Powerless', in Keane, J. (ed.), *The Power of the Powerless: Citizens against the State in Central Eastern Europe*. New York: M. E. Sharpe.

Havel, V. (1988) 'Anti-Political Politics', in Keane, J. (ed.), *Civil Society and the State: New European Perspectives*. London: Verso.

Hay, C. (2007) *Why We Hate Politics*. Cambridge: Polity.

Hebdige, D. (1979) *Subculture: The Meaning of Style*. London: Methuen.

Heelas, P., Lash, S., and Morris, P. (1995) *Detraditionalization*. Oxford: Blackwell.

Held, D., and McGrew, A. G. (2007) *Globalization/Anti-Globalization: Beyond the Great Divide*. 2nd edn, Cambridge: Polity.

Held, D., Moore, H. L., and Young, K. (ed.) (2008) *Cultural Politics in a Global Age: Uncertainty, Solidarity and Innovation*. Oxford: Oneworld.

Hindess, B. (1996) *Discourses of Power: From Hobbes to Foucault*. Oxford: Blackwell.

Hirst, P. (1997) *From Statism to Pluralism: Democracy, Civil Society and Global Politics*. London: UCL Press.

Hirst, P. (2001) *War and Power in the 21st Century: The State, Military Conflict and the International System*. Cambridge: Polity.

Hirst, P. (2006) *Space and Power: Politics, War and Architecture*. Cambridge: Polity.

Hirst, P., and Thompson, G. (1999) *Globalization in Question: The International Economy and the Possibilities of Governance*. 2nd edn, Cambridge: Polity.

Hobbes, T. ([1651] 1968) *Leviathan: The Matter, Forme and Power of a Commonwealth, Ecclesiasticall and Civill*. Harmondsworth: Penguin.

Hobden, S. (1998) *International Relations and Historical Sociology*. London: Routledge.

Hobden, S., and Hobson, J. M. (2001) *Historical Sociology and International Relations*. Cambridge: Cambridge University Press.

Hobsbawm, E. J. (1990) *Nations and Nationalism since 1780: Programme, Myth, Reality*. Cambridge: Cambridge University Press.

Hornqvist, M. (2004) 'The Birth of Public Order Policy', *Race & Class* 46(1): 30–52.

Ignatieff, M. (2000) *Virtual War: Kosovo and Beyond*. London: Chatto & Windus.

Isin, E. F., and Turner, B. S. (eds) (2002) *Handbook of Citizenship Studies*. London: Sage.

Isin, E. F., and Turner, B. S. (2008) 'Investigating Citizenship: An Agenda for Citizenship Studies', in Isin, E. F., Nyers, P., and Turner, B. S. (eds), *Citizenship between Past and Future*. London: Routledge.

Jenkins, J. C. (1983) 'Resource Mobilization Theory and the Study of Social Movements', *Annual Review of Sociology* 9: 527–53.

Jones, D., et al. (2001) *On Fire: The Battle of Genoa and the Anti-Capitalist Movement*. Edinburgh: One-Off Press.

Jordan, T. (2002) *Activism! Direct Action, Hacktivism and the Future of Society*. London: Reaktion Books.

Joxe, A. (2002) *Empire of Disorder*. New York: Semiotext(e).

Kaldor, M. (2006) *New and Old Wars: Organized Violence in a Global Era*. 2nd edn, Cambridge: Polity.

Kant, I. ([1795] 1970) 'Perpetual Peace', in Reiss, H. (ed.), *Kant: Political Writings*. Cambridge: Cambridge University Press.

Kapteyn, P. (2004) 'Armed Peace: On the Pacifying Condition for the Co-operative of States', in Loyal, S., and Quilley, S. (eds), *The Sociology of Norbert Elias*. Cambridge: Cambridge University Press.

Kaufman, S. J. (2001) *Modern Hatreds: The Symbolic Politics of Ethnic War*. Ithaca, NY: Cornell University Press.

Keane, J. (1988a) *Democracy and Civil Society: On the Predicaments of European Socialism, the Prospects for Democracy, and the Problem of Controlling Social and Political Power*. London: Verso.

Keane, J. (ed.) (1988b) *Civil Society and the State: New European Perspectives*. London: Verso.

Keane, J. (2003) *Global Civil Society?* Cambridge: Cambridge University Press.

Keane, J. (2009) *The Life and Death of Democracy*. London: Simon & Schuster.

Kellner, D. (1992) *The Persian Gulf TV War*. Boulder, CO: Westview Press.

Kellner, D. (1994) *Media Culture: Cultural Studies, Identity and Politics between the Modern and the Postmodern*. London: Routledge.

Kellner, D. (1997) 'Habermas, the Public Sphere and Democracy: A Critical Intervention', at: http://knowledgepublic.pbworks.com/f/Habermas_Public_Sphere_Democracy.pdf.

Klein, N. (2008) *The Shock Doctrine: The Rise of Disaster Capitalism*. London: Penguin.

Koselleck, R. (1988) *Critique and Crisis: Enlightenment and the Pathogenesis of Modern Society*. Oxford: Berg.

Krasner, S. D. (2001) 'Rethinking the Sovereign State Model', in Cox, M., Dunne, T., and Booth, K. (eds), *Empires, Systems and States: Great Transformations in International Politics*. Cambridge: Cambridge University Press.

Laclau, E. (ed.) (1994) *The Making of Political Identities*. London: Verso.

Lash, S., and Urry, J. (1994) *Economies of Signs and Space*. London: Sage.

Lassman, P. (2000) 'The Rule of Man over Man: Politics, Power and Legitimation', in Turner, S. (ed.), *The Cambridge Companion to Weber*. Cambridge: Cambridge University Press.

Lawson, S. (ed.) (2003) *Europe and the Asia-Pacific: Culture, Identity and Representations of Region*. London: RoutledgeCurzon.

Lefebvre, H. ([1968] 1984) *Everyday Life in the Modern World*. New Brunswick, NJ: Transaction Books.

Lenin, V. I. ([1922] 1964) 'The Question of Nationalities or "Autonomisation"', in *Questions of National Policy and Proletarian Internationalism*. Moscow: Progress.

Lenin, V. I. ([1918] 1992) *The State and Revolution*. London: Penguin.

Levy, D., Pensky, M., and Torpet, J. (eds) (2005) *Old Europe, New Europe, Core Europe: Transatlantic Relations after the Cold War*. London: Verso.

Linebaugh, P. (1991) *The London Hanged*. London: Allen Lane.

Lipset, S. M. (ed.) (1969) *Politics and the Social Sciences*. New York: Oxford University Press.

Lister, R. (2003) *Citizenship: Feminist Perspectives*. 2nd edn, Basingstoke: Palgrave Macmillan.

Lister, R. (2008) 'Inclusive Citizenship: Realizing the Potential', in Isin, E. F., Nyers, P., and Turner, B. S. (eds), *Citizenship between Past and Future*. London: Routledge.

Loader, I., and Walker, N. (2007) *Civilizing Security*. Cambridge: Cambridge University Press.

Lukács, G. ([1922] 1971) *History and Class Consciousness: Studies in Marxist Dialectics*. London: Merlin Press.

Luke, T. (1995) 'New World Order or Neo-World Orders: Power, Politics and Ideology in Informationalizing Glocalities', in Featherstone, M., Lash, S., and Robertson, R. (eds), *Global Modernities*. London: Sage.

Lukes, S. (2005) *Power: A Radical View*. 2nd edn, Basingstoke: Palgrave Macmillan.

McClure, K. (1992) 'On the Subject of Rights: Pluralism, Plurality and Political Identity', in Mouffe, C. (ed.), *Dimensions of Radical Democracy: Pluralism, Citizenship, Community*. London: Verso.

McDonald, K. (2006) *Global Movements: Action and Culture*. Oxford: Blackwell.

McKay, G. (1996) *Senseless Acts of Beauty: Cultures of Resistance since the Sixties*. London: Verso.

Mann, M. (1986) *The Sources of Social Power*, Vol. 1: *A History of Power from the Beginning to AD 1760*. Cambridge: Cambridge University Press.

Mann, M. (2003) *Incoherent Empire*. London: Verso.

Marinetto, M. (2007) *Social Theory, the State and Modern Society*. Maidenhead: Open University Press.

Marx, K. ([1844] 1992) 'On the Jewish Question', in *Early Writings*. London: Penguin.

Marx, K., and Engels, F. ([1845–6] 1987) *The German Ideology*. London: Lawrence & Wishart.

Melucci, A. (1989) *Nomads of the Present: Social Movements and Individual Needs in Contemporary Culture*, ed. J. Keane and P. Mier. London: Hutchinson Radius.

Melucci, A. (1996a) *The Playing Self: Person and Meaning in the Planetary Society*. Cambridge: Cambridge University Press.

Melucci, A. (1996b) *Challenging Codes: Collective Action in the Information Age*. Cambridge: Cambridge University Press.

Mertes, T., and Bello, W. F. (2004) *A Movement of Movements: Is Another World Really Possible?* London: Verso.

Meyer, D. S. (2001) 'Protest and Political Process', in Nash, K., and Scott, A. (eds), *The Blackwell Companion to Political Sociology*. Oxford: Blackwell.

Miller, P., and Rose, N. (2008) *Governing the Present: Administering Economic, Social and Personal Life*. Cambridge: Polity.

Mills, C. Wright (1956) *The Power Elite*. Oxford: Oxford University Press.

Modood, T. (2008) 'Multiculturalism, Citizenship and National Identity', in Isin, E. F., Nyers, P., and Turner, B. S. (eds), *Citizenship between Past and Future*. London: Routledge.

Mohanty, C. T. ([1988] 2003) 'Under Western Eyes: Feminist Scholarship and Colonial Discourses', in Mohanty, C. T., *Feminism without Borders: Decolonizing Theory, Practicing Solidarity*. Durham, NC: Duke University Press.

Mouffe, C. (1992) 'Democratic Citizenship and the Political Community', in Mouffe, C. (ed.), *Dimensions of Radical Democracy: Pluralism, Citizenship, Community*. London: Verso.

Mouffe, C. (2005) *On the Political*. Abingdon: Routledge.

Mukerji, C. (1997) *Territorial Ambitions and the Gardens of Versailles*. Cambridge: Cambridge University Press.

Mullard, M., and Cole, B. A. (eds) (2007) *Globalization, Citizenship and the War on Terror*. Cheltenham: Edward Elgar.

Munck, R. (2006) 'Global Civil Society: Royal Road or Slippery Path?', *Voluntas: International Journal of Voluntary and Nonprofit Organizations* 17(4): 324–31.

Münkler, H. (2005) *The New Wars*. Cambridge: Polity.

Murray, C. A., et al. (1989) *Charles Murray and the Underclass: the Developing Debate*. London: IEA Health and Welfare Unit.

Nash, K. (2000) *Contemporary Political Sociology: Globalization, Politics and Power*. Oxford: Blackwell.

Nash, K. (2001) 'The "Cultural Turn" in Social Theory: Towards a Theory of Cultural Politics', *Sociology* 35(1): 77–92.

Nash, K., and Scott, A. (eds) (2001) *The Blackwell Companion to Political Sociology*. Oxford: Blackwell.

Nederveen Pieterse, J. (1995) 'Globalization as Hybridization', in Featherstone, M., Lash, S., and Robertson, R. (eds), *Global Modernities*. London: Sage.

Negri, A. (2008) *Reflections on Empire*. Cambridge: Polity.

Negri, A., with Scelsi, R. V. (2008) *Goodbye Mr Socialism: Radical Politics in the 21st Century*. London: Profile Books.

Neocleous, M. (2003) *Imagining the State*. Maidenhead: Open University Press.

Neocleous, M. (2008) *The Critique of Security*. Edinburgh: Edinburgh University Press.

Nicholson, L., and Seidman, S. (1995) *Social Postmodernism: Beyond Identity Politics*. Cambridge: Cambridge University Press.

Ong, A. (1999) *Flexible Citizenship: The Cultural Logics of Transnationality*. Durham, NC: Duke University Press.

Outhwaite, W. (2008) *European Society*. Cambridge: Polity.

Owen, D. (2001) '"Postmodern" Political Sociology', in Nash, K., and Scott, A. (eds), *The Blackwell Companion to Political Sociology*. Oxford: Blackwell.

Pappe, I. (2006) *The Ethnic Cleansing of Palestine*. Oxford: Oneworld.

Pateman, C. (1988) *The Sexual Contract*. Cambridge: Polity.

Pickering, M. (2001) *Stereotyping: The Politics of Representation*. London: Palgrave Macmillan.

Plant, S. (1992) *The Most Radical Gesture: Situationist International in a Postmodern Age*. London: Routledge.

Poggi, G. (1978) *The Development of the Modern State*. New York: HarperCollins.

Poggi, G. (2001) *Forms of Power*. Cambridge: Polity.

Purkis, J., and Bowen, J. (eds) (1997) *Twenty-First Century Anarchism: Unorthodox Ideas for the New Millennium*. London: Continuum.

Rancière, J. (1995) *On the Shores of Politics*. London: Verso.

Rancière, J. (2006) *Hatred of Democracy*. London: Verso.

Raunig, G. (2007a) *Art and Revolution: Transversal Activism in the Long Twentieth Century*. Los Angeles: Semiotext(e).

Raunig, G. (2007b) 'The Monster Precariat', *Translate*, at: http://translate. eipcp.net/strands/02/raunig-strands02en (accessed 22 July 2009).

Ray, L. (2001) 'Civil Society and the Public Sphere', in Nash, K., and Scott, A. (eds), *The Blackwell Companion to Political Sociology*. Oxford: Blackwell.

Richards, P. (1996) *Fighting for the Rainforest: War, Youth and Resources in Sierra Leone.* Oxford: James Currey.

Rose, N. (1991) *Governing the Soul: Shaping of the Private Self.* London: Routledge.

Rousseau, J.-J. ([1755] 1973) *The Social Contract and Discourses.* London: Dent.

Said, E. (1988) *Orientalism.* New York: Vintage.

Said, E. (1998) *Culture and Imperialism.* 2nd edn, New York: Vintage.

Saramago, J. (2007) *Seeing.* London: Vintage.

Sassen, S. (2006) *Territory, Authority, Rights: From Medieval to Global Assemblages.* Princeton, NJ: Princeton University Press.

Sayer, D. (1990) *Capitalism and Modernity: Excursus on Marx and Weber.* London: Routledge.

Scott, A. (1990) *Ideology and the New Social Movements.* London: Routledge.

Scott, A. (ed.) (1997) *The Limits of Globalization: Cases and Arguments.* London: Routledge.

Scott, J. C. (1998) *Seeing Like a State: How Certain Schemes to Improve the Human Condition Have Failed.* New Haven, CT: Yale University Press.

Seidman, S. (ed.) (1996) *Queer Theory/Sociology.* Oxford: Blackwell.

Sennett, R. (1976) *The Fall of Public Man.* New York: Knopf.

Sennett, R. (1998) *The Corrosion of Character.* New York: Norton.

Sennett, R. (2006) *The Culture of the New Capitalism.* New Haven, CT: Yale University Press.

Shaw, M. (1988) *Dialectics of War: An Essay in the Social Theory of Total War and Peace.* London: Pluto.

Shaw, M. (1991) *Post-Military Society: Militarism, Demilitarization and War at the End of the Twentieth Century.* Cambridge: Polity.

Shaw, M. (2005) *The New Western Way of War: Risk-Transfer War and its Crisis in Iraq.* Cambridge: Polity.

Skeggs, B. (1997) *Formations of Class and Gender: Becoming Respectable.* London: Sage.

Skinner, Q. (1978) *The Foundations of Modern Political Thought.* Cambridge: Cambridge University Press.

Sklair, L. (2000) *The Transnational Capitalist Class.* Oxford: Blackwell.

Smith, A. D. (1995) *Nations and Nationalism in a Global Era.* 2nd edn, Cambridge: Polity.

Smith, A. D. (1998) *Nationalism and Modernism.* London: Routledge.

Smith, A. D. (1999) *Myths and Memories of the Nation.* Oxford: Oxford University Press.

Smith, A. D. (2001) *Nationalism: Theory, Ideology, History.* Cambridge: Polity.

Smith, A. D. (2004) *The Antiquity of Nations.* Cambridge: Polity.

Smith, J., and Eisenstadt, S. N. (2006) *Europe and the Americas: State Formation, Capitalism and Civilizations in Atlantic Modernity.* Leiden: Brill.

Sofsky, W. (2003) *Violence: Terrorism, Genocide, War.* London: Granta.

Solomos, J., and Back, L. (1994) 'Conceptualising Racisms: Social Theory, Politics and Research', *Sociology*, 28(1): 143–61.

Somers, M. R. (2005) 'Citizenship Troubles: Genealogies of Struggle for the Soul of the Social', in Adams, J., Clemens, E. S., and Orloff, S. (eds), *Remaking Modernity: Politics, History and Sociology*. Durham, NC: Duke University Press.

Spruyt, H. (1994) *The Sovereign State and its Competitors: An Analysis of Systems Change*. Princeton, NJ: Princeton University Press.

Stewart, A. (2001) *Theories of Power and Domination: The Politics of Empowerment in Late Modernity*. London: Sage.

Strange, S. (1997) *Casino Capitalism*. Manchester: Manchester University Press.

Tester, K. (1992) *Civil Society*. London: Routledge.

Thompson, E. P. (1970) *The Making of the English Working Class*. 2nd edn, Harmondsworth: Penguin.

Thomson, J. E. (1996) *Mercenaries, Pirates and Sovereigns: State Building and Extraterritorial Violence in Early Modern Europe*. Princeton, NJ: Princeton University Press.

Tilly, C. (1978) *From Mobilization to Revolution*. London: Addison-Wesley.

Tilly, C. (1992) *Coercion, Capital and European States, AD 990–1992*. Oxford: Blackwell.

Tilly, C. (1995) *European Revolutions, 1492–1992*. Oxford: Blackwell.

Tilly, C. (2004) *Social Movements, 1768–2004*. Boulder, CO: Paradigm.

Tismanaenu, V. (1999) *The Revolutions of 1989*. London: Routledge.

Toscano, A. (2009) 'The War against Pre-terrorism: The Tarnac 9 and *The Coming Insurrection*', *Radical Philosophy* 154.

Traugott, M. (ed.) (1994) *Repertoires and Cycles of Collective Action*. Durham, NC: Duke University Press.

Trend, D. (ed.) (1995) *Radical Democracy: Identity, Citizenship and the State*. London: Routledge.

Trentman, F. (2006) 'The "British" Sources of Social Power: Reflections on History, Sociology, and Intellectual Biography', in Hall, J. A., and Schroeder, R. (eds), *An Anatomy of Power: The Social Theory of Michael Mann*. Cambridge: Cambridge University Press, pp. 285–305.

Trotsky, L. ([1906] 2007) *Permanent Revolution: Results and Prospects*. London: IMG.

Turner, B. S. (1992) 'Outline of a Theory of Citizenship', in Mouffe, C. (ed.), *Dimensions of Radical Democracy: Pluralism, Citizenship, Community*. London: Verso.

Turner, B. S. (1995) *Medical Power and Social Knowledge*. 2nd edn, London: Sage.

Urry, J. (2003) *Global Complexity*. Cambridge: Polity.

Vaneigem, R. (1979) *The Revolution of Everyday Life*. 2nd edn, London: Rising Free Collective.

Viénet, R. (1992) *Enragés and Situationists in the Occupation Movement, France, May '68*. Brooklyn, NY: Autonomedia; London: Rebel Press.

Virilio, P. (1986) *Speed and Politics*. New York: Semiotext(e).

Virilio, P. (1989) *War and Cinema: The Logistics of Perception*. London: Verso.

Virilio, P. (1998) *The Virilio Reader*, ed. J. Der Derian. Oxford: Blackwell.

Virno, P., and Hardt, M. (eds) (1996) *Radical Thought in Italy: A Potential Politics*. Minneapolis: University of Minnesota Press.

Vogel, A. (2006) 'Who is Making Global Civil Society? US Philanthropy and Empire in World Society', *British Journal of Sociology* 57(4): 635–55.

Walby, S. (1994) 'Is Citizenship Gendered?', *Sociology* 28(2): 379–95.

Wallerstein, I. (2004) *World-Systems Analysis: An Introduction*. Durham, NC: Duke University Press.

Walzer, M. (1992) 'The Civil Society Argument', in Mouffe, C. (ed.), *Dimensions of Radical Democracy: Pluralism, Citizenship, Community*. London: Verso.

Weber, M. (1946) *From Max Weber: Essays in Sociology*, ed. H. H. Gerth and C. Wright Mills. New York: Oxford University Press.

Weber, M. (1978) *Economy and Society: An Outline of Interpretive Sociology*. Berkeley: University of California Press.

Weber, M. (1994) *Political Writings*, ed. P. Lassman. Cambridge: Cambridge University Press.

Weiss, L. (1998) *The Myth of the Powerless State: Governing the Economy in a Global Era*. Cambridge: Polity.

Willis, P. (1977) *Learning to Labour: How Working Class Kids Get Working Class Jobs*. Farnborough: Saxon House.

Young, I. M. (1990) *Justice and the Politics of Difference*. Princeton, NJ: Princeton University Press.

Zald, M., and McCarthy, J. D. (eds) (1987) *Social Movements in an Organizational Society*. New Brunswick, NJ: Transaction Books.

Žižek, S. (1992) 'Ethnic danse macabre', *The Guardian*, 28 August.

Žižek, S. (2004) *Plague of Fantasies*. 2nd edn, London: Verso.

Žižek, S. (2006) *How to Read Lacan*. London: Granta.

Index